JUNIUS AND ALBERT'S
Adventures in
THE CONFEDERACY

JUNIUS AND ALBERT'S
ALBERT'S
Adventures in
THE CONFEDERACY

A CIVIL WAR
☆ ODYSSEY ☆

PETER CARLSON

PUBLICAFFAIRS
New York

Published in the United States by PublicAffairs™,
a Member of the Perseus Books Group

PublicAffairs books are available at special discounts for bulk purchases in the
U.S. by corporations, institutions, and other organizations. For more information,
please contact the Special Markets Department at the Perseus Books Group,
2300 Chestnut Street, Suite 200, Philadelphia, PA 19103, call (800) 810-4145, ext.
5000, or e-mail special.markets@perseusbooks.com.

Book Design by Cynthia Young

Library of Congress Cataloging-in-Publication Data
Carlson, Peter, 1952–
Junius and Albert's adventures in the Confederacy : a Civil War odyssey
/ Peter Carlson. — First Edition.
     pages cm
Includes bibliographical references.
ISBN 978-1-61039-154-2 (hardcover : alk. paper) — ISBN 978-1-61039-155-9
(e-book)   1. Richardson, Albert D. (Albert Deane), 1833–1869.   2. Browne,
Junius Henri, 1833–1902.   3. United States—History—Civil War,
1861–1865—Prisoners and prisons, Confederate.   4. Prisoners of
war—Confederate States of America—Biography.   5. Escapes—United
States—History—19th century.   I. Title.
E468.9.C347 2013
973.7'710922—dc23
[B]

                                        2012042886

10 9 8 7 6 5 4 3

To newspaper reporters, past and present,
who went off on adventures and came back with stories.

CONTENTS

PART 3: FLIGHT

JUNIUS BROWNE

ALBERT RICHARDSON

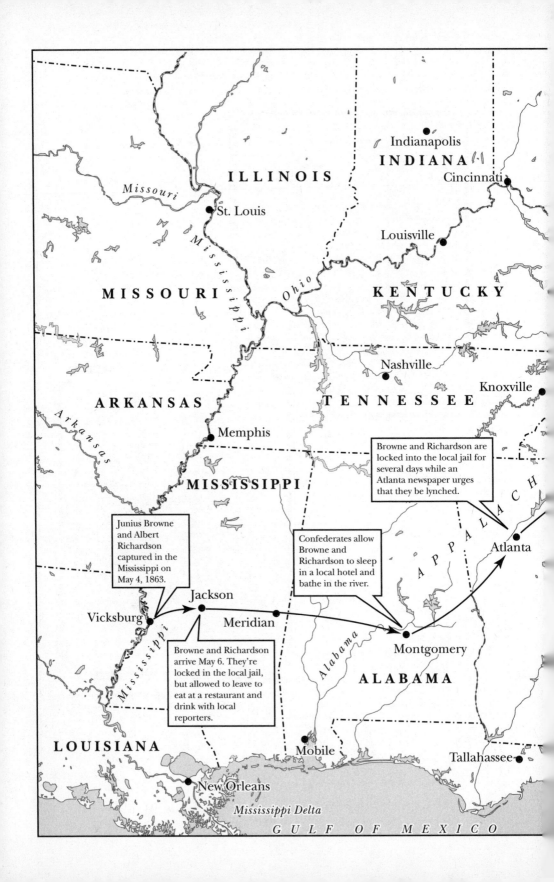

Indianapolis

INDIANA

Cincinnati

ILLINOIS

Missouri

St. Louis

Louisville

MISSOURI

Mississippi

Ohio

KENTUCKY

Nashville

Knoxville

Arkansas

ARKANSAS

TENNESSEE

Memphis

MISSISSIPPI

Browne and Richardson are locked into the local jail for several days while an Atlanta newspaper urges that they be lynched.

Junius Browne and Albert Richardson captured in the Mississippi on May 4, 1863.

Confederates allow Browne and Richardson to sleep in a local hotel and bathe in the river.

A P P A L A C H

Atlanta

Jackson

Vicksburg

Meridian

Browne and Richardson arrive May 6. They're locked in the local jail, but allowed to leave to eat at a restaurant and drink with local reporters.

Mississippi

Alabama

Montgomery

ALABAMA

LOUISIANA

Mobile

Tallahassee

New Orleans

Mississippi Delta

G U L F   O F   M E X I C O

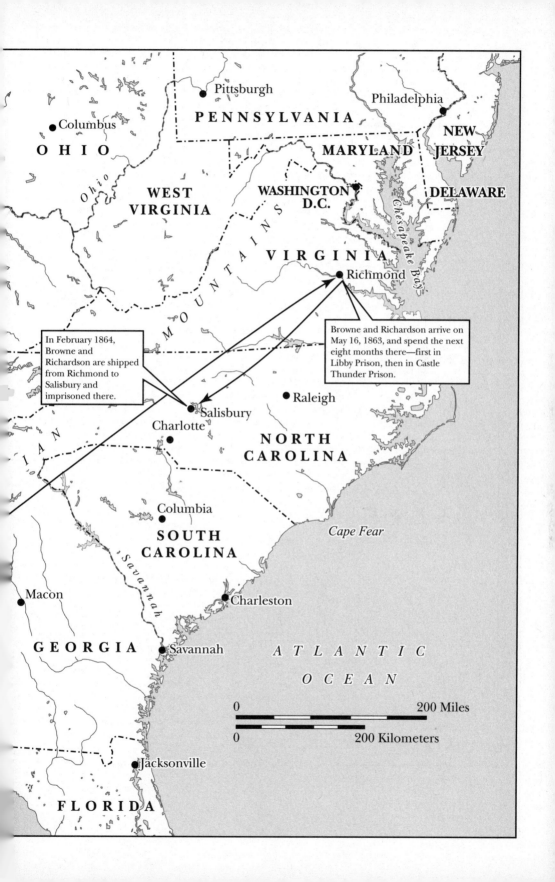

In February 1864, Browne and Richardson are shipped from Richmond to Salisbury and imprisoned there.

Browne and Richardson arrive on May 16, 1863, and spend the next eight months there—first in Libby Prison, then in Castle Thunder Prison.

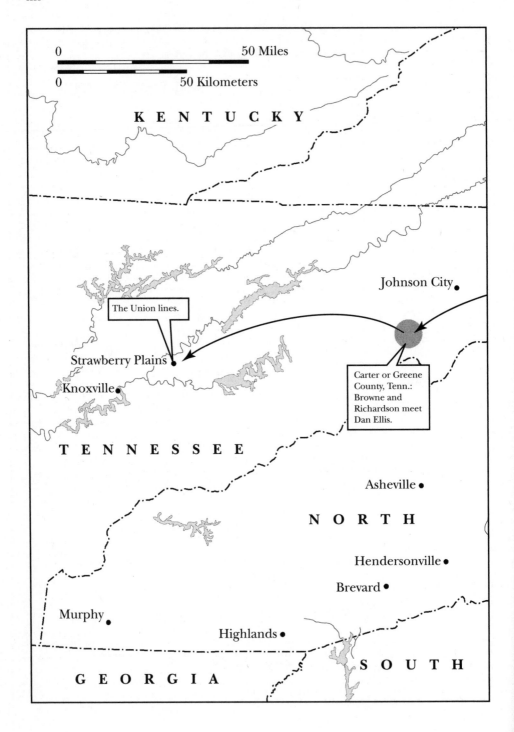

0 50 Miles

0 50 Kilometers

K E N T U C K Y

Johnson City

The Union lines.

Strawberry Plains

Knoxville

Carter or Greene
County, Tenn.:
Browne and
Richardson meet
Dan Ellis.

T E N N E S S E E

Asheville

N O R T H

Hendersonville

Brevard

Murphy

Highlands

S O U T H

G E O R G I A

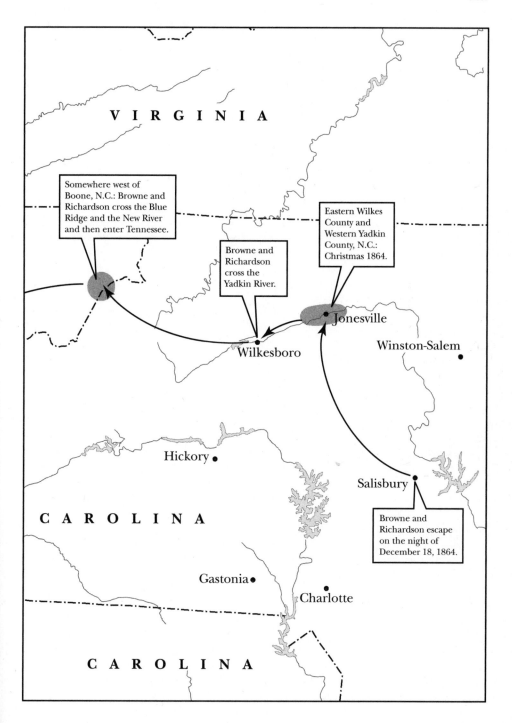

Somewhere west of Boone, N.C.: Browne and Richardson cross the Blue Ridge and the New River and then enter Tennessee.

Eastern Wilkes County and Western Yadkin County, N.C.: Christmas 1864.

Browne and Richardson cross the Yadkin River.

VIRGINIA

Jonesville

Winston-Salem

Wilkesboro

Hickory

Salisbury

CAROLINA

Browne and Richardson escape on the night of December 18, 1864.

Gastonia

Charlotte

CAROLINA

PART 1:
BATTLEFIELDS

1

A MAGNIFICENT MAN-TRAP

S OON THE GREAT BATTLE would begin, and Browne and
Richardson were determined not to miss it. They'd seen many
battles but they'd missed others, including Shiloh, arriving too
late to witness the fighting and reduced to writing moody descriptions of the forlorn battlefield—the trees pockmarked with bullet
holes, the ground strewn with hats, boots, broken guns, and, of
course, rows of fresh graves, some of them ripped open by animals
who dragged dead soldiers through the dirt and tore at their uniforms to get the fresh meat.

Albert Richardson and Junius Browne were reporters for the *New
York Tribune*, Horace Greeley's newspaper. Both were 29 years old,
and they'd been friends for a decade. Albert was stocky and strong,
with a close-cropped beard and a serious face that masked a droll wit.
Junius was scrawny and prematurely bald, a bookish intellectual with
jug ears and a caustic sense of humor.

On May 3, 1863, they linked up at the Union army encampment in
Milliken's Bend, a boggy backwater on the Mississippi, 25 miles north
of Vicksburg. A couple weeks earlier, General Grant's army had

marched to Grand Gulf, Mississippi, 50 miles south of Vicksburg, the Confederate stronghold that Grant was preparing to attack. As everyone on both sides knew, if Grant could capture Vicksburg the Union would control the Mississippi River, and cut the Confederacy in half.

Whatever might happen there, Vicksburg would be among the war's most important battles, so Richardson and Browne needed to get to Grand Gulf. The two possible routes were both exceedingly dangerous. They could walk 75 miles south through the swamps on the Louisiana side of the Mississippi, then cross the river to Grand Gulf, which would take three days, assuming they made it past the Rebel snipers hiding in the marshes, eager to shoot passing Yankees. The alternative was to hitch a ride on one of the boats that set out from Milliken's Bend at night, ferrying supplies to Grant's army. That route was quicker—only about eight hours—but the boats had to float past Vicksburg, where batteries of Confederate cannon were waiting to blow them to bits. .

Both routes were frightening, so Richardson and Browne tried to evaluate the odds. They'd heard that 15 Union boats had attempted to steam past the Rebel guns and that 10 or 12 of them had reached Grand Gulf unscathed, so they figured their chances were reasonably good. And there was another factor: Riding down the river past Rebel cannons would make a far more exciting story than plodding through the Louisiana mud. After two years of war reporting, they'd slogged through enough mud to last a lifetime. They located a tugboat captain who was planning to drag two barges of hay down the river that night and he invited them to come along. Another reporter—Richard Colburn of the *New York World*—agreed to accompany them.

As they waited for nightfall, the three reporters encountered Sylvanus Cadwallader of the *Chicago Times* and urged him to join their expedition. Cadwallader was skeptical. Floating past cannons on a barge packed with highly combustible hay bales seemed like an invitation to incineration. Cadwallader decided to take his chances with the mud. He borrowed an army mule and headed south through Louisiana. He spent the night listening as the cannons of Vicksburg boomed, and wondering if his friends would make it past them.

★

THE TUGBOAT LEFT Milliken's Bend a couple hours before midnight. The *Sturges* was a steam-powered tug that hauled two massive barges stuffed with bales of hay, as well as 32 soldiers from an Ohio infantry unit and the three reporters. A bright moon hovered overhead and a gentle breeze stirred the spring air. It was a perfect night for a romantic river cruise with a beautiful woman but a terrible one for sneaking past Confederate cannons under cover of darkness. There was precious little darkness and no cover: The full moon lit the sky and shimmered off the water, illuminating the *Sturges* as it chugged slowly south towards Vicksburg, dragging the barges behind.

Perched atop bales, the reporters made a disconcerting discovery: Although their barge was filled with hay that exploding shells could easily ignite, it carried only two small buckets for firefighting—and not even a single lifeboat.

"This is a magnificent man-trap," Browne said, before quickly shrugging off the danger. "But the greater the risk, the more interesting the adventure, I suppose."

The three lit cigars and started joking about their predicament. If they were killed, somebody suggested, maybe they could cover the story of their own deaths for a newspaper in heaven.

Scoffing at death was the code of the "Bohemian Brigade"—the tongue-in-cheek name that Junius Browne and other Northern war correspondents had coined to describe themselves. A self-conscious romantic, Browne reveled in the idea that they were "knights of the quill," swashbuckling poet-warriors living "a nomadic, careless, half-literary, half-vagabondish life." They traveled into the hell of battle and returned to tell the tale, risking their lives "purely from a love of adventure—to have the experience—which is a very natural desire of the poetico-philosophical temperament." During the tedious days between battles, Browne and his fellow reporters—most of them not quite as "poetico-philosophical" as he was—killed time drinking, telling stories, and concocting a semi-serious code for their fictitious Brigade: Bohemians would suffer all necessary privations without grumbling, laugh at danger, and try to extract as much fun as possible out of the grim business of war.

As the barge floated south, a Union officer produced a bottle of Catawba wine and ceremoniously sliced off the top with his sword. He poured the wine into a cup, and he and the reporters passed it around, drinking toasts to the success of their mission, to victory at Vicksburg, and to the women they loved. They drank and smoked and waited for the inevitable bombardment.

It began after midnight, as the tug and its barges rounded a peninsula just north of Vicksburg and the reporters noticed that the trees had been shaved from the shore to give the cannoneers an unobstructed view of their targets. First, Rebels on the Louisiana side of the river fired their rifles, signaling to the batteries downstream that a Yankee boat was approaching. Ten minutes later came the boom of the first cannon, then many more. The Confederate gunners had honed their aim on previous nights; one of the first shells slammed into the second barge—the one that wasn't occupied—and exploded with a blast that ignited the hay.

"Well done for the Rebels," Browne muttered.

More cannons roared, some so close that the reporters could see flames jump from the barrels. The Mississippi twisted like a snake outside Vicksburg, and as the tug chugged and puffed around the bends it seemed as if the cannon blasts were coming from left and right, front and rear, all at the same time.

Richardson burrowed into the hay, hoping the bales would cushion him from cannonballs, but he popped his head up periodically to watch the cannons firing and the shells shrieking across the sky. The spectacle reminded him of Tennyson's popular ode to the Crimean War's doomed Light Brigade:

> *Cannon to right of them,*
> *Cannon to left of them,*
> *Cannon in front of them*
> *Volley'd and thunder'd;*
> *Storm'd at with shot and shell,*
> *Boldly they rode and well,*
> *Into the jaws of Death,*
> *Into the mouth of Hell*
> *Rode the six hundred.*

Squatting in the hay, Richardson watched Browne boldly standing atop the highest bale, his slender body and bald head exposed against the bright sky. *Why didn't Junius take cover? Was he brave or crazy?* A shell exploded nearby, and Browne collapsed. Albert attempted to ask his friend if he was all right, but his voice failed to function. He thought about reaching for Browne in the darkness but feared that his fingers would find only mutilated flesh. Finally, Junius spoke, announcing sheepishly that he'd slipped and fallen, and Richardson relaxed.

On shore, the cannons kept firing, their muzzle flashes now shrouded in the acrid smoke that hung over the riverbank like a morning fog. Between blasts, the reporters listened for the wheezing, puffing sound of the tug chugging down the river. As long as they could hear it they dared to think they might survive. They were south of Vicksburg now, almost beyond the range of the cannons. In ten minutes, they'd be safe, and could start joking about how scared they'd been. But a shell streaked out of the sky and smashed into the tug, exploding in its steam engine, killing the captain and spewing boiling water over his crew. As the burned men shrieked, fiery coals blasted out of the boiler and ignited the hay in the barges. From the shore came the sound of Rebels cheering.

Scalded soldiers leaped into the river, and the reporters threw them bales of hay to use as life rafts. Richardson and Colburn tried to stomp out the fires, but the flames, spitting sparks, leaped in great sheets. Richardson could see Browne, still standing atop the highest bale like a statue on a pedestal, observing the bombardment with the careless ease of a man watching a Fourth of July fireworks display. Albert hollered to his friend to come down to a safer perch, but Browne, who liked to think of himself as a stoic fatalist, calmly pointed out that in the present circumstances no safe places seemed to be available.

The Rebels' cannons kept blasting, and the barge, no longer pulled by the tug, spun in slow circles. The men had no idea where to seek safety.

"Which direction is Vicksburg?" Richardson yelled.

"There," Browne said, pointing into the smoke.

Richardson disagreed. "I think it must be on the other shore."

"Oh, no," Browne insisted. "Wait a moment and you'll see the flash of the guns."

He was right. A moment later, the cannons sent more shells arcing towards them. Richardson dropped behind a bale for safety, and found himself worrying whether his voice had betrayed how frightened he was. Around him, burned and wounded soldiers groaned and leaped into the river.

"Let's take to the water," Richardson yelled.

He climbed onto the railing and looked down. The muddy Mississippi was 10 or 12 feet below. He threw himself in and climbed aboard the bale Browne and Colburn tossed him. He yanked off his boots, tied them to the bale with his watch chain, and began floating south.

Lying on his back, Richardson stared into the sky and watched a shell arching towards him. The sight amazed him. He'd heard wounded soldiers swear they'd seen the shots that hit them, but he had never believed it. Now he saw it himself: A round, smooth, shining black cannon ball was heading right for him. It plunged into the water just a few feet away, the splash knocking him off his bale. Astonished to be alive, he scrambled back on.

Still on the barge, Browne and Colburn watched all this in horror. Then they hurled a couple of bales into the river, jumped in after them, and soon all three reporters were floating slowly downstream. Colburn and Browne, who were close enough to talk about their next move, decided to ride the bales until they were out of danger, then swim to the Louisiana shore and hike south. Richardson, separated from his friends, began tearing up the letters he carried with him, some of them from high-ranking Union officers, so that he wouldn't be caught carrying them if he were captured.

WHEN THE CANNONS STOPPED FIRING, the Confederates dispatched a boat to capture any Yankees who might have survived the bombardment. The Rebels quickly scooped up Richardson and a half-dozen soldiers. They deposited their captives on shore, under guard, then rowed back to pick up more survivors. When the boat returned, Richardson was relieved to see that Browne and Colburn were aboard.

The reporters counted the survivors and learned that only 16 of the 32 soldiers were still alive, and several were badly burned, their scalded skin hanging off their faces as they moaned in agony.

It was past two o'clock in the morning as the Confederate soldiers marched their prisoners through the darkness towards Vicksburg, two miles away. The reporters were soaking wet but unharmed, although Browne hobbled along bare-footed because he'd lost his shoes in the river. It was a pathetic parade of dirty, dripping, forlorn men, and Browne, whose thoughts turned often to classical allusions, joked that they looked like "Charon's ferrymen on a strike for higher wages."

Plodding along, Browne and Richardson conferred in hushed whispers about what to tell their captors. Should they admit that they were

Tribune reporters or should they pretend to work for a less loathed journal? The *New York Tribune* was the most famous and controversial newspaper in America, despised by Confederates for its tireless abolitionist crusading and its famous editorial, printed not long after the war began, demanding that President Lincoln immediately dispatch the army to conquer the Confederate capitol: "TO RICHMOND! TO RICHMOND ONWARD!" A few months earlier, Richardson had interviewed three captured Confederate officers and asked, "What would you do with a *Tribune* correspondent if you captured him?" Their reply was quick and unequivocal: "We would hang him upon the nearest sapling." Although the memory of that exchange was chilling, Richardson and Browne decided that their captors would soon discover their true identity, so they might as well admit it.

When they reached Vicksburg, a Confederate officer recorded their names and other pertinent information, and Colburn, playing the role of Bohemian jester, said, "I hope, sir, that you will give us comfortable quarters."

"We will do the best we can for you," the officer replied dryly.

Their best turned out to be the yard behind the city jail, a foul stretch of dirt bisected by a ditch that served as an open sewer. As the first rays of dawn illuminated their new home, the reporters met their fellow prisoners, a ragged collection of local miscreants, some white, some black, all of them filthy.

"What did you come down here for?" one young prisoner asked. "To steal our niggers?"

2

VERY PERILOUS BUSINESS

JUNIUS BROWNE AND ALBERT RICHARDSON were old friends who'd shared many adventures, in peace as well as war.

They met in 1853 when they were 19-year-old reporters for rival Cincinnati newspapers covering a Democratic Party gathering at Niagara Falls. They bunked in a hotel room so crammed with delegates and reporters that Browne slept on a table and Richardson stretched out on the floor. Waking the next morning, Richardson noticed that Browne was traveling with a copy of Dante's *Divine Comedy*. He struck up a conversation, and the two men headed off to breakfast to continue it. They had much in common: They were both born in the same month, October, of the same year, 1833; they both loved literature, art, and theatre. And they'd both become newspapermen because they longed for lives more adventurous than the ones their fathers had envisioned for them.

"Before the end of the first day of our acquaintance," Browne later recalled, "we felt as if we'd known each other for years."

Junius Henri Browne grew up in Cincinnati, a skinny, gawky kid who loved to read. The son of a prosperous banker, he attended

St. Xavier College, a Jesuit institution for boys aged 8 to 16. The family was Protestant, but Junius's father wanted his son to receive a classical education and he believed that the famously rigorous Jesuits would provide it. They did. At St. Xavier, the school day began at eight in the morning and concluded at 7:15 in the evening with a "moral lecture." Classes included calculus, chemistry, astronomy, surveying, bookkeeping, ethics, metaphysics, Greek, Latin, and French. Students read Cicero and Tacitus in Latin, Homer and Demosthenes in Greek. Classes in moral philosophy were conducted in Latin. Browne served as recording secretary of the Philopedean Society, a debating club that helped prepare him for a lifetime spent expressing his opinions frequently and forcefully. If the Jesuits had hoped to convert Junius to Catholicism, they failed; they produced instead a devout skeptic who questioned nearly everything from the Holy Bible to holy matrimony. When Junius graduated at 16 with honors in chemistry, mathematics, and moral philosophy, he went to work at his father's bank, a job he detested. Like most young men who describe their temperaments as "poetico-philosophical," he found banking dreary. He quit after two years to work in a trade that has traditionally served as a refuge for the skeptical, the curious, the opinionated, the semi-adventurous, the quasi-literary, and the vaguely talented—journalism.

At St. Xavier, Junius was known by his family's name—Brown—but when he became a reporter, he changed the spelling to Browne, the extra "e" adding a little panache, a certain savoir faire that set him apart from the hordes of prosaic non-e Browns who were so common across America.

Junius was among the few reporters—in Cincinnati or anywhere else—who studied philosophy for fun. He read the Stoics of ancient Greece and the essayists of the French Enlightenment, and even the Vedas, the ancient Hindu scriptures. His friend Albert Richardson had memorized huge swaths of Shakespeare, but he thought the idea of voluntarily reading the Vedas was hilarious, and he loved kidding Junius about it.

Albert Deane Richardson was a handsome, tawny-haired, idealistic young man who grew up in Franklin, Massachusetts, on a farm that had been tilled by seven generations of his ancestors—"the straightest sect of Puritans," as he called them. His parents hoped that Albert would become a farmer, but the boy was more interested in reading than in plowing or harvesting. Inspired by romantic tales of pioneers exploring the mountains, forests, and deserts of the American frontier, Albert left home at 17, and headed west. His first stop was Pittsburgh, where he found work as a reporter and wrote comic skits for a local theatre group. After a year, he continued west, to Cincinnati, where he grew a beard and worked for the *Sun,* covering murder trials, political campaigns, and other gloriously unsavory spectacles.

Cincinnati, a feisty port city on the Ohio River, supported several newspapers, and young reporters like Richardson and Browne bounced from one to another. After work, they hung around taverns to drink with their cronies, talk shop, swap books, and argue about politics, literature, and women. The most controversial political issue of the day was slavery, particularly in Cincinnati, where escaped slaves fleeing Kentucky frequently sought refuge, and where the slave-catchers sent to retrieve them sometimes battled with local abolitionists. Browne and Richardson argued passionately for abolition. It was something else they had in common.

Browsing in a local bookshop one day, Richardson met Mary Louise Pease, the 19-year-old daughter of the shop's owner. Nicknamed "Lou," she was pretty and sharp and funny, and she loved books as much as he did. Albert was smitten. So was Lou. Soon after they began keeping company, Lou was pregnant. On October 6, 1855, they married in Cincinnati's First Unitarian Church. Four months later, Lou gave birth to a son and the young parents named him Leander Pease Richardson.

Browne, who seldom missed an opportunity to joke about the similarities between matrimony and imprisonment, no doubt teased Richardson about his new role as paterfamilias. But Richardson didn't let marriage imprison him or curtail his longing for western adventure. In 1857, he took a job as a correspondent for the *Boston Journal* and moved his family to Kansas so he could cover the most important story of the era—the battles between pro-slavery and "Free Soil" settlers in what became known as "Bleeding Kansas."

THE BLEEDING RESULTED from the Kansas-Nebraska Act of 1854, which gave citizens of the two territories the right to vote on whether to permit slavery. The act sparked an influx of immigrants into Kansas. First came slaveholders from the Southern states, including the so-called "Border Ruffians" from Missouri. Then

New England abolitionists bankrolled thousands of antislavery settlers. Both sides were armed. Henry Ward Beecher—the famous abolitionist preacher and brother of Harriet Beecher Stowe, author of
Uncle Tom's Cabin—raised money to provide the Northerners with
Sharps rifles, which became known as "Beecher's Bibles." Inevitably,
fighting erupted, with massacres and atrocities on both sides. Soon,
Kansas split and two rival governments formed, one pro-slavery, one
"Free Soil," each claiming legitimacy, each with its own legislature,
constitution, and governor.

Richardson settled Lou and Leander in a two-room cottonwood
cabin in the tiny settlement of Sumner and traveled the state on
horseback, searching for stories. He found plenty. Bleeding Kansas
was paradise for an ambitious reporter. Richardson covered countless
speeches, rallies, and conventions, some of them ending in shootouts
between pro- and antislavery mobs. In Leavenworth, in 1857, he
watched a mob batter down the door of a jail, drag out a prisoner, and
hang him from a cottonwood tree. "For a moment, the poor wretch
clutched the rope above his head, lifting himself up," Richardson reported, "but a heavy ruffian caught him by the feet, his grasp gave
way, and he never struggled again."

Richardson didn't merely report the story of Bleeding Kansas, he
also served as secretary to one of the state's two legislatures, the one
controlled by "Free Soil" forces. In those days, such political moon-
lighting was not considered an outrageous violation of journalistic
ethics because the concept of journalistic ethics had not yet been invented; the idea that a reporter might support a political cause surprised nobody. When the legislature repealed the pro-slavery laws
enacted by the state's rival legislature, Richardson rejoiced. "The bogus laws are formally repealed and wiped from our statute books,
thank God!" he wrote to his brother Charles, who edited a religious
publication called *The Congregationalist* in Boston. "A huge bonfire of
tar barrels was kindled in front of the Eldridge House, and a copy of
them was publicly burned amid the jubilant shouts of the crowd."

Chasing news, Richardson rode back and forth through sweltering
days, freezing nights, rain, snow, and the wind that seemed to blow
constantly across the prairie. He spent so much time on horseback
that he learned to take naps in the saddle, while his horse ambled
along. When night fell, he frequently found himself far from home, or a
hotel, so he followed the custom of the territory and knocked on the

door of a farmhouse. Farmers on the frontier were usually eager for guests who could entertain them with news of the outside world. One cold, rainy night when he knocked at a log cabin, he found it occupied by a family of Indians. They welcomed him. As he warmed his wet body by the fire, he watched a young mother, her baby feeding at her breast, light a foot-long pipe. She took a few puffs, and then passed it to the baby's grandmother. It wasn't the kind of thing he had seen while growing up among the Puritans of Franklin, Massachusetts. A few weeks later, traveling in the same area with his wife and son, Richardson stopped at the same cabin and his whole family spent the night with his Indian acquaintances.

Richardson liked the people of the West. They were warmer, more outgoing and demonstrative than the taciturn, poker-faced New Englanders he'd grown up among. "The New England ways are cold ways," he wrote in a letter to his brother's wife, Jennie. "New England is like a wet blanket to me." But he knew—because his wife frequently reminded him—that he, too, was a taciturn New Englander who seldom exhibited much emotion.

"I wish you would manifest a little excitement on *some* subject," Lou would tease him, "just for variety's sake."

☆

IN 1858, PROSPECTORS DISCOVERED gold near Pikes Peak, in the Rocky Mountains and thousands of Americans headed there, many in wagons bearing signs reading "Pikes Peak or Bust." Smelling a good story, Richardson boarded a westbound stagecoach in Leavenworth on May 25, 1859, eager to cover the gold rush.

For two days, Richardson was the only passenger in the coach, but when the stage stopped in Manhattan, Kansas, a strange-looking gentleman stepped aboard. His bespectacled face was clean-shaven, but a fringe of white whiskers hung from the underside of his chin, making him look a bit like a billygoat, albeit a professorial one. He wore a white suit, a white hat, and a long white linen coat. He was the most famous, influential, and controversial newspaperman in America— Horace Greeley.

Greeley was the editor of the *New York Tribune*, but his fame and fortune came not so much from the daily edition of the paper, which could be purchased only around New York, but from the weekly edition, which circulated across the country. The newspaper was particularly popular in the West, where settlers papered the walls of their cabins with its pages, a practice that encouraged visitors to indulge in a custom known as "reading the walls." Many of the words in Greeley's papers were Greeley's own. The editor was a man of endless opinions, most of them idealistic, many of them eccentric. Over the years he had crusaded against slavery, alcohol, and gambling, and in favor of vegetarianism, spiritualism, and the use of human manure as a fertilizer. To his many detractors, he was a blowhard and a crackpot. To Albert Richardson, he was a hero, the man who published America's best newspaper.

Famous for popularizing the phrase "Go west, young man," Greeley was making his first western trip when he settled himself into the stagecoach and shook Richardson's hand. For the next nine days, the two men traveled across the plains at the rate of about 50 miles a day. When they stopped for the night in small towns, the residents inevitably asked the visiting sage to make a speech, and Greeley, a natural ham, was happy to oblige.

One afternoon, three Cheyenne braves on horseback raced up to the stagecoach. They were friendly, but they spooked the mules pulling the stage. In a panic, the mules galloped down a steep hill and the coach flipped over and crashed. Richardson and the driver leaped to safety, but Greeley, trapped, bounced around until the carriage hit the dirt. He crawled out, bleeding from his head, arms, and legs.

When the stage reached Denver a few days later, Greeley decided to rest his battered body. Denver was a scraggily gold rush boomtown where about 150 crude shacks housed a few hundred scruffy prospectors, most of whom wore knives and guns dangling from their belts. Greeley and Richardson took a room in The Denver House, the best hotel in town. The log building was topped with a canvas roof and contained six bedrooms separated by cotton walls, and a larger room that served as a bar and gambling emporium. Greeley reported that he found sleeping there difficult due to frequent outbursts of gunfire.

When the locals learned of the celebrity in their midst, they urged Greeley to make a speech. Despite his wounds, the editor bowed to popular demand and delivered an impromptu oration in the Denver House barroom. "On one side, the tipplers at the bar silently sipped their grog," Richardson reported. "On the other, the gamblers respectfully suspended the shuffling of cards and the counting of money from their huge piles of coin, while Mr. Greeley, standing between them, made a strong anti-drinking and anti-gambling address, which was received with perfect good humor."

Richardson was a charming traveling companion, and by the time he and Greeley parted ways, the venerable editor had hired the young reporter to cover the West for the *Tribune*. Thrilled to write for America's most important newspaper, Richardson escorted his wife and son to his family's farm in Massachusetts, then turned around and headed back to the West. He spent nearly a year roaming Texas, Oklahoma, Colorado, and New Mexico, writing about prospectors, Comanches, three-card monte hustlers, land swindlers, wagon trains, Kit Carson, prairie dog towns, and antelope, which he described as "the best living illustration of poetry in motion."

Albert also noted the amazing ability of American pioneers to look at their scruffy, dusty little outposts and see the glorious cities of the future: "Congregate a hundred Americans anywhere beyond the settlements," he wrote, "and they immediately lay out a city, frame a State constitution and apply for admission to the Union, while twenty-five of them become candidates for the United States Senate."

IN THE FALL OF 1860, Richardson returned to his family's farm in Massachusetts to spend the winter months with Lou and Leander and his newborn daughter, Maude. Abraham Lincoln had just been elected president, and the Southern states began seceding from the Union—South Carolina on December 20, then Mississippi, Florida, Alabama, Georgia, and Louisiana in January. By the time Texas seceded on February 1, Richardson was itching to end his family holiday and head out to cover what he knew would be the biggest story of his lifetime. He wrote to Greeley, volunteering to go south to report on the secession crisis. It was a dangerous assignment for any Northern reporter, particularly one from the hated abolitionist *Tribune*, and Albert traveled to New York to plead his case in person.

It was his first trip to the *Tribune*'s Manhattan headquarters, a five-story building topped with a huge *Tribune* logo and an American flag. Inside, he climbed the circular iron staircase to the third floor, where a sign read "Editorial Rooms of the Tribune. Ring the Bell." He rang, somebody peeked through a grated window, the door opened, and Richardson entered the city room, where men toiled at a dozen green desks. The walls were plastered with maps and the air reeked of printer's ink, paste, sweat, and cigar smoke. Greeley was away on a lecture tour, so Richardson poked his head into the office of Charles Dana, the *Tribune*'s managing editor, who ran the paper's day-to-day operations while Greeley pondered utopian ideas and scribbled his editorials.

Dana was a thin man with a thick black beard. When Richardson arrived, he was flipping through his daily mail, perusing letters at the rate of about one a minute.

"I received your letter," he told Richardson, without pausing in his perusing. "I suppose you know it is a rather precarious business."

"Oh, yes."

"Two of our correspondents have come home within the last week, after narrow escapes," Dana said. "We still have six in the South and it would not surprise me, this very hour, to receive a telegram announcing the imprisonment or death of any of them."

"I have thought about all that and decided."

"Then we shall be very glad to have you go," Dana said.

Dana's fears for his correspondents' safety were well founded. In November, he'd sent reporter Charles Bingham to Charleston, the hotbed of the secession movement. Eager to continue breathing, Bingham hid his connection to the *Tribune*. After his anonymous dispatches were published, the Charleston *Mercury* advocated that the *Tribune* reporter ought to be identified and lynched. In February, Charleston police arrested Bingham and interrogated him for 12 hours before expelling him from the city.

By then, Dana had already sent another reporter to Charleston. He'd also dispatched correspondents to other southeastern cities, so he sent Richardson farther west, to Memphis and New Orleans. Albert devised a cover story to conceal his identity: He was a merchant from New Mexico, traveling through the South before sailing to Vera Cruz on business. New Mexico was neutral territory in the quarrel over slavery and Richardson figured he'd spent enough time there to feign residency. He just had to remember to stifle his New England accent and his habit of using the Yankee phrase "I guess" instead of the Southern "I reckon." Like the paper's other undercover correspondents, he would mail his dispatches to a New York bank, which would forward them to the *Tribune*.

When Richardson reached Memphis, he looked up an old friend, a Northern reporter now working as an editor at a Memphis newspaper.

"What are you doing down here?" the editor asked.

"Corresponding for the *Tribune*," Richardson replied.

"How far are you going?"

"Through all the Gulf states, if possible."

"My friend, do you know you are on very perilous business?"

"Possibly," Richardson said. "But I shall be extremely prudent when I get into a hot climate."

"I don't know what you consider a hot climate," the editor replied, before pointing out how heated Memphis had become. A week earlier, a mob had shaved the heads of two Northerners suspected of being abolitionists. Before that, a man accused of helping slaves escape was lynched. "If the people in this house, and out on the street in front, knew you to be one of the *Tribune* correspondents, they would not leave you many minutes for saying your prayers."

On March 4—the day Abraham Lincoln and his vice president, Hannibal Hamlin, were inaugurated in Washington, DC—Richardson took a train to New Orleans and eavesdropped on his fellow passengers as they discussed the news of the day.

"I hope to God he will be killed before he has time to take the oath."

"I have wagered a new hat that neither he nor Hamlin will ever live to be inaugurated."

Richardson struck up a conversation with a Mississippi planter who said he'd recently spent six weeks in Wisconsin and was appalled by the ignorance of the people there. "They suppose, if war comes, we shall have trouble with our slaves," he said. "That is utterly absurd. All my negroes would fight for me."

In New Orleans, Richardson took a room at the St. Charles Hotel and strolled around town, delighting in the warm spring weather, the good strong coffee, and the friendly people. He had no trouble getting Louisianans to talk. They'd ask where he came from and he'd tell them about New Mexico and the Rocky Mountains. Within minutes they'd change the subject to the issue on everyone's mind—secession—and then all he had to do was sit back and listen. They told him that Hamlin was a mulatto, and that Lincoln was white trash, a vulgar common laborer, certainly no match for the scholarly aristocrat Jefferson Davis, who'd just become president of the Confederate States of America. They told him that slavery was necessary because only Negroes could pick cotton or cut cane in the sweltering Southern sun. And they informed him that the North couldn't survive without the South's cotton, and that the South would win any civil war because Yankees were too yellow to fight.

In the elegant barroom of the St. Charles Hotel, Albert watched a slave auction while waiters delivered drinks to the men bidding on human beings. The slaves stood in a row in front of the auctioneer's platform with numbers pinned to their clothes. The numbers corresponded to descriptions printed in a program. Number 7 was a young woman holding a baby: "7. Betty, aged 15 years, and child 4 months. No. 1. Field-hand and house servant, very likely. Fully guaranteed."

Betty and her baby sold for $1,165.

The light-skinned quadroon girls offered for sale attracted close attention from the tipsy gentlemen in the bar, who leered and snickered as they inspected the girls' arms, shoulders, and breasts.

"This girl, gentlemen, is only 15 years old," the auctioneer announced in stentorian tones. "Warranted sound in every particular. An excellent seamstress—which would make her worth a thousand dollars even if she had *no other qualifications*. She is sold for no fault, but simply because her owner must have money. No married man had better buy her. She is too handsome."

She sold for $1,100. The auction disgusted Richardson, who called it "the most utterly revolting spectacle that I have ever looked upon."

He walked to Lyceum Hall to observe Louisiana's secession convention. A pudgy former governor presided, sitting on a platform, flanked by oil paintings of George Washington and Jefferson Davis. Hanging nearby was a freshly painted portrait of the delegates to the convention, which struck Richardson as funny. "The delegates," he joked in a dispatch to the *Tribune*, "have made all the preliminary arrangements for being immortalized." The convention had already voted to secede from the United States; now the delegates debated whether to ratify the Confederate Constitution. Some delegates proposed that the people of Louisiana be permitted to vote on the new Constitution, but that democratic proposal was quickly defeated. Richardson mocked the Southern aristocrats' haughty scorn for democracy: "The idea that a laboring man with rough hands, who does not own even a single 'nigger,' should wield as much power at the ballot box as a 'high-toned' gentleman in broadcloth, who was born to govern, is utterly repugnant to their sense of the fitness of things."

Next, Richardson traveled to Jackson to observe Mississippi's convention. He wasn't impressed there, either. The delegates sprawled in their chairs, their boots propped on their desks, munching apples, smoking cigars, reading newspapers, and paying scant attention as their fellow delegates delivered long, florid orations denouncing Lincoln and the "Black Republicans." Albert didn't linger long in Jackson, fearing that the locals were getting suspicious. A traveler could sojourn in New Orleans without attracting attention, but in Jackson people distrusted strangers who hung around the convention for no apparent reason.

Back in New Orleans, Richardson chatted with a secessionist who told him there were three people he thought deserved lynching. The first was the governor of Ohio, who had refused to return a runaway slave. The second was Senator Andrew Johnson, the Tennessee Democrat who opposed his state's secession.

"And the third?" Richardson asked.

"Some infernal scoundrel who is writing abusive letters to the *Tribune* about us."

"Have you no suspicion who he is?"

"Some think it is a Kentuckian engaged in the cattle trade, but I suspect it to be a man employed at *The Picayune*. We are keeping a sharp eye on both. If we *do* catch him, I don't think he'll write many more letters."

Richardson recorded the conversation in his final dispatch from New Orleans, and added a few lines of comic commentary: "I ventured to plead a little for the Governor and the Senator, but quite agreed with my friend that the audacious scribbler ought to be suppressed. It struck me as one of those cases in which acquiescence was the better part of valor. But when you *do* catch him, Colonel, will you be good enough to let me know?"

On April 12, Confederate artillery in Charleston began shelling the Federal garrison at Fort Sumter, and Richardson decided it was time to head home. He boarded a boat bound for Mobile and noticed that three of his fellow passengers were Confederate officers traveling to Pensacola to join General Braxton Bragg's army, which was besieging the Federal forces at Fort Pickens. In a Mobile hotel, Richardson climbed the stairs to his room and encountered the same three officers. When they spotted him, they began loudly denouncing the *Tribune* and suggesting that if they caught one of its reporters they'd happily hang him from the nearest tree.

Richardson considered fleeing, but that would only confirm their suspicions, and besides, where could he go? He was on a staircase, three floors from the street. So he tried to stay calm and keep his face from showing any emotion—exactly the kind of behavior that his wife liked least. He pulled a cigar from his pocket, turned to the loudest soldier, who happened to be smoking, and casually asked for a light. Surprised, the soldier removed his cigar from his mouth, knocked the ash off with his forefinger, and handed it to Richardson, who calmly ignited his own Havana and thanked him. The soldiers walked off, and Albert retreated to his room, a good deal less serene than he had pretended. He figured he'd been unmasked, and expected to be arrested at any minute. He left the hotel, booked passage on a riverboat to Montgomery, and disappeared into his stateroom. In the afternoon, a cabin boy knocked on his door to report that Fort Sumter had surrendered. Church bells rang, cannons boomed, and crowds gathered to cheer the great victory. Richardson hunkered in his room, hoping to be overlooked.

In Montgomery, he caught a train to Atlanta, where he learned from the local newspapers that a reporter for the *New York Times* had been arrested in Charleston. In Atlanta, he boarded a train heading north. In Charleston, he saw the Confederate flag flapping over Fort Sumter and watched jubilant crowds celebrating. In Wilmington, North Carolina, somebody announced that Virginia had seceded from the Union, and the passengers cheered. Sitting alone and silent, Richardson aroused suspicions. Three men approached him.

"We have news," one of them said, "that Virginia has seceded."

"Good!" Richardson replied. "That will give us all the border states."

As the train rumbled north, a drunken passenger fired his pistol out a window, yelling "Hurrah for Jeff Davis!" Richardson stared morosely at the Confederate flags that flew in every town and listened to a passenger bloviate about how the gallant Southerners would easily crush the Yankees: "We can whip them any morning before breakfast! Throw three or four shells among those blue-bellied Yankees and they will scatter like sheep."

That did it. Until then, he'd hoped for a peaceful solution to the crisis, but now he'd heard one too many diatribes about the cowardly Yankees. He was sick of the South, sick of the threats of lynching, and disgusted with arrogant slave owners who fancied themselves aristocrats. Let the war come, he thought. It was time to find out if these Confederates really were anything more than bluster and swagger.

After several days of travel, the train crossed the Potomac and entered Washington. Richardson saw the American flag flying over the Capitol, and he realized, much to his amazement, that the sight of it had brought tears to his eyes.

Washington seethed with panic. Wild rumors circulated. Rebel armies were said to be outside the city, ready to attack, and residents fled to the countryside. President Lincoln issued a call for troops to defend Washington, and when the 6th Massachusetts Volunteer Militia passed through Baltimore en route to the capital, a mob opened fire on them, killing four soldiers and wounding 36. The soldiers fired back, killing 11 rioters.

Richardson caught a night train to Baltimore, and found the city swarming with bands of armed Rebels. Union supporters were hiding or fleeing. A Rebel mob had torn up the railroad tracks that led north, so Richardson hired a carriage to take him to York, Pennsylvania, where he managed to catch a train to New York.

When he arrived in Manhattan, he hustled to the *Tribune* office and learned that he was the last of the newspaper's undercover Southern correspondents to reach New York. Somehow, they'd all made it back safely.

Now that the Civil War was a reality, Greeley and Dana devised a new assignment for Richardson: He would be the *Tribune*'s chief correspondent in the western theatre of the war, covering stories himself while leading a team of other reporters. Richardson set up an office in Cairo, Illinois, and started hiring correspondents. Among the first he picked was his old friend from Cincinnati—Junius Henri Browne.

3

NO ONE HERE SEEMS TO HAVE ANY KNOWLEDGE ABOUT ANYTHING

DISPATCHED BY ALBERT RICHARDSON, Junius Browne arrived in Jefferson City, Missouri, in September 1861. He wandered around, slogging through streets slathered with a thick slush of mud and horse manure churned by the hooves of the Union cavalry that galloped back and forth, trying desperately to look like a fearsome fighting force. Aside from the cavalry, and some infantry training nearby, nothing was happening. Jefferson City was the capital of Missouri, but the governor had fled and so had the legislature and many of the residents.

Browne wondered what he was supposed to do. He failed to see anything that might interest the readers of his new employer, the *New York Tribune*. Unlike Richardson, Junius was not a natural reporter. Albert could walk into any situation, effortlessly mingle with all types of people, and come away with whatever information he needed, but Browne was an intellectual who would rather read a French philosopher than interview a provincial politician, and he was too shy to master the art of mingling. He tended to stand back and watch, then describe what he observed in ironic essays packed with classical allusions. He self-mockingly described this style as "sesquipedalian fustian"—a pompous, polysyllabic way of saying that his writing was pompous and polysyllabic.

Browne was an esthete who delighted in the higher pleasures of cosmopolitan life—literature, music, drama, and opera. He also delighted in women, particularly beautiful, cultivated women who enjoyed discussing literature, music, drama, and opera. In Jefferson City, he found none of these pleasures. He couldn't locate a single book worth reading, and if there were any beautiful women in town, they were keeping themselves well hidden. Within days, he was bored, lonely, and depressed.

He considered quitting his job and slinking back home, but his pride kept him in Jefferson City. Soon, other reporters drifted into town, all of them hoping to cover a battle between the Union army and the state's Confederate militia.

Missouri was a slave state, and early in 1861, its pro-Confederate governor, Claiborne Jackson, called a secession convention. In a hall surrounded by rowdy mobs of armed Union and Confederate partisans, the convention surprised Jackson by voting not to secede—at least not "at present." A month later, when Rebels shelled Fort Sumter, President Lincoln asked America's governors to send troops to suppress the rebellion. Jackson angrily refused and instead created a pro-Confederate state militia. In June, when Federal troops seized Jefferson City, the governor fled with his militia to the southwestern corner of the state to set up a Confederate government-in-exile. On August 10, Union forces commanded by General Nathaniel Lyon attacked Jackson's militia at Wilson's Creek, but the Rebels defeated them; Lyon was killed and the Federals retreated to Jefferson City. By September, reporters were flocking to the city because they figured that the Union army, now commanded by General John C. Fremont, would soon attack the Rebels.

It didn't happen. Fremont holed up in a house in St. Louis, pondering strategy, while Browne and the other correspondents wandered Jefferson City in a fruitless search for news. Day after day, thousands of Union soldiers marched and drilled, and drilled and marched, then marched and drilled again. The reporters yawned.

Only one of the reporters had witnessed a real battle. Franc B. Wilkie, of the *New York Times*, had covered the battle of Wilson's

Creek, as well as a subsequent Confederate victory in Lexington, Missouri, where Wilkie, his belly full of wine, had walked up to a Rebel soldier, handed him his *Times* business card and, after a night in the brig, came away with an exclusive interview with Confederate General Sterling Price. Wilkie was a gruff, tough former blacksmith, and when he met Junius Browne in Jefferson City, he was appalled by the skinny little man from the *Tribune*, whom he described as "undersized, slender as a woman, with a pale, effeminate face, hands and feet as diminutive as those of a child, a sensitive mouth, and with an expression of helplessness." To Wilkie, Browne was the milquetoast son of a Cincinnati banker, a pathetic excuse for a war correspondent who was likely to fall apart at the first sign of battle.

Browne might not have disputed that assessment. As he watched a funeral procession rumble through Jefferson City—the dead man a soldier who'd succumbed to some camp-borne illness—Browne found himself getting teary at the thought of how the poor lad had died far from home without his loving mother there to smooth his pillow or kiss his fevered brow. He realized his reaction was pathetic: If the mere sight of a closed coffin could reduce him to blubbering sentimentality, what would happen when he saw scores of soldiers blown to bits in battle?

The problem was hypothetical, though, because no battle was imminent. The correspondents had little to do but sit around drinking, smoking, playing cards, and telling stories. "We had considerable leisure, and amused ourselves as best we could," Browne reported. "We smoked pipes, played whist, discussed Poetry, Metaphysics, Art, the Opera, Women, the World, the War and its future."

Bored, the correspondents began jokingly calling themselves the "Bohemian Brigade." Browne may not have coined the phrase but he embraced it, writing a semi-serious definition of the Bohemian: "an ill-fated fellow of aesthetic and luxurious tastes, born out of place, and in opposition to his circumstances—who assumes indifference to all things and scoffs because he cannot smile."

Browne loved the notion of the Bohemian Brigade, and he adopted a world-weary cynicism that the more perceptive Bohemians recognized as a mask designed to hide a sensitive soul. When the talk turned to women, as it often did, Browne proclaimed himself a man of the world, uninterested in domestic bliss. Women were "works of art," he said, but marriage ruined them, turning charming creatures into

"domestic drudges." He noted sardonically that the married Bohemians seemed to be enjoying their escape from the so-called pleasures of
hearth and home. Browne thought about women frequently. In the
male world of war, they were scarce, and he missed them: "I often wondered how men fond of women managed to endure." He seldom passed
up an opportunity to talk to women, and when that wasn't possible, he
talked *about* them—their beauty, their fickleness, their frightening
ability to beguile a man's mind. He often sounded like a wounded romantic, a man who'd somehow been injured in *amour*. Had some two-
timing Jezebel broken his heart? Or was it simply that the belles of
Cincinnati failed to swoon for scrawny, balding intellectuals who enjoyed reading French philosophers and mocking marriage?

One day in Jefferson City, Browne interviewed a forlorn young soldier who revealed that his fiancé had informed him that she'd fallen in
love with another man. The soldier told Browne that at first he'd
planned to kill himself, but now he'd devised a more creative ploy: In
his first battle, he would charge the Rebels in a manner certain to result in death, thus ending his heartache while ensuring that he'd be
forever remembered—by relatives, friends and, of course, his wayward
fiancé—as a courageous war hero.

Browne smiled and told the soldier that he was crazy to think of
dying for a silly, fickle woman. Instead, he should rejoice because he'd
managed to escape the horrors of matrimony.

The soldier asked Browne how he'd become so cynical so young.

"Through observation and reason," Junius replied.

E ARLY IN OCTOBER 1861, Albert Richardson arrived in Jefferson
City, convinced that he "smelled" the coming of battle. His nose had
failed him: The army remained idle, and Richardson was compelled to
join Browne and the other Bohemians in their ceaseless pursuit of
amusement. Now numbering more than a dozen, the bored reporters
rented six rooms in what Richardson described as "a wretched little tavern" and behaved "like boys let out of school." They drank. They sang.
They wrestled. They raced their horses across the rolling hills outside
the city and inevitably some of them tumbled off their mounts and
knocked themselves silly. One reporter dislocated a shoulder and went
home injured before he'd heard a single shot fired in battle.

With nothing else to write about, some reporters penned comic accounts of their high jinks, which explains how the *Cincinnati Gazette* happened to cover a pillow fight sparked by one of Junius Browne's periodic rants about marriage:

> Happening to drop in the other night, I found the representatives of *The Missouri Republican*, *The Cincinnati Commercial*, *The New York World*, and *The Tribune* engaged in a hot discussion upon matrimony, which finally ran into metaphysics. *The Republican* having plumply disputed an abstruse proposition of *The Tribune*, the latter seized an immense bolster, and brought it down with emphasis upon the glossy pate of his antagonist. This instantly broke up the debate, and a general melee commenced. *The Republican* grabbed a damp towel and aimed a stunning blow at his assailant, which missed him and brought up against the nasal protuberance of *Frank Leslie's Weekly*. The exasperated *Frank* dealt back a pillow, followed by a well-packed knapsack.

At the time, this pillow fight was the closet thing to battle that Browne, and most of the other reporters, had yet experienced.

Finally General John C. Fremont rode out from St. Louis to take command of the army. Nicknamed "The Pathfinder" for his famous explorations of the West in the 1840s, Fremont became the Republican Party's first candidate for president, running in 1856 on the slogan "Free Soil, Free Men and Fremont." In his St. Louis mansion, plotting strategy, "he sat in a room in full uniform with his maps before him," recalled Fremont's most able underling, Ulysses S. Grant. "When you went in, he would point out one line or another in a mysterious manner, never asking you to take a seat. You left without the least idea of what he meant or what he wanted you to do."

In August, Fremont issued a proclamation freeing all slaves owned by Confederate sympathizers in Missouri. The proclamation delighted abolitionists, but angered Abraham Lincoln, who hoped to retain the loyalty of slave owners in the border states. Lincoln ordered Fremont to rescind it. Fremont refused, and sent his wife to Washington to negotiate with the president.

In early October, Fremont emerged from his mansion and traveled to the Jefferson City encampment. After a week of preparations, he marched his army towards southwestern Missouri, presumably to attack the Confederate militia there.

Eager to witness warfare at last, Richardson, Browne, and the other Bohemians tagged along, traveling on horseback and sleeping in tents provided by the army. Browne, an urban creature fond of civilized comforts, failed to appreciate the charms of camping.

One rainy night, a reporter in Browne's tent began to itch. He scratched, then scratched again and again. He yanked off his shirt and spotted dozens of little black dots that turned out to be fleas. He ripped off the rest of his clothes and slapped furiously at the pests. At this point, the other Bohemians noticed that they, too, were itching. Soon, they were all naked, swearing and slapping. Outside the tent, thunder crashed and heavy rain fell, which gave Browne an idea. Naked as a newborn, he fled the infested tent, hopped on his horse, and galloped off through the countryside, letting the downpour wash the fleas from his body. It was a grand operatic gesture and it worked—at least for a while.

ON OCTOBER 25, Fremont's cavalry captured the town of Springfield in a brief skirmish that surprised not only the Confederates but also the Bohemians, who somehow missed it. The disappointed reporters reassured themselves that they couldn't possibly miss the grand clash of armies that would surely come within days. But a week passed and Fremont still hadn't attacked.

He never would.

A few days later, on November 2, a courier arrived at Fremont's tent bearing a message from the White House: The president had fired the general. The next day, Fremont's replacement, General David Hunter, arrived and marched the army back towards Jefferson City.

The abrupt retreat incensed the Bohemians, who grumbled that the damn generals were spoiling their chance to cover the damn war. On the long ride back to St. Louis, Browne and a reporter for the *St. Louis Democrat* encountered two women. They were young and educated and adventurous enough to be riding alone across what was, at least theoretically, a war zone. They, too, were heading for St. Louis, so they all traveled together.

"Quite Bohemianish, and certainly fond of adventure were these fair girls, who frequently regretted they were not men, that they might be emancipated from the narrowness Society imposed upon them," Browne wrote. "My journalistic companion and myself explained to them the character of the Bohemian Brigade, and with their full permission, elected them honorary members of that unique society. The girls and we duo of Bohemians had a good deal of amusement in riding, walking, fording creeks and rivers, and exploding, to our satisfaction, the multifarious shams of modern society and present-day custom. Our journeying was romantic, and certainly agreeable after our long absence from feminine society."

Despite that pleasant interlude, Browne and the other reporters reached St. Louis in a morose mood. Once again there was nothing to do. Not surprisingly, the Bohemians began drinking and misbehaving.

"The idleness of the place was demoralizing," Wilkie recalled.

> People drank who never drank before. I remember on one occasion that the gentle, inoffensive Junius Henri Browne— the very incarnation of all the milder virtues, who would go a long distance around rather than step on a fly—became a trifle excited after a rather bountiful dinner, and at once became transformed into a pirate, a John L. Sullivan, a would-be shoulder-hitter. He doubled his hands into fierce fists as large as those of a ten-year-old child. He braced back his shoulders, drew his little slouch hat down so that it covered one eye, and with savagely set jaws, swaggered about, clamoring for someone to tread on his coat-tail, and announced his ability to "mop" the boulevards with anybody and everybody in the hateful city. If it be true that *in vino veritas*, then at heart the suave, inoffensive, exquisitely polite little gentleman is a fighter, a belligerent.

★

IN FRANKLIN, Massachusetts, on January 26, 1862, Albert Richardson's wife, Lou, gave birth to the couple's third child. She named the boy Albert Deane Richardson Jr. The proud father was not in attendance and had little time to celebrate. A week later, he and Browne and a gaggle of Bohemians set off from Cairo, Illinois, to cover

General Ulysses S. Grant's attack on two Confederate forts in northern Tennessee, Fort Henry and Fort Donelson.

Grant's army traveled down the Tennessee River in an armada of warships, and Richardson and Browne managed to finagle their way aboard the general's vessel. Grant landed his army just out of range of Fort Henry's cannons, and his troops marched towards the fort while Union gunboats bombarded it from the river. Recognizing that he couldn't defend the fort, Confederate General Lloyd Tilghman ordered his infantry—about 3,000 men—to retreat to Fort Donelson, some 12 miles to the east. To cover his infantry's escape, Tilghman's artillery blasted away at the Federal fleet.

Browne and Richardson went ashore with Grant's troops, slogging through swampy, flooded woods. Browne accompanied the soldiers on their march, while Richardson climbed a tall oak tree on the riverbank for a better view of the artillery battle. For an hour, the ships and the fort pounded each other with shells until the air was so full of smoke that Richardson could no longer see the gunships. When the Confederates ran up a white flag of surrender, Albert shinnied down the tree and joined the Union soldiers as they swarmed into Fort Henry.

"Our shots had made great havoc," he reported in the *Tribune*. "In the fort, the magazine was torn open, the guns completely shattered, and the ground stained with blood, brains and fragments of flesh. Under gray blankets were six corpses, one with the head torn off and the trunk completely blackened with powder, others with legs severed and breasts opened in ghastly wounds."

The retreating Confederate infantrymen had fled so abruptly that they'd left pots of stew cooking over campfires. Union soldiers helped themselves to the grub while grabbing guns, knives, books, whisky, and clothing that the Rebels had abandoned.

Richardson watched as Union soldiers delivered their highest-ranking captive, General Tilghman, to the conquerors of the fort— General Grant and Commodore Andrew Foote, commander of the Federal gunboats.

"How could you fight against the old flag?" Foote asked.

"It was hard," Tilghman replied, "but I had to go with my people."

A Chicago reporter interrupted to ask every journalist's most prosaic but necessary question: "How do you spell your name, General?"

"Sir, if General Grant wishes to use my name in his official dispatches, I have no objection," Tilghman replied. "But, sir, I do not wish to appear at all in this manner in any newspaper report."

"I merely asked it," the reporter said, "for the list of prisoners captured."

"You will oblige me, sir," Tilghman replied, "by not giving my name in any newspaper connections whatsoever."

Of course, Richardson included Tilghman's name in his story, as well as that absurd dialogue. He wrote his article aboard a Union ship heading back to Cairo, where he dispatched it to the *Tribune.*

Junius Browne remained with the Union soldiers outside the fort, although he'd been partially blinded when a box of ammunition exploded during the battle, sending debris into one eye, which swelled shut. Despite the injury, Browne stayed with the Union soldiers for the next ten days, as they marched 12 miles through swampy woods in a fierce, driving snowstorm, and then attacked Fort Donelson. Browne, who had brought neither tent nor blankets nor food, ate what he could cadge and slept on the frozen ground. The little man was tougher than he looked.

For four days, Union troops besieged Fort Donelson, battling the Confederate defenders along a five-mile arc west of the fort. The fighting was Browne's long-deferred introduction to the grisly realities of war: "Poor fellows lay on the ground with their eyes and noses carried away; their brains oozing from their crania; their mouths shot into horrible disfiguration, making a hideous spectacle."

Browne wandered the battle lines, climbing hills in an attempt to get a panoramic view of the action. On one hill, he stood in a cornfield and listened to artillery blasts while watching calves calmly grazing in a snow-dusted field. He saw a farmhouse and thought it was deserted until a man walked out the door. Was he a Rebel soldier or a farmer? Browne got close enough to see that the man wasn't wearing a uniform. The farmer invited Browne to come in and warm himself by the fire. He accepted and huddled near the fireplace with the farmer's family as the booming of artillery shook windows and rattled crockery. The farmer's wife told Browne that her son had been taken prisoner at Fort Henry and she feared the Yankees would torture him. Browne assured her that the boy would be safe, which seemed to comfort her. The farmer's daughter—who was about 18 and, Browne thought, quite pretty—complained that the war had caused a shortage of calico. If the Yankees win this battle, she asked, will we be able to get some calico? Browne was unable to come up with an answer. *Calico? Men were dying by the dozens less than a mile away and this girl was worried about calico?*

After days of battle, the besieged Confederates launched a surprise counterattack that nearly broke the Union lines, but Grant rallied his troops and drove the Rebels back into the fort. The next day, Confederate General Simon Buckner sent a note to Grant, proposing to negotiate "terms of capitulation." Grant responded with a terse message informing Buckner that he would accept "no terms except unconditional and immediate surrender." Buckner reluctantly agreed to what he called Grant's "ungenerous and unchivalrous terms," and surrendered Fort Donelson and its 12,000 men. It was the Union's first major victory of the war, and it earned the general the nickname "Unconditional Surrender Grant."

After Buckner surrendered, Browne joined the Union forces occupying the fort and interviewed captive Confederates. He was amused to learn that some Rebels went to war accompanied by their slaves, and were now imprisoned with them: "A young officer from Nashville had his black servant with him. The Negro took his master's leg into his lap, and like a washerwomen rubbed the mud out of his pantaloons." Later, at dinner, the young officer became incensed when his servant, perhaps emboldened by the presence of Yankee soldiers, failed to serve his master's meal promptly enough.

"I wish I had that nigger at home," the officer muttered. "I'd blow him to hell."

"We don't blow Negroes to hell," Browne told him. "We're not in that line at all."

Browne caught a boat to Cairo and wrote his account of the battle, weaving together notes he'd scribbled each night by the light of campfires. His story filled two full pages of the *Tribune* on February 22, 1862. By then, readers already knew the outcome of the battle, but Browne's first-person account, like any good feature story, revealed what it felt like to be there.

Sometimes Browne got a bit carried away and his prose veered into the more vivid shades of purple. When he described Federal soldiers cheering the news of the fort's surrender, he began reasonably enough: "Ever and anon a loud cheer went up for the Union and this was caught up at a distance and echoed by our soldiers and re-echoed by the surrounding hills." But his next sentence soared into the realm of pure poetry: "Many a brave warrior heard that glorious shout as his senses reeled in death and his spirit went forth embalmed with the assurance that he had not fallen in vain." In those days, readers enjoyed such flights of fancy, and even the *Tribune*'s crusty copy editors liked the line enough to let it stand.

Unlike many correspondents, who wanted to appear omniscient in their dispatches, Browne was willing to admit that he frequently had no idea what was happening in the battle, and neither did anybody else. "Everything was so confused," he wrote. "The different divisions of the army were so far removed from each other that it was impossible to determine in one part of the field what was happening in another." Early in his story, he wrote a line that sums up the "fog of war" so well that it could be included in nearly every battle dispatch in every war ever fought: "No one here seems to have any knowledge of anything, the leading officers having little more information than the privates."

The battle of Fort Donelson made Junius Browne a legend among his fellow Bohemians—not for his writing, but for the kind of stunt that reporters recount over drinks for decades. It happened on the last day of the battle, when Browne and several other reporters were hunkered behind rocks and fallen trees with a group of Union sharpshooters who were trying to pick off a Confederate artillery crew. The Rebel cannon was hidden behind a wall of logs a couple hundred yards away. Periodically, the Rebels would fire at the Yankees, then duck behind their breastworks, and the Union snipers would fire back. But they kept missing their targets.

"Are you a good shot?" one frustrated sniper asked Browne. "If you are, here is as good a rifle as ever killed a Rebel, and if you'll pepper that fellow over there at that gun, I'll give you anything I've got."

Browne had no confidence in his marksmanship but he was willing to try. He took the sniper's rifle, crouched into a firing position, aimed at the Rebel battery, and waited. When the cannon blasted, he pulled the trigger.

The Rebel cannon ceased firing.

"I think you fixed him that time," the sniper said, eyeing Browne with admiration.

"I wouldn't be surprised," Browne replied, although he was completely surprised. He walked away, feigning nonchalance, before anybody could test his dubious shooting prowess again.

Franc Wilkie of the *New York Times* was impressed by the man who'd seemed so unimpressive in Jefferson City five months earlier: "The sharpshooters were enthusiastic over the result, and were emphatic in declaring that he had laid out the cannoneer. They urged him to try some more; he had, however, the good sense to stop while his credit stood thus high, and went away. It is my conviction that it was the first and last gun he ever fired."

★

SOON, BROWNE BECAME FAMOUS AGAIN, at least among the Bohemians. In St. Louis a couple weeks later, he heard that a Union army was marching into Arkansas. He headed south, accompanied by Richard Colburn of the *New York World*, but by the time they reached Rolla, Missouri, they learned that the battle was over: Union forces had defeated a Confederate army in a fierce fight now known as the Battle of Pea Ridge. Browne and Colburn realized that Thomas Knox of the *New York Herald* would scoop them in a rival New York newspaper. Frustrated, they devised a simple solution: They would wing it—simply concoct accounts of the battle based on the brief reports and wispy rumors that had reached Rolla.

It was unethical, of course, but hardly unprecedented. Journalists in the nineteenth century were not finicky about facts and did not permit them to ruin a good story. Newspapers routinely enlivened their meager supply of facts by garnishing them with rumors, exaggerations, political rants, vicious invective, and the kind of pseudo-poetic prose that escaped the gravitational pull of truth and soared into fantasy. During the Civil War, reporters routinely made soldiers' dying words sound as lofty and eloquent as a Shakespearean soliloquy. The dead soldiers never complained, nor did their kin. All these habits contributed to a slang insult that became popular during the war: "He lies like a newspaper." But even by the lax standards of the day, what Browne and Colburn did was outrageous: They wrote long, vivid, eyewitness accounts of a battle that occurred 200 miles beyond their eyesight. The pieces were so ludicrously overblown that perhaps the two men were competing to out-do each other in the art of fiction. It seems quite possible that alcohol was involved.

Colburn's story reads like a parody of the style of first-person journalism that stars the reporter as the main character: "Even now, while I attempt to collect my blurred and disconnected thoughts," he began, "the sound of booming cannon and the crack of rifle rings in my ear, while visions of carnage and the flame of battle hover before my sight. Three days of constant watching, without food or sleep, and the excitements of the struggle, have quite unstrung my nerves."

That was hard to top, but Browne topped it with a heart-pounding, you-are-there style of prose that reads like fiction—which of course it was. Browne had learned that the Union won its victory with a dramatic charge lead by General Franz Sigel, so he cast Sigel as the hero of his yarn:

> Sigel was at last cut off, but his energy and that of his men hewed a passage through the serried ranks of the Rebels, and once more the scale of victory hung in equal balance. . . . Never was better fighting done—never ground more closely contested. Bayonet, musket, sword and cannon all did their bloody work, and the earth was stained and slippery with human gore. Every loyal soldier kept his eye fixed on his fearless leader. . . . Wherever they saw his streaming hair and flashing sword, they knew all was safe—that there was hope of victory while he survived.
>
> Strange that Sigel was not killed. He was well known to the Rebels, and a hundred rifles sought in vain to end his career. The balls wheeled about his head, but none touched him, though one carried away his spectacles and a second pierced his cap.

While Browne concocted his purple fiction, reports reached Rolla that the Confederate forces at Pea Ridge had included three regiments of Indians, and that some of them had scalped dead Yankees. Browne seized those facts with gusto, spinning out a gloriously lurid fantasy:

> The savages indeed seemed demonized, and it is said that the Rebels did everything in their power to excite them to frenzy, giving them large quantities of whisky and gunpowder a few minutes previous to the commencement of hostilities.
>
> The appearance of some of the besotted savages was fearful. They lost their sense of caution and fear, and ran with long knives against large odds, and fell pierced by dozens of bullets.

> With bloody hands and garments, with glittering eyes and hor-
> rid scowls, they raged about the field with terrible yells.

And so on. This preposterous hoax filled an entire page in the *Tri-bune*. It proved so popular that it was widely reprinted across the North and in England. Greeley praised it in an editorial, urging that a copy of the story "should be placed in every National soldier's hands."

A month later, the *New York Herald*, which had published Knox's authentic eyewitness account of the battle, charged that the correspondents for the *Tribune* and the *World* had "described with frenzied enthusiasm incidents which they invented." That was true but few people seemed to care, probably because the *Herald* and the *Tribune* were always carping at each other in print. The controversy faded away; Browne and Colburn remained employed and, apparently, unpunished.

Browne never explained his actions, at least not in print. Knox later wrote a memoir about his war years but never mentioned the hoax. Apparently, it didn't bother him: He and Browne remained friends for the rest of their lives. Wilkie, who had never liked Browne, grumbled about the bogus stories, calling them "eminently offensive," but the other Bohemians seemed to appreciate the sheer audacity. When the *Times* of London proclaimed that Browne's story was the best battle report of the war, his Bohemian friends couldn't help but smile. The little fellow had even bamboozled the haughty British.

4

SLOUCHING TOWARDS VICKSBURG

IN MARCH 1862, BROWNE AND RICHARDSON shipped out
for another adventure aboard Commodore Foote's flotilla, this
time heading down the Mississippi to attack the Confederate
stronghold at Island Number 10. The island sat in a tight bend in the
river in southern Missouri and was fortified with 52 cannons capable
of shelling any Union ship that dared try to enter Confederate waters
in Tennessee.

For three weeks, the Union fleet bombarded Island Number 10
while a Union army commanded by General John Pope occupied the
Missouri shore below the island, then crossed the river into Tennessee, thus surrounding the Confederates. On April 7, the Rebels
surrendered the island and its 7,000 defenders.

It was a great victory for the Union, and Browne and Richardson
were on hand to chronicle it for the *Tribune*. Unfortunately for them,
the capture of Island Number 10 was overshadowed by the news of a
surprise attack 200 miles away in Pittsburg Landing, Tennessee—the
Battle of Shiloh.

Early on Sunday morning, April 6, thousands of Confederate soldiers attacked Grant's army, surprising the sleepy men and driving the
Yankees to the banks of the Tennessee River. That night, Confederate
General P. G. T. Beauregard sent a telegram to Richmond, bragging
that he'd "gained a complete victory." He spoke too soon. The next morning, Grant—reinforced with 25,000 men who'd arrived overnight—coun-
terattacked and drove the Rebels back into Mississippi. The toll was
horrendous: During the two days of fighting, 20,000 men were killed or
wounded—double the casualties at Bull Run, Wilson's Creek, Fort
Donelson, and Pea Ridge combined.

Shiloh was the biggest battle of the war thus far and the *Tribune*
had missed it. Compelled to reprint an account of the battle from the
rival *Herald*, Horace Greeley was livid: *Where was Browne? Where was
Richardson?* "I was on duty at the siege of Island Number 10,"
Richardson wrote to his editor, "and wanted to see it finished."

Richardson quickly hustled to Shiloh, arriving while Union soldiers
were still burying the dead. Touring the battlefield, he counted 60 bullet holes in one tree, 90 in another. To piece together what had happened at Shiloh, he interviewed eyewitnesses. He even managed to get
an interview with General William Tecumseh Sherman, who detested
reporters and occasionally threatened to shoot them. But Richardson
possessed a rare talent for charming powerful men, and soon he was
bivouacking with Grant's staff and playing whist with his generals.
Grant smoked constantly, spoke rarely, and "bore himself with undis-
turbed serenity," Richardson noted, while Sherman talked incessantly
and seemed perpetually nervous. Watching the staff officers who
swarmed around the generals, trying to curry favor, Richardson
reached a wry conclusion: "Military men seem to cherish more jeal-
ousies than members of any other profession, except physicians and
artistes."

While Richardson consorted with generals, Browne, back at Island
Number Ten, was consorting with prostitutes. He discovered 20 of the
painted ladies encamped on the Tennessee shore near the island, some
of them quite young and pretty. They said they were "friends" of the
Confederate officers, but they didn't seem particularly distraught that
their friends were now prisoners. "Quite cosmopolitan in character,"
Browne noted, "they were unquestionably as willing to extend their
gentle favors to the National officers as to their late Rebel protectors,
knowing that Love makes friends of enemies."

Browne spent the next eight weeks aboard Commodore Foote's flotilla as it floated slowly towards Memphis. There was occasional combat with a Rebel ship or shore battery, but mainly the Yankees fought mosquitoes, which swarmed over the ships every night, sucking the invaders' blood. Worse than the mosquitoes was the monotony. Every day was precisely as dull as every other, except for Sundays, which were even duller. On Sundays, Commodore Foote summoned his men to a Christian service, at which he delivered a lengthy sermon. The sermons caused many sailors to slump into slumber, a sight that inspired Browne to write a sardonic theological observation: "It is certainly a virtue of many religious exercises that, if they do not convince, they cause sleep, and thus give rest to the body, though they furnish no consolation to the soul."

Occasionally, Browne and the other Bohemians would borrow a boat and row to the Arkansas shore in search of amusement and female companionship. They did manage to encounter some women, but Browne found them distressingly unladylike: "They drank whisky and smoked as freely as men, often chewed tobacco, and went about swearing in discordant tones and expectorating skillfully."

THOUSANDS OF TENNESSEANS gathered on the bluffs overlooking the Mississippi River, just north of Memphis, on the morning of June 6, 1862, to watch a magnificent spectacle: Eight Confederate warships steaming up the river to attack the invading Union fleet.

The spectators had a splendid view, but they weren't as close to the action as Browne, who was aboard the U.S.S. *Benton* along with Richardson, who'd returned from Shiloh in time to witness the battle. When the Confederate ships chugged into view, the Union fleet retreated long enough to allow the sailors to finish breakfast. Convinced that the Yankees were scared, the Rebels steamed ahead, firing their cannons. The Federals fired back and soon the river was so shrouded in blue smoke that it was difficult to tell friend from foe. Out of the smoke steamed two of the Union's newest warships—rams equipped with long, fortified prows. Crude but effective, the rams smashed into Rebel ships, ripping holes in their hulls. On the *Benton*, Browne watched sailors fire a cannon at the Confederate ship *General Lovell,* blowing a huge hole in its side. The *Lovell* started sinking. Her crew leaped into the water, and the *Benton*'s captain dispatched a lifeboat to rescue them.

When the shooting stopped and the smoke cleared, all but one of the Confederate warships had been destroyed or captured, and the other had fled south. The Federals lost only one ship.

That afternoon, Federal forces occupied Memphis, and Browne and Richardson went ashore with the Union sailors, strolling past local citizens, who seemed dazed at the unexpected sight of Yankees in their city. The *Tribune* reporters rented rooms at the city's best hotel, the Gayoso House. Remembering how he'd been forced to conceal his occupation while traveling incognito through Memphis during the secession winter of 1861, Albert signed his name on the register and then added, in large letters, "The New York Tribune."

Browne wrote the story of the river battle and, as usual, he did not stint on the verbal pyrotechnics, waxing lyrical in his description of how the *Benton*'s sailors gallantly saved the drowning Rebels who'd leaped off the *Lovell* as it sank: "It was a beautiful and humanizing spectacle to witness the efforts of the Unionists to snatch the Rebels from a watery grave." He also felt compelled to describe the women of Memphis—"often young and comely."

The Yankee correspondents spent the next week exploring Memphis and drinking with reporters from the city's Rebel newspapers. "One could have seen the *New York Tribune* and the *Memphis Appeal* sitting in pleasing converse over a bottle of champagne at the dinnertable of the Gayoso," Browne wrote. "Who, after that, could say journalists were not an amiable and a forgiving race, and that the people of the North and South were not a band of brothers?"

The occupying army permitted Memphis newspapers to continue publishing, but soon Union General Lew Wallace—who would later achieve immortality by writing *Ben Hur*—grew weary of the pro-Confederate editorials in the *Memphis Argus*. In a letter to the editor, he announced that the paper was henceforth under new management: "As the closing of your office might be injurious to you pecuniarily, I send Messrs. Richardson, of *The New York Tribune*, and Knox, of *The New York Herald*—two gentlemen of ample experience—to take charge of the editorial department of your paper."

It was a grand joke: General Wallace found it amusing to put a reporter from the abolitionist *Tribune* in charge of a Rebel newspaper, and even more amusing to pair him up with a reporter from the *Tribune*'s hated rival, the *Herald*. But Richardson and Knox were old friends and they had great fun writing editorials denouncing secession and predicting that the Confederacy would soon be crushed. Not surprisingly, this new editorial policy did not prove popular with *Argus* readers. "The publishers said their subscribers were rapidly falling off, on account of the change of editorial tone," Knox recalled dryly. "Like newspaper readers everywhere, they disliked to peruse what their consciences did not approve."

After ten days of merriment in Memphis, Browne rejoined the Union flotilla as it steamed up the White River into Arkansas. The Rebels had constructed a fort on the bluffs outside the town of St. Charles, and Union gunboats shelled it from the river. The Rebels fired back and one Confederate artillery shell sailed right through an open porthole on the gunboat *Mound City* and exploded in a steam engine, killing several sailors. Men leaped into the river from the doomed boat. As they flailed in the water, Rebels picked them off with rifles and blasted them with grape and canister. More than 125 sailors died, 43 of them in the river.

Browne watched the scene with horror and lambasted the Confederates in his dispatch to the *Tribune*:

> Shooting scalded, struggling, drowning men! Is this the nineteenth century? Live we in the freest and most enlightened country in the world?
>
> What a contrast, what a commentary upon the character of the Rebellion and its supporters, when we remember the heroic conduct of the sailors of the *Benton* opposite Memphis on the 6th, who periled their lives to preserve those of the enemy that leaped into the Mississippi from the sinking *Lovell*! Such is Rebel gratitude!

Browne wrote his story on a Mississippi riverboat, dispatched it to the *Tribune*, and then proceeded to St. Louis, where he fell ill with typhoid fever and sank into delirium.

★

WHEN RICHARDSON LEARNED that Junius was sick, he rushed to St. Louis to take care of him.

"Browne was lying here delirious and very ill with fever," he wrote to Sydney Gay, the *Tribune*'s new managing editor. "I arrived here yesterday and found him very sick with typhus fever, which seems partially settling upon the brain. He is in a critical situation. His terrible campaign of five months, shut up in one of our boats in that hot climate without exercise and eating the fearful fare is the cause of it. He was unable to take the [railroad] cars for Cincinnati—his home—and is here among strangers. As he is not only my associate, but one of my oldest and most intimate personal friends, my first duty is with him until this crisis of his disease passes."

Richardson had friends in St. Louis—he seemed to have friends everywhere—and he convinced an elderly married couple to allow Browne to convalesce in their house. "Their home is in a cool, airy, quiet part of town, almost in the country, and they have treated him like a son or a brother," Richardson wrote to Gay in early August. "It has undoubtedly saved his life. He is still utterly prostrate but I think the worst has passed. I can do nothing but stay right here with him until he is entirely safe."

Two weeks later, Richardson reported to Gay that Junius was recovering. "I read your inquiry, 'Where is Browne?' to him & he said that he must make the reply of Goethe's grandmother, who in her last hours received an invitation to a party & replied with her compliments that she would be most happy to be present, but was just then busily engaged in dying."

Browne might be the only war correspondent in history to describe his near-death experience by quoting Goethe's grandmother. But his sense of humor had returned. A few days later, he was strong enough to travel home to Cincinnati.

Richardson remained healthy, but he, too, longed to spend some time at home. "I should like a vacation of about two weeks or so, for though I have not worked hard of late, I am worn and weary," he wrote to Gay on September 5. "Can I spend two or three weeks with my family near Boston or have them meet me in Northern Ohio, as soon as there seems to be no special need of my remaining here?"

I T WAS A REASONABLE REQUEST—Richardson hadn't seen his family in more than eight months—but it arrived at an inopportune moment. On the previous day, General Robert E. Lee had marched his

Army of Northern Virginia across the Potomac and invaded Maryland. Gay's answer came in a telegram: "Repair to Washington without any delay."

Two hours later, Richardson boarded a train traveling east. He disembarked in Washington, at ten in the morning on September 12, purchased a horse, and rode 60 miles to Frederick, Maryland, arriving on the afternoon of September 14. Chasing the sound of gunfire, he caught up with the Union army in the village of Keedysville. He located the headquarters of General George McClellan, the commander of the Army of the Potomac, where he rendezvoused with another *Tribune* reporter, George Smalley. Richardson somehow convinced McClellan's chief of staff, General Randolph Marcy, to let him sleep in the farmhouse that Marcy had commandeered as his headquarters. Naturally, Richardson touted this coup in a letter to Gay: "I took tea last night & breakfast this morning, at a farmer's table, with Gen. Marcy & several others of McClellan's staff. I think McClellan's policy will be to treat correspondents courteously—at least for the present."

On September 16, the Union and Confederate armies jostled into positions facing each other across a field outside the town of Sharpsburg. That evening, Richardson and Smalley rode along the Union lines with General Joe Hooker, who was mounted on a bright white horse that stood out in the deepening dusk. They heard a single musket shot, then another. A band of Rebels stepped out of a clump of trees and fired. Bullets hissed past their heads. From somewhere out of sight, Confederate artillery boomed and a cannonball ripped into the ground, spewing dirt on Richardson. Hooker took off, spurring his white horse over a fence, and Richardson and Smalley galloped after him.

By then, it was dark. Richardson tied his horse to an apple tree and spent the night lying on the floor of Marcy's farmhouse, his head propped on his saddle, listening to the sporadic pops of distant gunfire.

The next day, September 17, 1862, Richardson watched the battle of Antietam through field glasses from a hill behind the Union lines. It began at dawn with a ferocious barrage of Union artillery. Richardson took out his watch and in one minute counted more than 60 blasts. Then he watched Hooker's troops charge, only to be attacked by Rebels, who surged forward, wailing like banshees. Union artillery blasted the charging Rebels, and from his hilltop perch Richardson could see fragments of human bodies flying through the air.

All day the battle raged and Richardson watched a panorama of carnage: "Riderless horses and scattering men, clouds of dirt from solid shot and exploding shells, long dark lines of infantry swaying to and fro, with columns of smoke rising from the muskets, red flashes and white puffs from the batteries—with the sun shining brightly on all this scene of tumult."

Richardson had witnessed the bloodiest day in American history—3,654 men killed on the battlefield, another 19,000 wounded or missing. The Federal forces pushed the Rebels back towards the Potomac and gained a few hundred yards of blood-soaked dirt, but McClellan could have destroyed Lee's army if only he'd launched another attack with the thousands of troops he'd held in reserve. He didn't. "It would not be prudent," he told his underlings.

That night, Richardson, Smalley and two other *Tribune* reporters huddled around a flickering candle in a farmhouse filled with wounded Union soldiers, writing notes on what they had seen that day. Around midnight, Smalley gathered their accounts, climbed on Richardson's horse, and rode to Frederick in search of a telegraph office. He found one, but it was closed. He sat on a log outside the door and waited, scribbling out a news story. "Fierce and desperate battle between two hundred thousand men has raged since daylight, yet night closes on an uncertain field," it began. "It is the greatest fight since Waterloo."

At seven in the morning, an employee opened the telegraph office and began transmitting Smalley's story. Smalley caught a train bound for Baltimore, and from there, an overnight train to New York. Standing beneath a dim oil lamp in the jostling train, he wrote all night long, weaving the notes of the four *Tribune* reporters into a long, narrative account of the battle. When he walked into the *Tribune* office at six the next morning, his clothes still reeking of gun smoke, the compositors waiting to set his copy cheered. Within a few hours, the *Tribune* was on the street with the first, and perhaps the best, account of the battle of Antietam.

Back in Sharpsburg, Richardson wandered the battlefield, struck by the endless variety of positions that dead bodies assume: "There were forms with every rigid muscle strained in fierce agony, and those with hands folded peacefully upon the bosom; some still clutching their guns, others with an arm upraised, and one with a single open finger pointing to heaven. Several remained hanging over a fence, which they were climbing when the fatal shot struck them."

Like nearly everyone else at Antietam, Richardson expected that McClellan would attack that day and finish off the Rebels. But McClellan again hesitated. That night, Lee and his men slipped safely across the Potomac.

Four days later, when McClellan still showed no signs of chasing Lee, Richardson wrote to Sidney Gay, pleading again for time off to visit his family. "Pardon me for reminding you that in my application to come East, I asked for a season at home. I desire to spend fully 3 weeks there to recoup. I have only been there four days since last Nov."

Not yet, replied Gay, who believed another major battle was imminent. It wasn't, but Richardson accompanied Union soldiers to Harpers Ferry, the scene of John Brown's famous raid three years earlier, and there he heard Lincoln's newly issued Emancipation Proclamation read to the troops.

In New York, the *Tribune* celebrated the news of the proclamation: "GOD BLESS ABRAHAM LINCOLN!"

A few days later, Lincoln arrived to meet with McClellan. The president was "unusually thin and silent and looks weary and careworn," Richardson reported. "The troops everywhere cheered him with warm enthusiasm."

Lincoln ordered McClellan to stop stalling and start chasing Lee's army, but the general continued to dally. On October 13, Richardson reported that J. E. B. Stuart's Confederate cavalry rode within five miles of McClellan's headquarters, which was so lightly guarded that the Rebels could have captured the general. Richardson couldn't resist adding a snide joke at McClellan's expense: "Stuart knew the interests of the Rebels too well to capture our commander."

The *Tribune*'s editors shared Richardson's disgust with McClellan's timidity and urged Lincoln to replace him with a general who wanted to fight. On November 5, shortly after the mid-term congressional elections, Lincoln fired McClellan.

On December 6, Richardson finally got the vacation he'd been begging for, and he traveled to Massachusetts to see Lou and their children. His oldest son, Leander, was now six years old, his daughter, Maud, was three, and the baby, Albert Jr., was ten months. Richardson looked forward to spending a traditional New England family Christmas with them before returning to the war.

★

I**T WASN'T TO BE.** Five days later, Gay summoned Richardson back to work. It was an emergency: A major battle had erupted in Fredericksburg, Virginia.

On December 13, 1862, the Union army, now commanded by General Ambrose Burnside, attacked Lee's Confederates near Fredericksburg and marched into a massacre. Shielded behind a high stone wall, the Confederates pounded the oncoming Yankees with artillery and musket fire. It was, as one union general put it, "murder, not warfare." After losing more than 10,000 men, Burnside gave up and retreated back across the Rappahannock River.

By the time Richardson arrived from Massachusetts, the battle was over. When he interviewed Burnside, he found the general visibly shaken: "As he spoke to me about the brave men who had fruitlessly fallen, there were tears in his eyes, and his voice broke with emotion."

Two weeks after the debacle at Fredericksburg, another Union army launched another frontal assault against another entrenched Confederate position, this one in the swamps of Chickasaw Bluffs, Mississippi, just north of Vicksburg. The result was similar: The Rebels mowed down the Yankees and drove them back. The Union army lost 1,700 men; the Confederates, about 200. Several reporters who had witnessed the catastrophe described it in letters sent to their newspapers via a military boat. But William Tecumseh Sherman, the general who'd lost the battle, ordered an aide to fish the reporters' letters out of the mailbag. Sherman hated reporters, and he perused the purloined letters with rising anger. Reading Thomas Knox's dispatch to the *Herald*, which blamed Sherman for the defeat, the general exploded and ordered Knox court-martialed as a spy. In February 1863, Knox was arrested, tried, convicted, and expelled from army lines with a warning "not to return under penalty of imprisonment."

The arrest angered Richardson. Knox was his old friend—and had been his editorial-writing colleague at the *Memphis Argus* the previous June—but his reasons were not merely personal. Richardson believed in the rights of reporters. "An accredited Journalist, in the legitimate exercise of his calling, has just as much *right* in the army as the Commander himself," he proclaimed in a letter to Gay. He drew up a petition supporting Knox and circulated it around Washington, collecting signatures from newspapermen and sympathetic politicians. On the evening of March 20, he walked to the White House, accompanied by James Winchell of the *New York Times*, to present the petition to President Lincoln.

Lincoln looked weary and despondent, but he greeted Richardson warmly, reminding him that they'd met before, on a cold day in Kansas in 1859, when Richardson had covered one of Lincoln's speeches. The two men swapped reminiscences for a few minutes, then Richardson launched into a defense of freedom of the press, and asked the president to issue an order permitting Knox to return to the army.

Lincoln listened, then began pacing around the room. He would issue the order, he said, if Grant agreed.

That was unlikely, Richardson replied, because Grant and Sherman were close friends.

"I should be glad to serve you or Mr. Knox, or any other loyal journalist," Lincoln said. "But, just at present, our generals in the field are more important to the country than any of the rest of us—or *all* of the rest of us. It is my fixed determination to do nothing whatever which can possibly embarrass any one of them."

Richardson found that logic impossible to refute.

"Let us see what we can do," Lincoln said. "I will write something to put our ideas into shape."

The president began searching for a pen and paper on his table, which was, Winchell recalled, "littered with documents lying in complete disorder." Lincoln's nine-year-old son, Tad, helped his father find a pen and the president began to write. First, he noted that "Mr. Knox's offense was technical, rather than willfully wrong." Then he ordered that Knox's sentence be revoked. This delighted Richardson and Winchell. But the president wasn't finished yet.

"I had better make this conditional on the approval of General Grant," Lincoln said. "I will just add a few words."

Those few words went a long way towards negating his previous words: "Now, therefore, said sentence is hereby revoked as to allow Mr. Knox to return to General Grant's head-quarters, and to remain if General Grant shall give his express assent, and to again leave the department if General Grant shall refuse such assent."

It was a deft maneuver by a masterful politician: Lincoln gave the reporters exactly what they had requested by revoking Knox's punishment, but then he affirmed Grant's right to revoke that revocation.

Lincoln handed the letter to Richardson with what the reporter re-called as "a little sigh of relief." Then the three men sat back and discussed the progress of the war. After extracting a promise that nothing he said would be quoted, the president admitted that his armies were stalled in Virginia and outside Vicksburg and that he had no idea how to proceed.

"God knows that I want to do what is wise and right," he said, "but sometimes it is very difficult to determine."

★

WHEN JUNIUS BROWNE RECOVERED from his bout of typhus he returned to work, but nothing seemed to go right.

He traveled to Kentucky, which had been invaded by Braxton Bragg's Confederate army, but he missed the Battle of Perryville, where General Don Carlos Buell's Union army defeated the invaders in a fight that killed 1,426 men.

"I went to Frankfort, Kentucky to reach Buell but could not possibly get through; a Rebel column being between myself and the Union army," Browne explained in an embarrassing letter to Gay. "While trying to 'make the connection,' the battle of Perryville was fought and I was forced to return to Louisville."

In November, Browne traveled to LaGrange, Tennessee, where Grant's army was encamped, but nothing was happening. He kept sending dispatches to the newspaper, but he received no replies.

In Memphis in January 1863, Browne received a package of *Tribunes* from Gay, but none contained any of his articles. He'd been sending dispatches regularly, he informed Gay by return mail. "Are they regularly received? If so, I regret they are too uninteresting for inclusion." Out of touch with his office and unable to find any battles to cover, Browne was frustrated, nervous, and worried. "Whenever you are dissatisfied with my labors, please inform me promptly," he wrote to Gay. "I should be deeply pained to occupy any position my employers did not think me competent to fill. Thus far I have been left all in the dark as to your wishes."

Browne had become a figure familiar to newspaper editors then and now—an insecure, depressed, needy reporter out on the road alone and desperate for a few words of encouragement from his bosses.

★

RICHARDSON WAS LUCKIER. He assigned himself to go to Murfreesboro, Tennessee, to interview General William Rosecrans, who had recently replaced Buell as head of the Union's Army of the Cumberland.

Rosecrans treated him like a visiting dignitary, inviting him to dinner and spending hours discussing military strategy. Never too bashful to inform the boss of his triumphs, Richardson wrote to Gay: "Rosecrans professed to know all about me as a journalist and received me with great kindness. I have never been so warmly received at any Army headquarters. I hope I have sense enough not to puff anybody on that account."

Richardson liked Rosecrans, but he was more excited about an obscure colonel named Abel D. Streight, who was gathering volunteers for a daring guerrilla cavalry raid from East Tennessee into Georgia—an attack designed to tear up railroad tracks, assault Atlanta, and burn its factories. "Won't it make a sensation down in Dixie if fortune smiles upon it!" Richardson wrote to Gay. "If it goes and ever gets back, it will be a stirring chapter in the history of the war."

Richardson wanted to cover Streight's raid, but a more pressing story beckoned. Grant's army was moving towards Vicksburg, and he decided to meet Browne in Milliken's Bend to cover that battle instead.

En route, he stopped in Memphis on May 1, and received a letter from Gay, who said the *Tribune* wanted stories with more color and excitement. Richardson scribbled a reply that reads as if he were humoring his boss: "Your suggestion about more of the Romance & picturesqueness of the war, & less of the commonplace will be of great service to me. I will endeavor to have them acted upon by all our correspondents."

Two days later, the Rebels captured Richardson, Browne, and Colburn as they floated down the Mississippi on hay bales.

"Pretty lively night, boys, isn't it?" Richardson said in his usual deadpan fashion, as the three Bohemians stood on the riverbank, dripping wet. "I thought several times, Junius, that there was a fair prospect of a couple of vacancies on the *Tribune* staff."

PART 2:
CAGES

5

IMPUDENT SCAMPS

RICHARDSON, BROWNE, AND COLBURN huddled around a fire in the Vicksburg jail yard, trying to dry their drenched clothes and gazing around at their miserable surroundings.

In the soft light of dawn, the reporters watched as prisoners began to rise from the ground where they'd slept. There were more than 150 of them. They coughed and spat, they scratched at the lice that infested their ragged clothes, and then they cooked breakfast by holding sticks tipped with bacon over smoky campfires. As the sun rose higher, it warmed the contents of the open sewer in the middle of the yard, and soon not even the homey aroma of crackling bacon could mask the stench of human waste. The Bohemians strained to come up with jokes about their accommodations:

After a few days in this jail, Hades might seem like a good place to vacation.

If a man took very good care of himself, he might be able to live for five or six days in this place. But then again who would want to live for more than five or six days in this place?

They chuckled sardonically because that's what Bohemians did in such situations. They were relieved to be alive after the previous night's terrifying bombardment, and they felt confident they wouldn't be in this wretched jail for long. After all, they were civilians, noncombatants, *reporters*, so it made perfect sense that they'd be released, perhaps soon enough to catch up with Grant's army and cover the battle of Vicksburg.

Around noon, soldiers marched the three reporters through the streets of Vicksburg to the courthouse. Browne hobbled along on his bare, bleeding feet, having lost his shoes and socks in the river. Inside the courthouse, they were led into the office of Major N. G. Watts, the Confederate agent of exchange, who announced that he'd be happy to parole them.

Parole was a curious process during the Civil War. In 1862, the two warring governments signed the Dix-Hill Cartel, agreeing that captured soldiers would be sent home after making a solemn promise not to fight again. When the two sides had repatriated an equal number of prisoners, the "paroled" men would be declared officially "exchanged," and they'd be free to rejoin their armies and start fighting again. It was a quaint system, built on the sanctity of a gentleman's word of honor. Later, it broke down in mutual mistrust, but it was still in effect on May 4, 1863, when the three reporters were captured. They weren't soldiers, but Major Watts agreed to parole them anyway. He drew up the official documents with their boilerplate language proclaiming that each man "is hereby paroled with full leave to return to his country on the following conditions, namely: that he will not take up arms again, nor serve as military police or constabulary force in any fort, garrison or field-work, held by either of said parties, nor as a guard of prisoners, depots, or stores, nor discharge any duty usually performed by soldiers, until exchanged . . . "

The reporters read the document, savoring the phrase *"is hereby paroled,"* and gladly signed. But Major Watts informed them that there was one little problem: Grant had announced that he was temporarily suspending all prisoner exchanges at Vicksburg, presumably because it would soon be a battlefield. There was only one other officially designated place for prisoner exchanges—Richmond—and Watts promised to send them there on the next available train. In the meantime, rather than return to the jail yard, they could make their quarters on the top floor of the courthouse.

"Gentlemen, you are a long way from home," the major said, his face lit with the smile of a man who believes he is about to say something very funny. "However, do not despond. I have met many of your people in this condition. I have paroled some thousands of them. In fact, I confidently expect within the next ten days, to see Major General Grant, who commands your army, a prisoner in this room."

The reporters smiled back, and told the major that they had no doubt he'd soon see Grant in Vicksburg, but probably not as a prisoner.

It was all very jolly, a bit of good-natured teasing, and then Confederate soldiers escorted the reporters to their new home on the top floor of the courthouse, a little room under a dome, high enough to catch cool breezes, and offering a panoramic view across the river to Louisiana. They could see Union army camps there, and they joked about being nearly within rifle range of their friends. They were still prisoners—a soldier guarded the door—but this room was far more pleasant than the jail yard, and the reporters had to admit that these Confederates were not so bad after all.

Rumors spread rapidly through Vicksburg about Yankee reporters captured in the river, and soon visitors arrived. Several Vicksburg newspapermen dropped by to chat, as did local officials and Confederate officers. They all asked lots of questions. *How long do you think the war will last? Do people in the North support Lincoln? Which Union generals are the best? What would happen if the Yankees won? Would they really free the slaves—and what would they do with them?*

After listening politely to the reporters' answers, the visitors launched into little speeches of their own, informing the Bohemians that the Confederate army had the best generals and the bravest soldiers, and that it was impossible for *any* army to conquer seven million proud people on their own soil.

"We will fight to the last man!" they kept saying. "We will die in the last ditch!"

So many people used that line—*die in the last ditch*—that it became a running joke among the Bohemians. Where is this ditch? How deep is it? They're going to need a very big ditch to hold all these Rebels who keep promising to die in it.

The reporters spent two days in their courthouse penthouse. While they were there, a local woman who'd watched Browne limping down the street on bare feet sent him a pair of shoes and some socks she'd knitted herself. The guards gave Browne a Union uniform coat and a cap from a dead Yankee soldier. When he put them on, this man who liked to think of himself as unsentimental found to his surprise that he was proud to wear the uniform of a common Union private.

★

ON THE AFTERNOON OF MAY 5, the Rebels marched the Bohemians to a train heading east to Jackson. About forty captured Union soldiers were also aboard, including the Ohio infantrymen who'd leaped into the river with the Bohemians. The Yankee soldiers were getting along quite well with their Rebel guards, passing around a whisky bottle and playing euchre. The train stopped when it came upon a regiment of Confederate soldiers who were marching off to fight Grant, and the captive Yankees, their tongues lubricated by whisky, leaned out the windows to razz them.

"Look out, Rebs, the Yankees are coming! Keep on marching if you don't want old Grant to catch you!"

"How are times in the North?" the Rebels responded. "Cotton a dollar and twenty-five cents in New York!"

"How are times in the South? Flour $175 a barrel in Vicksburg—and none to be had for that."

When the two sides had finished taunting each other about wartime inflation, the Yankees broke into song, belting out booze-fueled renditions of "Yankee Doodle," the "Star-Spangled Banner," and "John Brown's Body."

In Jackson, the Bohemians were locked in a local prison with no beds, no blankets, and no pillows. But that was merely an inconvenience, they told each other, because they'd already been paroled, and they would soon be free. Certainly the jailers seemed to take their parole status seriously—even permitting the Bohemians to leave the jail and stroll to a restaurant for dinner.

Jackson's streets seethed with frenzied activity. Grant had unexpectedly marched his army towards Jackson and people were hustling to get out of town before the Yankees arrived. Horses strained to pull wagons filled with entire families and their most prized possessions, including their furniture, their silverware, and their slaves. Richardson was amused by the frantic exodus. He remembered his visit to Jackson in early 1861, when he had listened to delegates at the secession convention bloviating about how Yankees couldn't fight. Apparently, they'd changed their minds about that.

Browne watched the fleeing families and studied the faces of their slaves, who seemed to be enjoying the sight of white folks panicking.

After dinner, the Bohemians set off in search of local reporters, and found them at the Bowman House hotel, where the *Memphis Daily Appeal* had set up a temporary headquarters. Known as "The Bible of the Confederacy," the *Appeal* was a fiery Rebel journal edited by John Reid McClanahan, a convivial drunk whose face was decorated with a scraggily goatee that resembled a furry sloth dangling from his chin. The Bohemians had imbibed with McClanahan in Memphis on the day Union forces occupied it. Now, he was delighted to crack open a bottle and regale them with tales of his adventures in exile.

Just before the Yankees conquered Memphis, McClanahan had loaded his printing press into a boxcar and shipped it 90 miles to Grenada, Mississippi, and began publishing the *Appeal* from there, vowing in a fiery editorial that he'd never "submit to a censorship under Lincoln's hireling minions." Five months later, in November 1862, the Yankees captured Grenada and McClanahan shipped his press to Jackson, where he wrote an editorial vowing to continue fighting for "the great ends and glorious objects for which our armies are struggling in the field." Now, with Grant marching towards Jackson, McClanahan was preparing to move the *Appeal* again, this time to Atlanta. He was a stubborn Rebel firebrand willing to do anything to keep the damn Yankees from censoring his newspaper, but he was only too happy to pour a drink for three captured Yankee reporters—and to give them clothing and loan them money.

The reporters spent two days in Jackson, hoping that Grant would quickly conquer the city and liberate them so they could cover the battle for Vicksburg instead of taking a long, slow trip to Richmond. But the Confederates shipped them out of town on an eastbound train, along with the 40 captured Union soldiers and a load of ammunition the Rebels wanted to keep out of Grant's hands. The train was guarded by such a small squad of Confederate soldiers that some of the Union prisoners thought they could overpower the Rebels, hijack the train, blow up the ammunition, and then march 20 miles west to meet Grant's army before the Confederates could catch them. They begged their commanders to endorse the plan, but the officers refused, explaining that fighting would violate the solemn promise they'd made in their parole documents. If they violated their parole and were then recaptured, the Rebels would have every right to hang them. So the prisoners abandoned their bold plan and sat quietly as the train rumbled towards Alabama.

On May 14, Grant's army marched into Jackson and hoisted the American flag over the state capitol. Grant sauntered into the Bowman House and rented the room occupied the previous night by Confederate General Joe Johnston, who had fled with his army. When Grant and General Sherman strolled through Jackson that afternoon, they ordered their men to tear up railroad tracks and burn whatever the Rebels could use to make war—foundries, factories, and a textile mill where women wove gray cloth for Confederate uniforms. Then Grant turned his army west and headed towards Vicksburg.

T HE TRAIN CARRYING the Yankee prisoners rattled through pine forests and past cotton plantations. Near Meridian, Mississippi, the prisoners' eastbound train passed a train filled with Confederate soldiers heading west, and one of the Rebels reached out the window and snatched Albert Richardson's hat right off his head. The Rebels no doubt thought that was hilarious, but Richardson was not amused. This was the nineteenth century, and a gentleman simply did not venture outdoors without a hat. Now bereft of headgear, Richardson tied a handkerchief on his head, much to the amusement of his friends.

The train moved slowly and stopped frequently, and everywhere people wanted to talk to the Yankees. Some whispered words of support but most lectured the prisoners about how the South could never be subjugated, how they'd fight to the last man, and die in the last ditch. Browne, who did not suffer fools happily, tried to avoid the lecturers, grumbling that he'd rather run the guns at Vicksburg again than listen to these idiots prattle on about dying in a ditch.

Richard Colburn adopted a different policy towards the prattlers. A droll Bohemian wag and a master of the deadpan put-on, he amused himself by humoring Rebels who hectored him. A brawny Texan, one of the guards on the train, informed the Bohemians that he'd personally lynched three abolitionists, hanging them all from the same oak tree near his house. Then the Texan launched into the standard lecture about how the Confederacy could never be defeated, ending with the now familiar refrain:

"We will fight to the last man! We will die in the last ditch!"

Colburn listened patiently, his face as somber as a pallbearer's, and then, after a thoughtful pause, he spoke. "Well, sir, if you should do that, and all be killed, we would regret it extremely!"

Richardson and Browne stifled giggles, but the Texan detected no humor.

"We shall do it, sir!" he vowed. *"We shall do it!"*

"Well, sir," Colburn said, his face still utterly serious, "as I said before, if you do, and all happen to *get* killed, including the very last man himself, of course we of the North shall be quite heartbroken."

When the Texan finally realized he was being mocked, he looked as if he wanted to tear Colburn's head off. But he refrained, and he never lectured them again.

In Montgomery, Alabama, the Confederate officers allowed the Bohemians to sleep at the Exchange Hotel and take a swim in the Alabama River. As they strolled through town, the reporters happened upon a bizarre scene: A white man leaned off his porch to speak to a light-skinned black girl, obviously of mixed race, who was standing on the sidewalk.

"Mary, God damn your soul!" the man yelled. "Have you said your prayers today?"

"No, master," the girl answered.

"Well, by God, if you don't do it before tomorrow, I'll lash the skin off your back, God damn you!"

Amazed at this strange dialogue, the reporters looked at each other, wondering if they'd really heard what they thought they heard. Apparently, they had. Browne was appalled and, in a perverse way, delighted: To him, this brief moment exhibited all the features of the much-lauded "Southern way of life"—slavery, miscegenation, brutality, vulgarity, hypocrisy, and bogus piety.

When the train reached Atlanta, the Rebels marched the Union soldiers to a military prison but left the reporters sitting under a tree near the railroad depot. After a while, they got up and wandered around the city, finally arriving at the prison. They stepped inside to ask their captors for advice on where they might spend the night.

That was a mistake. They were promptly locked into a cell. It was a dirty, nasty place, but they didn't let that bother them because, after all, they'd already been paroled and were confident they would be free soon enough.

They remained there for several days. Their only visitor was an obnoxious Irishman who served as a jailhouse runner, offering to procure whiskey or anything else the prisoners might desire. The Bohemians passed up the whisky, but Richardson, still devoid of headgear, asked the Irishman to get him a hat. For $50 in Confederate money, the Irishman sold Richardson a hideously ugly, crudely made, shapeless, dingy cotton hat. When he put it on his head, his friends laughed. Wearing a hat that ugly could bewitch his brain, Browne joked, and turn him into the kind of maniac who'd horsewhip his father or murder his grandmother. Richardson tolerated his friend's teasing, but he kept the hat. What else could a gentleman do?

Seeking convivial Bohemian companionship, the reporters sent their business cards to local newspapers, hoping for a visit, or at least a free paper. But the Rebel editors of Atlanta were not as sociable towards Yankee journalists as the Rebel editors of Memphis, Vicksburg, and Montgomery. They didn't visit or send reading matter, and the editor of one paper, the *Southern Confederacy*, denounced them in a wildly vitriolic editorial.

"Last evening some correspondents of *The New York World* and *New York Tribune* were brought here among a batch of prisoners captured at Vicksburg," the writer began, explaining that the "impudent scamps" had the audacity to send notes requesting a complimentary newspaper.

> Yankees are everywhere more impudent than any honest race of people can be, and a Yankee newspaper-man is the quintessence of all impudence. . . . The unheard-of effrontery that prompted these villains who, caught in company with the thieving, murdering vandals who have invaded our country, despoiled our homes, murdered our citizens, destroyed our property, violated our wives, sisters and daughters, to boldly claim of the press of the South the courtesies and civilities which gentlemen of the press usually extend to each other, is above and beyond all the unblushing audacity we ever imagined. . . . They are our vilest and most unprincipled enemies—far more deeply steeped in guilt, and far more richly deserving death, than the vilest vandal that ever invaded the sanctity of our soil and outraged our homes and our peace.

Richly deserving death? After blithely advocating murder, the editorial writer volunteered to join the lynch mob. "We would greatly prefer to assist in hanging these enemies to humanity than to show them any civilities or courtesies," he continued. "They deserve a rope's end, and will not receive their just desserts till their crimes are punished with death."

After reading that editorial, the Confederate lieutenant running the prison told the reporters that the editors of the *Confederacy* were a couple of transplanted Yankees from Vermont, which made him a little suspicious of their fire-breathing rhetoric.

"I am not very fond of Yankees myself," the lieutenant said. "I am as much in favor of hanging them as anybody. But these Vermonters, who haven't been here six months, are a little too violent. They don't own any niggers. 'Tisn't natural. There's something wrong about them. If I were going to hang Yankees as a venture, I think I would begin with them."

6

FRESH FISH! FRESH FISH!

THEY ARRIVED IN **RICHMOND, VIRGINIA**, at dawn on May 16, 1863, after a long, tedious train ride from Atlanta. In the railroad depot, Confederate soldiers lined up Richardson, Browne, Colburn, and the other prisoners from Vicksburg and marched them through the streets to a place that was already infamous among Union soldiers—Libby Prison. It was a three-story brick warehouse, and as the prisoners marched up to the front door, on Cary Street, they heard inmates on the top floors laughing and hooting at them, yelling, "Fresh fish! Fresh fish!"

Browne looked up at them, appalled and irate. Why would these prisoners take such delight in mocking their fellow Union men? What had happened to their dignity, their decency? Anybody who would behave in such stupid fashion, he thought, *deserves* to be locked up.

Inside the building, the Vicksburg prisoners shuffled into an office decorated with the trophies of war—American flags and Union regimental colors confiscated from previous prisoners. A Confederate clerk recorded each man's name, rank, and regiment number. Confronted with three reporters who had no rank or regiment number, the clerk grumbled and muttered a sarcastic inquiry about the health of Horace Greeley. When the reporters showed the clerk their parole documents, he informed them that prisoners were exchanged when a flag-of-truce boat steamed up the James River from Fortress Monroe, the Union naval base located near Hampton, Virginia. The boat wasn't due for a few days. In the meantime, they'd remain right where they were—at Libby.

After that, each man was stripped and searched, his boots and clothes removed by a guard who carefully checked soles and seams and confiscated money, pocket knives, watches, canteens, and anything else he deemed contraband. When that process was completed, the enlisted men marched off for transport to Belle Isle—an island prison in the James River where Union privates were incarcerated outdoors. The officers—and the reporters—trudged up three flights of stairs to Libby's top floor, and found themselves in an enormous room with no furniture. Prisoners swarmed around them, eager to hear where they'd come from, how they were captured, and how the war was going.

Surrounded by men hungry for news, the reporters told their story of running the batteries, and reported that Grant was tearing up Mississippi and would no doubt soon take Vicksburg. When they had finished, the crowd dispersed and the prisoners went back to their usual morning routine. Many of them stripped off all their clothes, sat naked on the bare floor, and proceeded to carefully examine every inch of their clothing, particularly their underwear painstakingly picking off lice and crushing them between their fingernails, a process that sometimes resulted in a tiny popping sound and a little spurt of blood.

It's called "skirmishing," the prisoners informed the reporters, and they did it every morning. Disgusted by the spectacle, the Bohemians gave silent thanks that they'd been paroled and would soon be released from this miserable place.

★

LIBBY PRISON BEGAN as a warehouse for tobacco, but the war transformed it into a warehouse for men.

It was built in the late 1840s by a tobacco baron named John Enders, who fell from a ladder during construction and died instantly. His slaves were not altogether sad to see him go: They'd been led to believe that he'd arranged to free them in his will. But the will *didn't*

free them, and in retaliation they torched the place. In 1861, businessman Luther Libby bought the building and hung a sign: "Libby and
Son, Ship Chandlers and Grocers." A year later, the Confederate government expropriated the warehouse as a space to store Yankee prisoners, but Libby's sign remained and gave the place its name.

The prison took up most of a city block near the James River. Outside, the lower half of the red brick building was painted a bright
white so that a prisoner attempting to shinny out the windows on a
rope could be easily seen—and shot. Inside, the top two floors were divided into three large rooms, each measuring 105 by 44 feet. These
were the prisoners' bedrooms, although they contained no beds, or
even chairs. The Yankees slept on the floor, on a blanket only if they
happened to have one. The building's ground floor was also divided
into three rooms—an office for the guards, a sick bay, and a kitchen.
Prisoners cooking in the kitchen could look through a hole in the floor
and peer into the cellar below, a dark dungeon where the Confederates
locked captives deemed unworthy to live with military officers on the
top floors—deserters, common criminals, and black prisoners. The
cooks sometimes dropped food through the hole to the poor starving
wretches in the dungeon, who would fight each other for each castoff
crust of bread.

On the top floors, life was not quite so brutal. Light streamed
through the windows and the food was adequate, if not appetizing. Every morning, guards distributed the daily allotment—usually pork or
beef and cornmeal—and the prisoners cooked it themselves on three
smoky stoves in the kitchen. When Junius Browne arrived, he grumbled that it was outrageous that officers and gentlemen were forced to
work as common cooks and dishwashers, but he was quickly informed
that the prisoners had *asked* to prepare their own meals after tasting
the slop served up by Libby's staff.

Cooking was an unpleasant chore, but at least it gave prisoners
something to do. Otherwise, they sat on the floor, talking or reading or
playing cards or staring out the windows. Libby's windows, which contained bars but no glass, offered beautiful views. A man could gaze out
and watch the James River rolling past bridges and islands, and beyond them, hills, fields, and farmhouses. It was a bucolic panorama,
particularly on a sunny morning, and it reminded a man that there
was a world outside the prison, that it was beautiful, and that some-
day he might return to it. But prisoners had to remember not to step

too close to the windows when looking out. Touching the bars—or even standing within three feet of them—violated a prison rule, and guards patrolling on the streets below enforced that rule by shooting at anyone they saw in the windows. They called this pastime "sporting for Yankees." A prisoner named George Forsyth was shot dead while reading a newspaper near a window, and fragments from his shattered skull splattered around the room.

Two men named Turner ran the prison. The commandant, Major Thomas Pratt Turner, was a thin, clean-shaven Virginian who resigned from the United States Military Academy at West Point in 1860 after refusing to "swear allegiance to a government I despise and abhor." Second in command was the warden, Richard "Dick" Turner, who was not related to his boss. A husky man who formerly worked as a plantation overseer, Dick Turner seemed to enjoy tormenting prisoners. He punched one inmate in the face when the man protested a guard's theft of his property. He routinely confiscated prisoners' blankets if he caught them lying on them during daylight hours. And when several black women were seen giving bread to Union prisoners as they marched though town, he ordered the women stripped to the waist and whipped.

Nearly as hated as Dick Turner was the prison clerk, Erasmus Ross, a little man who wore elegant suits and affected an air of arrogant pomposity. Ross conducted the prison's two daily roll calls and seldom missed a chance to display his contempt for the men he liked to call "damn Yankees." The prisoners feared him because he would occasionally summon an inmate to his office and the man would disappear, never to be seen again. One day, Ross punched a prisoner named William Lounsbury in the gut. "You blue-bellied Yankee, come down to my office," he said. "I have a matter to settle with you."

Terrified, Lounsbury arrived in Ross's office a few minutes later. Ross said nothing. He simply pointed behind a counter and then left the room. Confused, Lounsbury wondered what he was supposed to do. After a while, he looked behind the counter and found a Confederate uniform. He put it on and walked out of the office, then out of the prison. In the street, a black man walked up to him and said, "Come with me, sir, I know who you is." He led Lounsbury to the mansion of Elizabeth Van Lew, a wealthy Richmond woman and secret abolitionist who ran a Union spy ring in the Confederate capital and helped escaped prisoners flee the city.

Despite his carefully contrived appearance to the contrary, Ross was part of Van Lew's circle of pro-Union operatives. He used his job as Libby's clerk to funnel information to her, and occasionally help prisoners escape. His daily show of haughty disdain for the "damn Yankees" was pure performance, but it fooled his colleagues, as well as the prisoners, including Browne and Richardson.

"FRESH FISH! FRESH FISH!"

A few hours after the Bohemians arrived at Libby, the men on the top floors spotted another group of prisoners marching down Cary Street. This time the parade was much longer—more than a thousand forlorn figures in blue uniforms—but Libby's veterans greeted them with the same sarcastic chant that had irked Browne that morning.

"Fresh fish! Fresh fish!"

It took hours for the new men to go through the process of being stripped and searched and separated from their property. When it was over, the enlisted men were hauled to Belle Isle and the 95 officers traipsed upstairs to Libby's top floor.

Richardson recognized the leader of the group. He was Colonel Abel Streight, a tall, brawny, bearded officer who Richardson had met in Tennessee, while Streight was promoting a wild plan for a cavalry raid deep into Georgia to tear up railroad tracks and burn Atlanta's factories. In April, Richardson had touted Streight's audacious plan in a letter to his editor, Sydney Gay, and expressed a desire to cover the raid: "It will be a stirring chapter in the history of the war." But Richardson had chosen to cover the battle for Vicksburg instead. Now, he realized with amusement that if he'd opted to ride with Streight, he probably would have ended up in the same prison on the same day.

Libby's inmates were eager to hear the story of the raid, but Streight and his men were not so eager to tell it because the bold invasion had quickly become a comedy of errors. Streight's plan was inspired by the exploits of Confederate General Nathan Bedford Forrest, who'd earned the nickname "the wizard of the saddle" for his daring cavalry raids behind Union lines in Tennessee. But Streight failed to heed Forrest's most elementary lesson: Cavalry assaults work best when the raiders ride fast horses. Streight's men were mounted on mules. Mules were slower than horses, but Streight figured they'd be more sure-footed on the rugged mountain terrain of northern Alabama and Georgia. It didn't work out that way. In mid-April, Straight's 1,700 men and their mules sailed down the Tennessee River to Eastport, Mississippi, and disembarked. Almost immediately, the mules stampeded and 400 of them skedaddled off into the countryside. Streight's men managed to catch about half of them—probably the slower half. Still, Streight pushed on, heading east across northern Alabama, with several hundred of his "cavalrymen" slogging through the mud on foot. For two weeks, they headed towards Georgia, skirmishing with Forrest's Confederate cavalry nearly every day. Finally, on May 3—the day Richardson, Browne, and Colburn set off to run the batteries of Vicksburg—Streight and his exhausted men surrendered to Forrest near Rome, Georgia. Only after the surrender did Streight realize that his force outnumbered Forrest's five hundred men nearly three to one. Irate, Streight demanded that Forrest return the Union men's weapons and let them fight it out. Forrest, unsurprisingly, refused.

And so, thirteen days later, Streight and his dejected men could be found trudging through the streets of Richmond to Libby Prison while jeering crowds hooted at them.

That night, Streight's officers and the Bohemians experienced their first attempt to sleep in Libby Prison. It wasn't easy. They stretched out on the bare floor, their heads perched atop a book or a knapsack or their rolled-up pants. They tried one position, then another, searching in vain for one that didn't make their hips and shoulders ache. They tried to ignore the smell from the latrine and the sound of scores of men coughing, groaning, snoring, and farting, plus the sound of the joker who thought it was funny to imitate a crying baby. If they managed to drift off to sleep, they were awakened every half-hour as guards patrolling outside hollered out their reports:

"Post number 1—all's well!"

"Post number 2—all's well!"

"Post number 3—all's well!"

Anyone still asleep after dawn was awakened by Old Ben, an elderly black man who came to the prison every morning hawking Richmond's daily newspapers: "Great news in de papers! Great news from the Army of Virginny!" Old Ben sold the papers for 25 cents each—five times the price on the street—but he found plenty of customers among the bored soldiers.

While the men read the papers, an old black prisoner, known as "The General," strolled through each room, fumigating it by waving a skillet of burning tar, which emitted a vile smoke that was supposed to kill bugs. "Here is your nice smoke, without money and without price," The General chanted, but his smoke didn't seem to bother the bugs. On their first full day in Libby, Richardson and Browne reluctantly joined the ranks of the skirmishers, picking through their clothes in search of lice. Browne joked that they were like jealous husbands—searching for evidence they hoped they wouldn't find.

That day, Richardson wrote his first letter from Libby to Sydney Gay, their editor in New York:

Dear Mr. Gay,

As the clown in the circus says (and there is great profundity in our quoting that source) here we are!

Junius, R.T. Colburn of The World, and myself arrived at 5 yesterday morning after a tedious journey.

We had been here just 8 hours when in came Col. Streight with all his officers—100 in number! He came to grief just as surely as we and not half so brilliantly. Singular, was it not, that we should wash up in the same harbor?

We, the journalists, hold paroles from the regular Confederate Agent of Parole at Vicksburg, certifying that having given our pledge not to take up arms again, until exchanged, etc., we are at full liberty to return to our country. They are dated the 4th. But we have no information when we are to be sent North. We trust that you will take all feasible steps to facilitate it.

Junius begs me to make his regards.

Faithfully yours,

Richardson

★

A WEEK AFTER THE VICKBURG prisoners arrived at Libby, Confederate officials agreed to send them north on a flag-of-truce boat—all of them, that is, except Junius Browne and Albert Richardson.

The Union soldiers who'd been scooped out of the Mississippi with the Bohemians were going home, and so was Richard Colburn, but not the two *Tribune* reporters. No explanation was given. Everyone simply assumed the Rebels were punishing Richardson and Browne for the crime of working for America's most famous abolitionist newspaper.

Colburn protested to the Confederate authorities, and told his friends that he'd stay behind in solidarity with them. But they told him to go. He could help them more as a free man in the North than he could as a prisoner sharing their misery in Libby.

Colburn quickly wrote the story of their capture and the *World* published it on May 28, beneath a headline that ballyhooed it as the "Exciting Narrative of our Special Correspondent." Sydney Gay, the *Tribune*'s managing editor, read Colburn's story with trepidation, particularly the part that revealed that the Tribune reporters were still inexplicably detained. Gay had long worried about what might happen if Browne and Richardson were captured. He wrote to President Lincoln, asking him to do whatever he could to win their freedom.

Lincoln remembered Richardson, of course, and on June 1, the president sent a telegram to Colonel William Ludlow, the Union's official in charge of prisoner exchanges: "Richardson & Browne, correspondents of the Tribune captured at Vicksburg, are detained at Richmond. Please ascertain why they are detained, & get them off if you can."

The next day, Ludlow wrote to Robert Ould, the Confederate agent of prisoner exchange: "A. D. Richardson and Junius H. Browne, correspondents of the *New York Tribune*, captured about the 4th of May near Vicksburg, are said to be confined in the Libby Prison. Mr. Colburn, the correspondent of the New York World, who was captured with them, has been released. It has been the practice to treat attaches of the press as non-combatants and not to retain them. The release of Mr. Colburn is a partial recognition of this practice. Will you please inform me if you will release Richardson and Browne; and if not, why not?"

Ludlow's letter failed to move Ould, who was not inclined to sympathize with either Yankees or reporters. In 1859, when Ould was district attorney of Washington, DC, newspapers mocked his inept prosecution of Congressman Dan Sickles, who had killed his wife's lover in broad daylight in Lafayette Park and then became the first murder defendant in American history to win acquittal on the grounds of temporary insanity. Now, Sickles was a Union general; his defense attorney, Edwin Stanton, was Lincoln's secretary of war; and Ould was a Confederate bureaucrat in Richmond. A few months earlier,

Ould had displayed his attitude towards Union captives in a letter to a Confederate colonel: "Pay no regard to the Yankee prisoners. I would rather they should starve than our own people suffer. I suppose I can safely put it in writing: 'Let them suffer.'"

Ould's reply to Ludlow reeked of contempt. "When was the rule established that non-combatants were not to be retained?" he asked. Didn't the Union armies occupying Confederate territory in Virginia and Tennessee hold hundreds of non-combatants?

> What peculiar immunity should the correspondents of the *Tribune* have over an old gray-haired grandfather who never shouldered a musket or followed in the wake of an army? It seems to me that if any exception be made as to any non-combatants, it should be against such men as the *Tribune* correspondents, who have had more share even than your soldiery in bringing rapine, pillage and desolation to our homes. I have no compassion for such, even if their miseries were ten-fold greater. You ask why I will not release them. 'Tis because they are the worst and most obnoxious of all non-combatants.

☆

RICHARDSON AND BROWNE never saw those letters, but they guessed what was happening. They told each other that the Confederates were paying them a high compliment by singling them out for punishment: Obviously, the *Tribune* had gotten under the Rebels' skin. It was a crumb of comfort for two men locked in Libby prison.

One day, Browne reminded Major Turner, the prison commandant, that he and Richardson had been paroled, and that they had the parole documents right there in their pockets.

"Oh, that makes no difference," Turner said. "Your paroles do not go into effect until after you are on the truce boat."

"What in heaven's name do we want of paroles when we are on the truce boat?" Browne replied. "That is like telling a prisoner sentenced to execution that he is pardoned, but he is not to benefit by his pardon until after he has been hanged an hour."

It was insane, and the utter irrationality of their plight drove Browne to sputtering rage. *They'd been paroled! They had official documents stating that they were "hereby paroled," and the documents were signed by an official Confederate exchange agent! So why were they still prisoners?*

About a week after Colburn was released, another small group of Libby prisoners was sent north. When they heard the news they cheered wildly, and the sound of their celebration irritated Browne so much that he grumbled to Richardson that they should have the common decency to keep quiet and not torment the prisoners they were leaving behind.

Richardson tried to calm his friend. "You must remember, Junius," he said, "they have been prisoners for *three months.*"

Three months! It seemed like an eternity. Browne pondered the prospect of spending three months in Libby and concluded that he could never do it. Libby would kill him long before three months had elapsed.

Browne lost all hope. He figured he'd be stuck in this hideous hellhole until he died or the war ended. He sank into a deep depression. He said he felt as if his brain was on fire and his blood was boiling. Weak, sick, and feverish, he lay on Libby's bare floors for weeks, barely moving, just staring up at the window. He refused all medicine, and he even stopped reading, which had always been his greatest pleasure. But reading made him think, he said, and thinking made him brood, and brooding plunged him into a frightening state of dark despondency. As he lay there, words from the Book of Matthew kept running through his head: "I was a stranger and you did not welcome me, naked and you did not clothe me, sick and in prison and you did not visit me."

. . . sick and in prison . . .

. . . sick and in prison . . .

. . . sick and in prison . . .

Richardson watched Browne suffer and worried that he might die. Browne also worried that he might die—but feared even more that he would live long enough to go completely insane.

7

THE GENERAL'S DANCE

AS THE FOURTH OF JULY APPROACHED, the inmates of Libby Prison prepared to celebrate their country's 87th birthday. They formed a committee, which drew up a program of speakers and songs. But they needed a flag, and American flags were banned in the prison. So Captain Edward Driscoll of the 3rd Ohio Infantry, a tailor in civilian life, secretly sewed an American flag out of scraps of cloth donated by other prisoners—red flannel, white cotton, and a blue navy patch.

Driscoll and his fellow prisoners understood that the war wasn't going well for the United States of America. In Mississippi, General Grant was stalled outside Vicksburg. On May 19, 1863, he had ordered his men to charge the Confederates' trenches, but the Rebels drove them back. The Union lost nearly 1,000 dead and wounded, the Confederates, fewer than 100. Three days later, the Federals attacked again. This time, the Union lost more than 3,000 dead and wounded, the Confederates, fewer than 500. After that, Grant quit trying to assault Vicksburg and settled in for a siege.

In Virginia, the situation was even worse for the Union. In early May, Confederate General Robert E. Lee had outfoxed Union General Joe Hooker at Chancellorsville, and the outnumbered Rebels whipped the Federals decisively, driving them back across the Rappahannock River after inflicting 17,000 casualties. In mid-May—just as Browne and Richardson arrived at Libby—Lee began preparing for another invasion of the North. In mid-June, Lee's army, moving north through the Shenandoah Valley, defeated the Federals at Winchester, capturing 4,000 Yankee prisoners. Two weeks later, the Confederates were cutting a swath through Pennsylvania, seizing food, shoes, and clothing, tearing up railroad tracks, capturing several dozen free blacks and sending them south into slavery. From Harrisburg to Philadelphia, panicking Pennsylvanians packed up and prepared to flee.

In Libby prison, Richardson, Browne, and the other inmates were gripped by the news of Lee's invasion, reported in the Richmond papers. "The army of General Lee is still on its march Northward, and thus far has met with no opposition," the *Dispatch* reported on June 30. "Our cavalry have several times come upon large masses of Pennsylvania militia," the *Examiner* reported the same day, "who upon all occasions, take to their heels before our men can get a shot at them."

Flummoxed, General Joe Hooker couldn't decide how to counter the general who'd thrashed him at Chancellorsville. "I don't know whether I'm standing on my head or my feet," he said. Disgusted, Lincoln fired Hooker on June 28, replacing him with General George Meade.

In Richmond, Jefferson Davis dispatched his vice-president, Alexander Stephens, north on a flag-of-truce boat, hoping that Lee's success in Pennsylvania would force Lincoln to negotiate an end to the war on Southern terms. Smelling victory, Richmond's newspapers began to gloat: "A successful campaign by General Lee in the enemy's country will strike a terrible blow to the government at Washington," the *Dispatch* declared on July 3. "The next 30 days, should we continue victorious, may present an entirely new phase of the war, and draw us very near to its conclusion."

Libby's prisoners told each other that the Rebel papers lied, but that didn't stop the endless rumors spread by taunting guards: *Grant's been beaten at Vicksburg. Lee whipped Meade in Pennsylvania, and he's heading for Washington.* The news, the rumors, and the taunts combined to deepen the prisoners' despondency.

"The prison was gloomy and silent," Richardson wrote. "Our hearts were too heavy for speech."

Still, the prisoners vowed to celebrate the Fourth of July, and when the day came, they gathered on the prison's top floor and hung Driscoll's makeshift American flag from the rafters. A chaplain opened the celebration with a prayer, and somebody recited the Declaration of Independence. Then Colonel Abel Streight, who'd emerged as a defiant leader of the prisoners, delivered a fiery Independence Day oration that set the prisoners to cheering, clapping, and stomping their feet.

The noise attracted the warden, Dick Turner, who arrived, accompanied by a guard. When he saw the flag, he exploded with rage.

"Who put that thing up there?"

Nobody answered.

"Take it down at once."

Nobody moved.

Furious, Turner ordered the guard to get the flag. The guard climbed into the rafters and ripped it down. Turner announced that the party was over. There would be no more celebrations, and no more speeches. Then he left.

The guard stayed behind and watched as Streight led the prisoners in a debate about whether or not they should obey Turner's command to end the speeches. One by one, the men who'd been chosen to deliver speeches rose to say that they believed they had every right to speak on the subject, and then they specified in great detail exactly what they'd planned to say in their speeches. It was a clever ruse: The inmate orators delivered their speeches under the guise of pretending to discuss whether they should deliver them.

When this mock debate ended, the prisoners exhibited a wry sense of humor by voting to comply with Turner's order and skip the speeches. Then they concluded their celebration by singing "The Star-Spangled Banner" and "We'll Hang Jeff Davis from a Sour Apple Tree."

T WO DAYS LATER, on July 6, Libby's commandant, Thomas Turner, summoned all prisoners holding the rank of captain to an office on the first floor. The captains eagerly hustled downstairs, expecting that they might be paroled and sent home.

"Gentlemen," Turner said, "it is my painful duty to communicate to you an order I have received from General Winder, which I will read."

John Winder was the Confederate provost marshal of Richmond, whose duties included overseeing the city's prisons. His order referred to the much publicized story of two Confederate captains who had been captured behind Union lines in Kentucky, convicted of espionage by a military tribunal, and executed by firing squad. In retaliation, Winder was hereby ordering Commandant Turner to select two Union captains at random and execute them.

After reading Winder's order, Turner commanded the assembled Union captains—there were 74 of them—to line up around a table. The name of each captain was written on a slip of paper, carefully folded, and placed in a box on the table. Turner asked for a volunteer to draw the names of the two men who would be executed. Nobody volunteered. Turner summoned a Union chaplain, Reverend Joseph T. Brown, and ordered him to draw the names. Brown recited a short prayer and then, with tears running down his cheeks, he pulled two slips of paper from the box. A Confederate officer read the names— Henry W. Sawyer of the 1st New Jersey Cavalry, and John P. Flinn, of the 51st Indiana Infantry.

Turner announced that he would give Sawyer and Flinn ten days to get their affairs in order before their execution on July 16.

The captains trudged back upstairs, looking pale and stunned. Word of the macabre order spread quickly through the prison, horrifying the inmates, and inspiring endless speculation. *Would the Rebels really kill two innocent prisoners? Or was this some kind of cruel bluff?* Richardson talked to the two chosen victims. He found Flinn calm, but Sawyer was visibly nervous. Both men were certain that the Rebels were serious about killing them.

Richardson tried to convince them otherwise and cheer them up a bit. "There is not one chance in ten of their executing you," he told Flinn.

"I know it," Flinn answered. "But when we drew lots, I had one chance in 35—and then lost."

There was no answer to that.

Browne also tried to comfort the two men, predicting that not only would they escape execution, they'd be released—probably long before the two *Tribune* reporters. But the execution order hung heavy on Browne's mind. If the Rebels killed two prisoners in retaliation for a Union execution, wouldn't the Union retaliate by killing two Rebel prisoners? And if both sides kept retaliating, how long would it take before the Rebels decided to execute the two reporters from the hated *Tribune*? He joked with Richardson about which method of execution was preferable—hanging or shooting? Facing the firing squad, he said, seemed more manly and heroic. But after the joking ended, he brooded morosely. Even as a boy, he'd harbored an intense fear of being hanged. Was that, he wondered, some kind of premonition?

L ATE ON THE AFTERNOON of July 8, Browne lay under a blanket on the floor of one of Libby's upstairs rooms, sick and depressed. Around him, prisoners were killing time in the usual fashion—reading or talking or picking lice out of their underwear. Outside, a heavy summer rain lashed the ground. Inside, the men were despondent at the news in the morning papers: "MEADE'S ARMY ANNIHI-LATED," said the headline in the *Examiner*. "FORTY THOUSAND PRISONERS TAKEN."

Into this gloom stepped The General—the old black man who fumigated the rooms every morning and performed other menial tasks around the prison. He quietly entered the room, and shut the door behind him. Without saying a word, he walked to the center of the room and began to dance, exuberantly kicking up his feet and throwing out his arms.

Richardson watched this performance and wondered what was happening. He had talked to The General about the topic that everybody discussed endlessly—the war—and the man told him that it was a speculator's war, with both sides fighting for money, and he didn't give a damn who won. It was a sentiment frequently heard among the Northern antiwar Democrats known as "Copperheads," but Richardson had never heard a black man express it. Was The General lying, hiding his real views so he wouldn't get into trouble with the Confederates? Or was he really the only black man Richardson had ever met who wasn't rooting for a Union victory?

A crowd of prisoners gathered around, watching The General dance, until somebody asked, "General, what does this mean?"

"De Yankees has taken Vicksburg!" The General said, smiling broadly. "De Yankees has taken Vicksburg!"

He pulled a newspaper out of his pocket—an afternoon extra he'd swiped from one of the guards—and kept on dancing. The prisoners seized the paper and learned that The General was right: Grant conquered Vicksburg on July 4, capturing 30,000 Rebel soldiers. The Union now controlled the Mississippi, splitting the South in two. Hearing the news, the men in Libby cheered, whistled, stomped, shouted, and hugged each other. Some of them joined The General in his victory dance.

Junius Browne threw off his blanket, leaped to his feet, and joined the other prisoners in a spirited rendition of "The Star-Spangled Banner." When they finished, they could hear guards out on the street grumbling: "Did you hear that? Those damned Yankees must have got the news."

The prisoners celebrated long into the night, singing loud, raucous versions of their favorite patriotic songs, particularly "John Brown's Body," which was, Browne recalled, "especially obnoxious to the Rebels, and therefore particularly agreeable to us." During the celebration, Chaplain Charles McCabe of the 122nd Ohio Infantry, who entertained the men with hymns every night, stepped forward to sing new lyrics to that tune:

> Mine eyes have seen the glory of the coming of the Lord,
> He is tramping out the vintage where the grapes of
> wrath are stored.
> He hath loosed the fateful lightning of His
> terrible swift sword.
> His truth is marching on!

Before his capture, McCabe had read those lyrics in the *Atlantic Monthly*. They were written by Julia Ward Howe, an abolitionist poet who'd heard Union soldiers singing "John Brown's Body" while traveling near Washington. Her minister had suggested that she write new lyrics to replace the vulgar "John Brown's body lies a-mouldering in the grave" with something more uplifting. That night, she awoke from a deep sleep in Washington's Willard Hotel with new lyrics running through her head, and she climbed out of bed to write the song she called "The Battle Hymn of the Republic." Eighteen months later,

Chaplain McCabe taught the words to his fellow captives in Libby Prison as they celebrated the victory at Vicksburg.

> *In the beauty of the lilies, Christ was born across the sea*
> *With a glory in His bosom that transfigures you and me;*
> *As He died to make men holy, let us die to make men free,*
> *While God is marching on!*

As the prisoners belted out the chorus—*"Glory, glory Hallelujah! His truth is marching on!"*—Richardson thought he'd never seen men more filled with emotion.

Browne was among those singing with gusto. He felt good. His fever had disappeared, and his body surged with energy. He swore that the news of victory at Vicksburg had cured him. "That news, so glorious, proved more potent than any Arabian philter," he wrote. "I had no fever nor ailment of any kind for many a long month after."

Perhaps he was exaggerating for dramatic effect. Or maybe his fever had been psychosomatic, and thus susceptible to a quick cure provided by an injection of hope. Either way, the worst of Browne's long ailment was over and his depression lifted. He stopped spending his days lying on the floor and instead wandered the prison, smoking his clay pipe and chatting with other inmates. Recalling the Stoic philosophers he'd studied at Xavier, he vowed to take whatever punishments the prison dished out without complaining—and to live long enough to see the Confederacy die.

VICKSBURG WASN'T THE only source of heartening news for the Union. On July 3—the day before Grant conquered Vicksburg—Meade's army whipped the Confederates at Gettysburg, defeating the heroic but foolish frontal assault known as "Pickett's Charge" and sending Lee's army limping back towards Virginia. That news would have delighted the men locked in Libby Prison, but they were getting their information from the Richmond newspapers, which insisted that the Confederates had won the battle.

"OUR ARMY VICTORIOUS AT GETTYSBURG," the *Examiner* reported on July 7, four days after the battle. "THE YANKEE ARMY RETREATING." Elated by the alleged Rebel victory, the *Examiner*'s editors couldn't resist mocking the enemy: "Not even the Chinese are less prepared by previous habits of life and education for martial resistance than the Yankees. Scarcely a man can be found familiar with the use of a gun; few have any skill or experience in horsemanship, and the whole breed are as nervously fearful of gunpowder and bloodshed as women and negroes."

On July 8, both the *Examiner* and the *Dispatch* reported that Lee's army had mauled the Federals and captured 40,000 Yankee prisoners. But the following day, the *Examiner* revealed that its count of Yankee prisoners was "false in all things" and sheepishly admitted that it was Lee, not Meade, who had retreated. But the paper assured its readers that the retreat was merely tactical, not a sign of defeat: "General Lee was victorious in all the combats which have taken place. He has been engaged with the whole force of the United States and has broken its backbone."

The coverage became more bizarre on July 10, when the *Dispatch* printed excerpts from Northern newspaper stories that reported a Union victory, but added an editorial note: "The Yankee accounts, which we publish today, are a tissue of lies and exaggerations from beginning to end." The next day, the *Examiner* reprinted a *Philadelphia Inquirer* story that reported Lee's retreat, but added a parenthesis: "(It is well known in Richmond that this is a Yankee lie.)" Neither paper explained why it would print stories it believed to be bogus.

"We were not entirely victorious at Gettysburg," the *Examiner* finally admitted on July 15, a full twelve days after the battle. But the editors still couldn't bring themselves to concede defeat. "So far as the fighting went, all the Federal army did was prevent its own annihilation. The Confederates were repulsed but cannot, at present, with justice or candor, be said to have suffered defeat."

Reading both papers every morning in Libby Prison, Richardson and Browne watched gleefully as the Rebel reporters performed amazing verbal gyrations in their effort to turn defeat and retreat into glorious victory. Richardson was particularly amused by the newspapers' panic over the imminent arrival of those 40,000 Yankee prisoners who turned out not to exist: "It was entertaining to read the speculations of the Rebel papers as to what they could do with these forty-thousand Yankees—where they could find men to guard them, and room for them—how in the world they could feed them without starving the people of Richmond."

★

IN NEW YORK, NEWS OF the enormous casualties at Gettysburg arrived simultaneously with news of the North's first draft lottery. That unhappy juxtaposition ignited the bloody "draft riot," which killed at least 105 people over four days, and incinerated much of Manhattan.

The riot began on July 13, when a crowd of angry workingmen attacked the draft office, destroying the files and setting the building ablaze. The rioters were mostly Irish immigrants, many of whom had fled famine in their native land only to find themselves scorned and mocked by native New Yorkers and relegated to low-paying manual labor. For them, a war to end slavery meant that they'd have to compete with free black men for scarce jobs. And now the government was drafting Irish workingmen while their rich Yankee employers avoided military service by paying a $300 "commutation fee" or by hiring a substitute—the tactic employed by businessmen Andrew Carnegie and J. P. Morgan, future presidents Chester A. Arthur and Grover Cleveland, and the fathers of future presidents Theodore and Franklin Roosevelt.

Burning the draft office failed to sate the rioters' bloodlust. They swarmed through the streets of Manhattan, looting stores (including Brooks Brothers), trashing the homes of wealthy Republicans, and beating police commissioner John A. Kennedy nearly to death. The rioters looted and burned the Colored Orphans Asylum on Fifth Avenue and attacked any black person they saw, lynching a crippled black coachman, then setting his corpse on fire while chanting "Hurrah for Jeff Davis!"

That night, a mob marched into Printing House Square and besieged the office of the *Tribune*, threatening to lynch Horace Greeley, calling him "the niggers' friend." One man yelled, "Come out of there, you goddamned black-hearted abolitionist!" Another hollered, "Hang the damned son of a bitch!" Inside the building, managing editor Sydney Gay urged Greeley to sneak out the back door. Greeley refused, saying that he had an appointment for dinner with a friend and he intended to keep it. "If I can't eat my dinner when I'm hungry," he said, "my life isn't worth anything to me." As Gay watched from an upstairs window, Greeley walked out the front door and strolled through the mob. Nobody touched him.

While Greeley dined at a nearby restaurant, rioters shattered the *Tribune*'s windows and swarmed into the building, setting fire to papers before a squad of police drove them off. Upstairs, in the newsroom, reporters and editors continued to work on the next day's paper, which chronicled the riot in a story that filled the front page.

The mob returned the next night, eager to finish burning the *Tribune*, but when the rioters spotted men with rifles leaning out the upstairs windows, they fled. As it happened, the bullets Gay had obtained did not fit the rifles he'd procured, but the rioters didn't know that and so the *Tribune* survived to publish another day.

Browne and Richardson learned of the mob's assault on their newspaper by reading a gleeful account in the Richmond *Dispatch*: "Let us have more of these outpourings—a few more great cities on the mourner's bench—some more gutting and sacking of houses, and hanging and mutilating of men. It saves the Confederate troops a great deal of marching and fighting, and lops off many a dreary month of this war."

SAWYER AND FLINN, the two captains selected for execution, were locked in Libby's dungeon on a diet of cornbread and water, but they were permitted to write letters to their families.

"My Dear Wife, I am under the necessity of informing you that my prospects look dark," Sawyer wrote to his wife, Harriet. The Confederates had promised him that she and their five children could visit if they arrived before he was hanged.

> My situation is hard to be borne and I cannot think of dying without seeing you and the children. . . . You will proceed to Washington. My government will give you transportation to Fortress Monroe, and you will get there by flag of truce and return in the same way. Bring with you a shirt for me. . . . My dear wife, the fortune of war has put me in this position. If I must die, a sacrifice to my country, with God's will I must submit; only let me see you once more and I will die becoming a man and an officer; but for God's sake do not disappoint me.

Harriet Sawyer received the letter at her home in New Jersey and immediately set off for Washington, where she managed to arrange an audience with President Lincoln. He listened to her story, then devised a plan to save Sawyer and Flinn. He ordered William Ludlow, the Union's agent of prisoner exchange, to inform his Confederate counterpart, Robert Ould, that if Sawyer and Flinn were executed, the Union would retaliate by hanging two Confederate prisoners. One would be a captain selected at random. The other would be General William Henry Fitzhugh Lee, the captured son of Robert E. Lee.

When the Libby prisoners read that news in their morning papers, they celebrated, assuming that Jefferson Davis would do anything he could to prevent the execution of his best general's son. They were right. Davis countermanded the execution order and Sawyer and Flinn were released from the dungeon and permitted to rejoin the other officers on Libby's top floors.

Outraged, the editors of the *Richmond Examiner* demanded that Davis proceed with the execution, whatever the consequences: "It is hoped that the executive will see fit to give the order for the execution immediately; and as we now have over 500 federal officers in our hands, besides 5,000 or 6,000 privates, it is in the power of the government to carry retaliation to a very bitter extreme. The people call for the death of these two Yankees, and it is useless to delay their deaths any longer."

The *Examiner*'s editorial displayed a chilling callousness towards Union prisoners, but the *Dispatch* was even more bloodthirsty: "We confess to a special delight in hearing of piles of Yankee corpses, no matter how high or how broad or how long. For prisoners we have not the same weakness. They are troublesome to guard and must be fed. But dead men attempt no escapes, create no disturbances, eat no bread, cost no money. We had rather hear of one hundred thousand dead Yankees than of one single Yankee prisoner."

Both sides' threats to execute innocent captives showed just how bitter the prisoner issue had become. In the year between July 1862 and July 1863, the two warring governments had exchanged well over 100,000 prisoners. But in the summer of 1863, the exchange program broke down in mutual acrimony. The reason was race. After Lincoln's Emancipation Proclamation, the Union army recruited thousands of black soldiers, many of them escaped slaves. In response, the Confederate Congress passed a resolution stating that captured black soldiers would be returned to slavery and their white officers would be "put to death." Explaining this policy, Ould used the phrase that had often amused Richardson, Browne, and Colburn: The South would "die in the last ditch," he wrote, before it would relinquish "the right to send slaves back to slavery as property recaptured." In July, Lincoln announced that he would "permit no distinction as to color in the treatment of prisoners of war." But the South steadfastly refused to exchange black prisoners, and by the fall of 1863, the prisoner exchange program had effectively ended.

Of course, those decisions didn't affect the exchange of captured civilians, including newspaper reporters. In August 1863, S. A. Meredith, the Union's new exchange agent, attempted to arrange the release of Richardson and Browne. "When Vicksburg was captured, the editors of the Whig and Citizen fell into our hands, and were immediately paroled and sent away," Meredith wrote in a letter to Ould. "If you are sincere then, in your offers, I call upon you to give me evidence thereof by immediately releasing Messrs. Richardson and Browne."

Exhibiting a remarkable talent for legal hairsplitting, Ould rejected the notion that there was any similarity between Northern journalists captured at Vicksburg and Southern journalists captured at Vicksburg. "Your reference to the parole of the editors of the *Whig* and *Citizen* at Vicksburg has no sort of force," he replied. "They were paroled by the terms of surrender and not by any special grace of your authorities. You could not have retained them without a breach of the terms of capitulation. Their cases are in no respect analogous to those of Richardson and Browne, except in their avocation of driving the quill."

The *Tribune* reporters would be released, Ould added, when the Union army released every Southern civilian it held.

8

RAISE YOUR LEFT FOOT AND SWEAR

At night, Junius Browne escaped from Libby Prison.

Stretched out on the hard wooden floor, surrounded by scores of coughing, snoring men, Browne slowly drifted off to sleep, and then he left Libby and floated away to other places, other times—to his childhood home . . . to his family and his friends . . . to a city bustling with commerce and culture . . . to an elegant dining room where candlelight shimmered off silverware on a table piled with delicacies . . . to beautiful women with smiling eyes . . .

Only to awake, open his eyes, and find himself staring once again at the dusty wooden rafters of Libby Prison, where the men around him arose, groaning and cursing, their bones aching from the long night on the hard floor, many of them recently returned from their own dream voyages to other places, other times. Now they were all back in Libby Prison for another dull day destined to be much like yesterday and tomorrow.

Monotony was the enemy, and every man fought it his own way. Some played whist or euchre or poker or chess. Some used contraband knives to carve soup bones into rings or crosses or a brooch for a sweetheart back home. Some, including Browne and Richardson, read anything they could find that might transport their minds to some other place. But the main pastime at Libby, the main form of entertainment, was conversation. Richardson and Browne, being curious reporters, roamed the prison, chatting with inmates, listening to their stories. New captives arrived nearly every day—by the end of August, more than 550 officers squeezed into Libby's two upper floors—and they all had stories to tell. They told tales of battles on land and sea, accounts of victories and defeats, stories of courage and fear and folly. All the stories were different, of course, but they all ended the same way, with the teller captured by the damn Rebels and dragged off to this godforsaken prison.

One prisoner, who was captured at Vicksburg, had been shot in the eye during one of Grant's ill-fated assaults. The eye was gone, but otherwise the man was fine. "He walked about our room with a handkerchief tied around his head, smoking complacently," Richardson recalled, "apparently considering a bullet in the brain a very slight annoyance." The prisoners loved stories like that, freakish tales of men who had miraculously survived shots that should have killed them. There was the story of a soldier who was lying in the dirt, firing his rifle, when a Rebel cannonball hit the ground beside him and plowed a tunnel about six inches under him before it popped up on his other side like some kind of round metal gopher. And the story of the lieutenant who was shot in the mouth, which was open at the time, and the bullet knocked out three false teeth, which went flying into the thigh of the sergeant standing next to him—and both of them were barely scratched. And there were countless stories about men who found one, or two, or *nine* bullet holes in their clothes or their hats after a battle, but not a scratch on their bodies. And stories of men saved when the bullet that hit them was deflected by something in their pockets—a silver half-dollar, or a plug of tobacco, or, for one soldier, a little book of risqué song lyrics.

"I am sorry to say that I heard of no instance in which a life was saved by a Bible," Browne noted wryly, "and I'm bound to believe the fact is owing to the great scarcity of the sacred volume in the army, rather than to any want of preserving power in the Holy Book itself."

Of course, the prisoners did not talk only about the war. They spoke endlessly about the things they missed—their homes, their families, their wives and sweethearts. And they talked incessantly about food. The food at Libby was dismal and there wasn't enough of it, and the constant hunger inspired some men to engage in long detailed discussions about exactly what sumptuous delicacies they'd order if they happened to find themselves in some swanky restaurant. Richardson hated those conversations. They drove him mad with hunger, and he would flee the room so he wouldn't end up punching the obnoxious epicures in the nose.

What drove Browne mad was cooking. The prisoners had to cook all their meals and they hated the task, but Browne hated it more than most. The Cincinnati banker's son had grown up dining on food prepared by the family's cook. He joked that the only dishes he knew how to make were lobster salad and stewed oysters. Such delicacies were absent from the menu at Libby Prison, where the fare was far more plebian. Every day, prison workers plopped a pile of food in the kitchen for the day's meals—usually corn meal or rice, plus some stringy beef or greasy bacon, and maybe some dried beans or peas. The prisoners sometimes augmented that fare by purchasing black market fruits and vegetables from prison guards. Then they divided the ingredients up, with each "mess," or cooking group, receiving its share based on the number of men in the mess. Some messes contained 20 or more prisoners. Browne and Richardson belonged to Mess Number 21, which had only four members. They took turns: each man in Mess 21 cooked every fourth day. Browne dreaded his turn in the kitchen. "I would rather have attempted to capture Richmond," he grumbled, "or pay off the national debt."

The kitchen contained three wood-burning stoves, and they all leaked smoke, which filled the room with a hot, dry fog that stung the eyes. Water garnished with sand and twigs and bugs was pumped into the kitchen directly from the James River. Every day, dozens of prisoners swarmed over the kitchen and attempted the near impossible task of creating something reasonably edible for the men in their messes out of whatever ingredients happened to be available.

"There were very few dishes; the stoves were in a wretched condition; the wood was green; the bacon was tough; and my knife was dull," Browne wrote in a comic description of his first shift as a chef. "After laboring an hour, the perspiration streaming down my face, I succeeded in getting some pieces of bacon over the fire, and spilling the grease upon the only pantaloons I possessed. In another hour I had fried some bread in the pan, and at the close of the third I had boiled a little water impregnated with burnt corn, which the Rebels, with a delightful idealism, termed coffee."

That was breakfast, so he still had two more meals to cook.

Libby's kitchen was a smoky den of chaos, turmoil, and rage. There was never enough room on the stoves for all the cooks, so officers of the United States Army—captains, colonels, even *generals*—found themselves shoving and elbowing each other out of the way so they could place a skillet or pot or tin can filled with some dubious swill atop a barely functional stove. They bumped into each other, spilled food on each other, cursed each other, and occasionally punched each other over some momentarily momentous issue such as the moving of somebody's frying pan or the spilling of somebody's tepid ersatz coffee.

After a long day in the kitchen, a prisoner might start to think that life couldn't get much worse. But that feeling faded after the evening meal, when the cooks gathered up whatever scraps of food remained and brought them to the hidden hole they'd secretly cut in the kitchen floor, where they could peer into Libby's dungeon. Down there, in the perpetual darkness, hands were raised, hungry for even the most pathetic castoffs.

"When they saw the food coming," Richardson wrote, "they would crowd beneath the aperture, with upturned faces and eager eyes, springing to clutch every crumb, sometimes ready to fight over the smallest morsels, and looking more like ravenous animals than human beings."

EVERY MORNING, ONE OF THE guards would climb a ladder on Libby's top floor, open a scuttle in the ceiling, scamper up on the roof, and raise the Confederate flag. Every night, a guard would climb back up the ladder and lower the flag. One evening in late July, when the rooms inside Libby were sweltering ovens, some prisoners quietly ascended the ladder, opened the scuttle, and perched on the roof, basking in the cool breeze.

It was glorious up there, watching the sun go down and the blue sky turn slowly to black. Every night, groups of prisoners took their turns on the roof, escaping the foul, stifling air inside the prison and enjoying what Browne, an aficionado of the rooftop, called "the genial air of the evening."

Inevitably, the guards figured out what was going on, and Dick Turner showed up, enraged. He ordered the men off the roof, threatening that any prisoner caught up there would be sent down into the dungeon.

"It would be a desecration of Virginian atmosphere, I suppose, to be breathed by a hated Yankee prisoner," Captain Louis Beaudry wrote in his diary that day.

Beaudry was quite a character—a Vermont Yankee, a Methodist minister, a droll wit, and a go-getter who generated endless ideas. He was new to the prison, but he'd already enlivened the place. Chaplain of the 5th New York Cavalry, he was captured by Confederates outside Gettysburg and he arrived at Libby on July 18. Within a few weeks, he'd organized a debating society and recruited prisoners to argue such questions as "Resolved: That Intemperance Is a Greater Sin than Slavery," and "Resolved: That Fear of Punishment Has a Greater Influence on Mankind than Hope of Reward" and, for comic relief, "Resolved: That Men Ought Not to Shave Their Faces." Beaudry argued the antishaving position in that debate, and noted in his diary that he had "carried the day."

The rooms were so hot that the debaters frequently made their arguments while barefoot and naked above the waist. The prisoners in the audience didn't mind; many of them were wearing only underwear. The debates proved so popular that Beaudry decided to start a school. He called it the Libby Lyceum, but the prisoners quickly nicknamed it the "Libby Lice-I-See-'Em"—a nod to the pests that kept everybody scratching. Beaudry taught a French class. Federico Cavada, a Cuban-born colonel, taught a Spanish class. Other officers taught classes in Latin, Greek, algebra, military tactics, history, philosophy, physiology, and shorthand. One of the most popular classes was Major John Henry's lecture series on Mesmerism, a form of hypnosis based on the mystical ideas of Franz Mesmer, the German physician who coined the phrase "animal magnetism."

"The hitherto idle prisoners are *students* now," Charles McCabe, the singing chaplain, wrote in a letter to his wife.

Browne was among the best educated of the inmates, but he didn't volunteer to teach any classes. He claimed he wasn't in good "mental condition," but he was probably just too shy. Richardson was not so reticent. He loved the give-and-take of intellectual sparring, and on one hot August afternoon, he debated Major Henry on the topic "Is Mesmerism a True Science?"

Beaudry watched the debate and jotted a neutral description in his diary: "Most excellent thoughts advanced on both sides and brilliant speeches made." But Henry won the debate easily, arguing in favor of Mesmerism—not because the prisoners understood his mystifying metaphysics but because they were eager to be hypnotized, particularly if hypnosis could, as Beaudry put it, "make us believe that we are amply fed and clothed and delivered from the pesky varmints that are the *bete noir* of our existence here."

Soon, a craze for hypnosis spread through the prison, and for several weeks the sweltering summer afternoons were enlivened by the sight of sweaty men sitting on the floor in their underwear trying to hypnotize other sweaty men sitting on the floor in their underwear.

Results were, alas, disappointing.

The debates and classes unleashed the prisoners' dormant theatricality, and soon they began staging mock trials, complete with judge, jury, lawyers, bailiffs, and a defendant accused of some ludicrous crime, such as making too much noise at night while splashing around in the prison's only bathtub. Cases began with a bailiff chanting: "Hear ye! Hear ye! The honorable court for the county of Libby and the state of imprisonment is now opened!" Then the judge would swear in each witness by asking him to raise his left foot and answer the question: "Do you pompously swear that you will tear, tatter, transmogrify and torture the truth, the whole truth and everything but the truth, so help you Jeff Davis?"

On Friday morning, August 21, Beaudry summoned the prisoners to witness the debut of his latest creation—a weekly newspaper he called the *Libby Chronicle*. He solicited news, jokes, poems, and essays, and "published" what he received every Friday morning by reading it to a crowd of cheering, laughing prisoners.

On that first Friday, Beaudry announced the motto of the *Chronicle*: "A little nonsense now and then is relished by the best of men." Then he read his first editorial, a comic riff on mornings at Libby: The sun shining through the barred windows, waking men from "sweet dreams of home," followed by the arrival of Old Ben, hawking Rebel newspapers—"as innocent of literary taste as they are of reliable news"—and finally the day's first deadly skirmishes with the prisoners' most hated enemy, lice. "The casualties are many. The black flag is raised, and no quarters are given to these Rebel parasites that swarm as in the plagues of Egypt."

A week later, on August 28, the prisoners packed a room on Libby's top floor to hear Beaudry read the second issue of the *Chronicle*. It featured a long comic poem about Castle Thunder, a prison two blocks down Cary Street, an infamous and terrifying place where the Rebels kept captives who weren't worthy to live in Libby—deserters, draft dodgers, murderers, thieves, con men, runaway slaves, and some Yankee prostitutes captured when the Rebels seized Union-occupied Winchester. Beaudry announced that the poem was written by an anonymous Castle Thunder inmate and smuggled into Libby "through secret channels."

> *On Cary Street in Richmond, there is a mongrel den*
> *Of thieves, sneaks and cowards mixed up with gentlemen,*
> *Oh what a living shame to huddle in together*
> *Men and beasts, wild and tame, like birds of every feather!*
> *The Reb authorities scared up this greatest wonder,*
> *Made it a prison, and named it Castle Thunder.*

The poem went on for 96 more lines, mocking Castle Thunder's evil inmates, its drunken guards, its sadistic warden, its foul food, and its gargantuan vermin—"so big the lice themselves are lousy." The Libby prisoners loved the poem. Delighted to hear about a prison even worse than their own, they howled with laughter, and demanded that Beaudry read the poem again the following Friday.

Richardson and Browne missed Beaudry's second recitation of the poem. On September 2, the two *Tribune* reporters and Libby's 22 other civilian inmates were rounded up and marched down the street to another prison—Castle Thunder.

9

WHAT HAVE I DONE,
MR. ANTI-CHRIST?

T HE WALK DOWN CARY STREET from Libby to Castle Thunder
was only a few hundred yards but Albert Richardson and Junius
Browne felt faint and dizzy on the way. They figured it was because they hadn't walked down a street since arriving at Libby fifteen
weeks earlier. It was evening when they entered Castle Thunder, and
they were immediately locked into a dark, filthy room in the cellar.
They bedded down on the dirty floor, but barely slept because rats
kept scurrying over their hands and faces.

In the morning, guards led them upstairs to meet Castle Thunder's commandant, Captain George Washington Alexander. A theatrical man, Alexander cultivated an image designed for maximum
intimidation. He had long black hair, a long black beard, and fierce
dark eyes. He wore black pants, a black shirt, and a black leather belt
that held two huge pistols, a blackjack, and two pairs of handcuffs.
Sometimes he accessorized his somber ensemble with a bright red
sash, and he liked to strut around the prison accompanied by his huge
black Russian boarhound, Nero, who was said to weigh 182 pounds.

Captain Alexander looked like a pirate—and in fact he *was* a pirate, indicted for piracy by the United States government in 1861. He was also a playwright, a poet, a songwriter, an actor, and an escaped convict.

Alexander was 34 when Richardson and Browne encountered him. He'd spent 13 years in the United States Navy, sailing to Japan on Commodore Perry's historic mission in 1853. He resigned from the navy at the beginning of the Civil War and traveled to Richmond, where he joined a guerrilla band led by Richard Thomas, an adventurer who had fought for Garibaldi in Italy, where he took the name Zarvona. In June 1861, Zarvona, Alexander, and 16 other Rebels boarded the steamboat *St. Nicholas*, traveling from Baltimore to Washington. Zarvona wore women's clothing and posed as a French matron named "Madame LaForce." When the ship reached the Potomac, Zarvona changed into a Confederate uniform, and then he and his men pulled out guns and seized the ship. They sailed it into Chesapeake Bay, where they captured three other vessels and took them to Virginia. A month later, these Confederate pirates snatched another Northern ship before they were captured and locked in the guardhouse at Fort McHenry in Baltimore, charged with piracy and treason. Both crimes were punishable by death, but Alexander cheated the hangman by escaping from the prison, leaping from a rampart, and swimming to shore. After making his way back to Richmond, he joined the city's military police force. In June 1862, he became commandant of Castle Thunder.

"Without intending to inflict him with a compliment," the *Richmond Enquirer* noted in its account of Alexander's promotion, "we must add that he is not only one of the most gallant but one of the handsomest men in the Confederate service."

Soon, Alexander was displaying his gallant handsomeness on stage. He wrote a musical play called *The Virginia Cavalier*, which debuted in Richmond in March 1863. The play's toe-tapping showstopper was "The Southern Soldier Boy," sung by actress Sallie Partington, who played the devoted sweetheart of a Confederate soldier. The lyrics, written by Captain Alexander, included a rousing chorus:

> *Yo! ho! Yo! ho! Yo! ho! ho! ho! ho! ho! ho!*
> *He is my only joy.*
> *He is the darling of my heart*
> *My Southern soldier boy.*

But the most dramatic moment in *The Virginia Cavalier* came when the author, dressed in his usual black ensemble, galloped across the stage on his black horse, trailed by Nero, as the audience cheered.

Critics were less enthralled. "The dialogue is stupid, the incidents are stale, and the plot ridiculous," wrote the reviewer for the *Southern Illustrated News*. "As the plot began to unfold itself, some of the literary gentlemen groaned inadvertently, and despondingly moved towards the door."

But snooty theatre critics were hardly Alexander's worst problem. Two weeks after the play opened, the Confederate Congress voted to investigate rumors that Alexander tortured prisoners at Castle Thunder. For two weeks, a committee of five congressmen heard testimony from prisoners and prison workers who described the punishments at Castle Thunder. Inmates were flogged, handcuffed to pillars, stuffed into "sweat boxes" too small to stand in, forced to wear a ball and chain, and hung up by their thumbs.

"The prisoners were stripped and whipped on their bare back, each receiving ten or twelve lashes laid on by the strongest man," a prison employee testified. "The words Captain Alexander used while the whipping was going on were, 'Lay it on!'"

Several guards defended Alexander, telling the committee that Castle Thunder's inmates were so evil that only brutality could control them. And several prisoners testified that the commandant had treated them with extraordinary kindness, even permitting them to order food from local hotels—or to leave the prison to dine in restaurants. "I got my meals sent frequently from the hotels," said one prisoner "and always got more than I wanted."

After the witnesses testified, Captain Alexander made his closing statement. Summoning all his theatrical talent, he launched into a dramatic account of his heroics as a Confederate pirate. "I followed my unfortunate leader far within the enemy's lines, never questioning an order, but obeyed all, never asking, 'Where go we?' We fell. I suffered. But thank God I escaped from the tyranny of the 'usurper of rights,' and have tried to deal them some good blows." At Castle Thunder, he did what was needed to keep order among murderers, deserters, and traitors, he said, and if he should lose that job he promised to find some other way to fight for the Confederacy. "No matter what may be said or done, you cannot keep this strong right arm idle! It shall work, either as officer or private, until we achieve what we are all struggling for—the vindication of a sacred right, *self-government!*"

Who could resist such steadfast devotion to the glorious cause? Not the congressmen. They voted to allow Alexander to retain his post. The pirate commandant of Castle Thunder would survive to strut his hour on the prison's stage for at least a while longer.

Five months later, facing a pair of newly arrived prisoners—the two Yankee reporters for the *New York Tribune*—Captain Alexander was charming. He had just returned from two weeks of vacation, and he was in a jovial mood, willing to help a couple of fellow writers, despite their abolitionist heresies. It was almost as if he was a member of the Bohemian Brigade—or hoped to be. "The commandant of the Castle," Browne wrote, "happened to have some literary pretensions—they were purely pretensions—and therefore treated journalists with a certain degree of consideration."

Alexander assigned Richardson and Browne to the best quarters in Castle Thunder—the "citizens' room." Roughly 50 feet long and 30 feet wide, it was clean, freshly whitewashed, and fairly comfortable, with glass in the windows, gas lights, a small stove, chairs, and actual *beds*, the first they'd slept in since their arrival in Richmond.

The citizens' room was a kind of country-club prison, a little haven for about 50 educated, affluent, "respectable" inmates who had money and were willing to share it with the prison staff. Among the prisoners was Solomon T. Bulkley, a reporter for the *New York Herald*, who had been captured in June at the Battle of Brandy Station. Bulkley explained to the newcomers how the system worked: Captain Alexander allowed the citizens' room prisoners to receive money from home, and to use it to buy food from the prison staff. The food was very expensive—the workers took their cut and so, presumably, did Alexander—but it beat living on prison rations.

Two Union spies were also among the lucky residents of the citizens' room. Convicted of espionage and sentenced to hang, Pryce Lewis and John Scully seemed unlikely candidates for residency in the prison's most desirable room. But there was a reason for their presence. For months, they'd been languishing in a squalid cell for condemned prisoners, but then they received a package from their boss, Allan Pinkerton. Guards inspected the box and found that it contained not only clothing but Confederate money, U.S. greenbacks, and $20 in gold. Captain Alexander summoned the two spies to his office, showed them the confiscated booty, and announced that he was transferring them to the citizens' room. He also told Lewis and Scully that they were now eligible to use money sent from the North to purchase food—and even whisky if they wanted it.

"What a difference money makes," Lewis noted, "even in the case of condemned prisoners!"

The revelation of rampant corruption in the prison made the *Tribune* reporters very happy. They had feared that Castle Thunder would be worse than Libby, but now they were delighted to discover that it was far more comfortable—at least for inmates lucky enough to live in the citizens' room. The reporters mocked Alexander behind his back for his vanity, his pomposity, and his wretched writing, but they were happy to be among his favorites.

"Compared to those about us," Browne wrote, "we were the purple-robed patricians of the place."

MINGLING WITH OTHER PRISONERS in the exercise yard, Richardson and Browne soon learned how lucky they were. Castle Thunder was composed of three adjoining warehouse buildings, and by the fall of 1863, more than 1,500 inmates were packed into it, living in squalor and surviving on two meals a day—usually bread, a thin soup, and some stringy, greasy meat. The meat was billed as beef, but rumored to be horse or mule. A standing joke among the prisoners was that they always got more meat after major cavalry battles.

Worse than the food was the company. In Libby, all the inmates on the top two floors were Union officers—educated, disciplined men united in a common cause. But at Castle Thunder, the prisoners were a ragged collection of men with little in common—Yankee deserters, Rebel deserters, runaway slaves, Union spies, Confederate soldiers convicted of theft or murder or some other crime, and Southern citizens deemed disloyal to the Confederacy. Not surprisingly, these prisoners did not always get along, and they beat, maimed, robbed, and killed each other with some regularity. When they did, Captain Alexander and his guards responded with public floggings and the other, more baroque tortures described in the congressional hearings.

The prisoners regaled newcomers with stories of Alexander's brutality and his hair-trigger temper. But Alexander wasn't as feared or loathed as his deputy, John Caphart. A nasty old man with a long gray beard, shaggy eyebrows, and sunken eyes, Caphart served as the prison's hangman, and he seemed quite fond of that job.

In his daily duties at Castle Thunder, Caphart was so eager to crack skulls with his ever-present club that the prisoners dubbed him "the Anti-Christ." That nickname gave rise to a probably apocryphal tale: A black woman who'd heard Caphart called Anti-Christ assumed that was his name. When she passed him on a Richmond street, she greeted him politely as "Mr. Anti-Christ." Irate, Caphart whipped out his club and beat her while she begged for mercy, saying, "Oh, please, Mr. Anti-Christ, don't beat me! What have I done, Mr. Anti-Christ?"

Browne and Richardson soon witnessed Castle Thunder's routine brutality towards black inmates and the young black boys who worked running errands in the prison. "At the Castle, the negroes frequently received from five to 25 lashes," Richardson wrote. "I saw boys not more than eight years old turned over a barrel and cowhided. One woman upward of sixty was whipped in the same manner. This Negress was known as 'Old Sally.' She earned a good deal of Confederate money by washing for prisoners, and spent nearly the whole of it in purchasing supplies for unfortunates who were without means. She had been confined in different prisons for nearly three years."

Life was brutal for most Castle Thunder prisoners, but in the citizens' room, it was delightfully cushy. Soon, Richardson and Browne were receiving boxes from home, and from their friends at the *Tribune*. The boxes contained books and food—jams, pastries, sardines, and smoked meats—and carefully hidden American dollars. The price for receiving the boxes was to share the food with the prison staff, and to use the greenbacks to hire prison workers to buy food in the local markets, and cook it. While the rest of Castle Thunder's inmates ate maggot-ridden soup and mystery meat, the grandees of the citizens' room dined on chicken, potatoes, fresh bread and butter, vegetables, fruits, and pastries. At night, they stayed up as late as they wanted, playing hard-fought games of whist by the light of the room's gas lanterns, smoking good cigars, and drinking that rarity in wartime Richmond, real coffee.

Prisoners frequently departed the citizens' room and headed north on flag-of-truce boats, their exits greased by large legal fees paid to well-connected Richmond lawyers. Captain Alexander quickly replaced the departed with other inmates deemed likely to keep the money flowing. Among the new arrivals were two more reporters from the *New York Herald*—Leonard Hendrick and George Hart, captured by Confederate cavalry in the Shenandoah Valley. With their arrival there were five reporters in the citizens' room, turning the place into an unofficial Bohemian press club.

In late September, the two Union spies, Lewis and Scully, used money from the North to hire a lawyer named Humphrey Marshall. A former congressman from Kentucky, Marshall had served as a Confederate general until he resigned his commission in June 1863 and set up a legal practice in Richmond. Marshall mingled with Richmond's movers and shakers and was a friend of Robert Ould, the Confederate agent of prisoner exchange. He met with Lewis and Scully in Captain Alexander's office and informed them that he could arrange their release but it would cost them $500 apiece—$500 in U.S. currency, not inflation-debased Confederate dollars. They promised to get the money, and several days later, John Caphart, the Anti-Christ, came to the citizens' room and told them to gather their things. They were going home.

Richardson and Browne observed this miracle and immediately hired Marshall. If he could win the release of two Union spies who'd been sentenced to hang, surely he could arrange a speedy exit for two mild-mannered newspaper reporters who had, after all, been officially paroled five months earlier.

"THE STRAWBERRY PLANTS arrived in good condition," Louise Richardson wrote to Sydney Gay on September 23, 1863. "Please accept my thanks for them."

A few weeks earlier, Lou Richardson had given birth to her fourth child, Mary Louisa Richardson, conceived when Albert Richardson had made a brief visit home the previous winter, before heading back out to cover the war. Lou was living with Richardson's extended family in Massachusetts, struggling to raise her newborn and the three older kids—Leander, now seven, Maude, four, and Albert Jr., who was almost two. Her in-laws were generous and kind, but she missed her family and friends in Cincinnati and, of course, her husband. She and Richardson wrote letters back and forth, but those letters are lost to history. Her letters to Sydney Gay still exist, however, and they reveal that she was, not surprisingly, lonely, worried, and despondent.

"I have been watching the papers in vain ever since I saw the statement that a general exchange had been determined," she wrote to Gay on September 23. "What is the prospect of our friends being speedily released?" She informed him that she'd been ill after giving birth. "I have been confined to a sickbed for the last fortnight and have felt my desolation more than ever. I must hope the exchange will soon happen."

Three weeks later, she wrote to thank Gay for sending a check for $25, a portion of Richardson's salary, mailed to her at his request. "In case I need it, could I draw on the *Tribune* for money without an order from my husband? I have been supplied heretofore by my brother-in-law but he prefers that I should in the future get my supplies from you if convenient." She told Gay that she had read so many newspaper stories about possible prisoner exchanges that she didn't know what to believe anymore, and she was eager for any solid information he might possess. "Thank you again and again for your efforts in their behalf and for your assurances of sympathy," she added. "Separated entirely from my own friends, with three children sick and myself far from strong, I assure you sympathy is very dear to me."

Gay wrote back to tell Louise that he'd learned it might be possible to get prisoners released by paying a ransom. By then, Gay had communicated with Lewis and Scully, the released spies, and learned how they'd managed to buy their way out. His letter to Lou no longer exists, so it's impossible to determine exactly what he revealed to her, but apparently he asked how much ransom she might be willing, or able, to pay.

"In reply to your query, I hardly know what to say," Lou replied. "The Confederates have been so obstinate in regard to the exchange of the correspondents that if they were to set a price for their ransom, it would be in all probability so high that they could not afford to give it. It would be useless to try and get Mr. R. away unless the terms embraced the release of Junius as well. So Mr. Browne's friends must be consulted. All the ready money that I know of that my husband could command is about seven hundred dollars."

She didn't know whether Richardson would be willing to spend the family's savings to buy his freedom. "Would it be best for me to write to him anything about it?" she asked. She also expressed skepticism that the Confederates would ever agree to a deal. "Besides," she added, "I should not think our government would permit it, as it would be so much 'aid & comfort' to the Rebels."

Writing again a few weeks later, she revealed that she no longer cared whether Richardson or the United States government would approve of a ransom deal: If it could work, she was willing to try it. "If I could be assured that the plan you have in view was pretty certain to succeed, or that the money was to be paid only on condition that it was successful, I would not hesitate to pledge three, four or even *five* hundred dollars for its accomplishment."

Weeks passed with no further news about the ransom deal. "I am wondering how your plan is succeeding," she asked Gay on November 30. She told him that she'd received three letters from Richardson, who mentioned that he'd been sick with a fever but was recovering. "I received a note from a released prisoner who had been confined in Castle Thunder and who was released a couple of weeks since. He wrote a doleful story of the general suffering there." Then she asked again: "What is your private opinion in regard to the exchange?"

★

HUMPHREY MARSHALL, the Confederate lawyer, was a portly man with drooping jowls and a big barrel belly—a walking caricature of a prosperous attorney. Richardson and Browne met Marshall in Castle Thunder, showed him the official parole documents they had received in Vicksburg, and told him that everybody else who'd been paroled with them had already gone home. Marshall drafted legal papers on their behalf, requesting that the Confederate government "enforce their clear, legal, unquestionable rights under this parole."

The legal appeal didn't work. Neither did the lure of ransom money. Robert Ould—who had released the two Union spies and several of Marshall's other clients from the citizens' room—simply refused to set the *Tribune* reporters free. Apparently, Ould loathed *Tribune* reporters more than he hated Yankee spies.

"I consider your case hopeless," Marshall told his clients.

With that blunt assessment echoing in their ears, Browne and Richardson were left with only one road to freedom—escape. Fortunately, escape was a fairly common occurrence at Castle Thunder. Two men had escaped by digging a hole through a rear wall and squeezing out. Four convicted murderers managed to cut a hole in the floor of their cell and drop into the storeroom below, where they stole muskets, which they used to shoot their way past the guards. Several prisoners escaped by smearing their faces with croton oil, which produced skin lesions that resembled smallpox—at least if you didn't look too closely. Terrified of contracting the disease, the guards had no desire to look closely, so they simply shipped the stricken prisoners off to a local hospital. On the way, the fakers leaped out of the ambulance and scooted off.

But the most effective method of escape was to bribe guards. Bribery was commonplace, a staple of the prison economy and, of course, the source of the cushy lifestyle of the citizens' room. Money slipped to guards routinely bought tobacco and food. Sometimes it could also buy a door left conveniently unlocked at an opportune moment. The reporters knew which guards were willing to work for tips, and in the fall of 1863, they located a corporal who agreed to help them escape. He told them he had to line up other guards he could trust and station them in the right places at the proper time, and of course they would have to be paid, too. Solomon Bulkley cut a deal: The corporal would sneak the five reporters—three from the *Herald*, two from the *Tribune*—out of the building late one night in return for $70 in U.S. greenbacks and two gold watches.

On the chosen night, the Bohemians crawled into their beds and pretended to sleep. At one o'clock in the morning, as planned, the corporal arrived at the citizens' room.

"All things are ready," he whispered.

The reporters climbed out of bed and shuffled silently through the darkened room. The corporal assured them that he had all his conspirators stationed in the right places, and that the reporters could safely reach the street. After that, if they happened to encounter any of the sentries who patrolled Richmond, the password for the night was "Shiloh." The corporal was ready to proceed. All he needed was the money.

Bulkley handed him a bankroll. The corporal stepped down the hall to a light so he could count the bills. A few minutes later, he returned, angry, shoving money back at Bulkley, saying he'd been short-changed, given a wad of one-dollar bills, instead of fives. The deal was off.

The reporters retreated to their room, cursing and sputtering. Bulkley swore he'd given the corporal a roll of fives and the crooked guard came back with a roll of ones. Dammit, they'd been scammed.

But when the sun came through the windows, and Bulkley could actually see his money well enough to count it, he realized that he really *had* given the corporal the wrong bankroll. In the dark, he'd mistakenly given the man ones instead of fives.

The Bohemians had managed to botch their breakout with an idiotic blunder, and to make matters worse, they were charged with attempting to escape.

Captain Alexander seemed amused by the episode. "It's your duty to escape if you can," he told them, "and my duty to keep you if I can."

He announced their punishment—ten days in the dungeon.

HART AND HENDRICK were locked in one cell, Browne, Richardson, and Bulkley in another. "A dismal dirty place, that cell," Browne wrote. It was about twenty by twelve feet with one small window for light and air. The floor and the walls were encrusted with dirt and there was no furniture except a malfunctioning stove.

The Bohemians bribed a guard to bring a stool, a wash basin, and some wood for the stove, and tried to make themselves comfortable. The next day, seven more prisoners arrived in the cell, all of them Confederate soldiers charged with various crimes—desertion, theft, assault. Hard, scarred, rough-looking characters, they were not the respectable kind of inmate that one tended to meet in the citizens' room, and the reporters were wary of them. But they turned out to be friendly fellows, particularly after Browne agreed to ghostwrite a love letter for one of them, an illiterate burglar who was smitten with a local barmaid. Browne took to this task with gusto, producing a letter written in his usual purple prose, complete with *bon mots* in several foreign tongues, quotes from classical literature, and lyrical passages comparing the beauty of the burglar's moll to the fabled charms of various Greek and Roman goddesses. He read this overheated epistle to the burglar, who pronounced himself pleased, although he admitted he didn't understand a word of it.

Soon, the three reporters, all of them veteran interviewers, got their seven cellmates talking, telling their life stories. They weren't really soldiers, they admitted, they were con men using the war to run various scams, which they were happy to explain. One scam was common on both sides in the war—bounty jumping. A man volunteered for the army, collected his enlistment bonus, and deserted at the first opportunity. Then he traveled to another town, enlisted under another name, collected another bonus, and deserted again.

The reporters were familiar with bounty jumping, but not with some of their cellmates' more baroque scams, such as "running a kink" or "shoving a mick." Running a kink was fairly simple: It meant stealing a slave in one place—sometimes by convincing him you were helping him escape—and then selling him somewhere else. "Shoving a mick" was a bit more complicated: It involved finding a rich man willing to pay serious money to hire a substitute to take his place in the army, then getting an ignorant Irishman drunk enough to agree to enlist for far less than the rich guy had promised—and, of course, pocketing the difference.

Browne, whose taste in entertainment usually ran to classical and philosophical literature, reveled in the sordid revelations of his low-life cellmates. "They were a rare coterie of gentlemen, and I greatly admired the delicacy of their organization, and their sublimated ideas of honor," he wrote, tongue in cheek. "They furnished us with some knowledge of the corruption that existed in Secessia."

Richardson couldn't resist teasing Browne about his fascination with the con men. "What do these learned gentlemen think about Dante?" he asked. "Do they hold that Beatrice was an actual woman or only a type of the purely spiritual? I should like to hear what that fellow with the one eye knocked out had to say about the books of the Vedas. If he is a little befogged concerning them, that gentlemen with the end of his nose bitten off must have a clear conception of the subject. What the devil is the use of having a nose like his, Junius, unless it enables him to understand the Hindu mythology."

For ten days, the Bohemians languished in the dungeon and enjoyed an intensive seminar on the con games of the Confederacy, and then they returned to their more comfortable quarters in the citizens' room.

10

CAPTIVITY DRIES UP THE HEART

A
S THE YEAR 1863 NEARED ITS END, the great armies of the Union and the Confederacy retired to their winter quarters to huddle around campfires and await the arrival of spring, when flowers would bloom and birds would sing and the soldiers would once again march forth to slaughter each other.

For the Confederates, 1863 had begun with optimism but ended in gloom. The defeats at Gettysburg and Vicksburg were followed in September by the Federals' capture of Knoxville and Chattanooga. The Confederates had won a victory at Chickamauga Creek in Georgia in late September, but on November 25, the Union army in Chattanooga, now commanded by General Ulysses S. Grant, defeated the Rebels at Missionary Ridge and sent them fleeing south towards Atlanta. In Virginia, General Meade's Union army failed to crush Robert E. Lee's battered forces after Gettysburg, but it had killed and wounded thousands of Rebel soldiers that Lee could not replace.

As winter set in, the Yankees controlled large swaths of Confederate territory in Virginia, Louisiana, Mississippi, and Tennessee. The loss of land, coupled with the Union's naval blockade, caused food shortages in much of the South and the Confederate government was hard pressed to feed its armies. The value of Confederate currency plummeted and food prices soared. Richmond was hit particularly hard. Since the city had become the Confederate capital in 1861, its population had tripled from 40,000 to 120,000. In the spring of 1863, food shortages had led to a riot by angry housewives, who smashed store windows and stole whatever they could carry off. Since then the privations had only worsened.

"Poor women are begging for bread with tears in their eyes," Elizabeth Van Lew, the wealthy Richmond woman who was secretly spying for the Union, wrote in her diary that winter. "On Thursday, I went through the city for meals and I could not get a particle anywhere."

Richmond's food shortage was exacerbated by the need to feed the city's population of captured Union soldiers, which rose steadily after the breakdown of the prisoner exchange program. By December 1863, Richmond held more than 13,000 Yankee prisoners, including 1,200 officers packed so tightly into Libby's upper stories that the men slept on their sides, nestled like spoons on the hard floors. During the night, when the pain in their hips and shoulders woke them up, somebody would yell, "spoon over to the right" or "spoon over to the left," and dozens of men would turn from one side to the other. In October, Libby's daily rations were cut in half. By December, the prisoners were receiving only a few ounces of beef per month.

Conditions were worse on Belle Isle, the James River island where the Confederates held more than 8,000 captured Union enlisted men. There, prisoners lived outdoors, the lucky ones in ragged tents, the unlucky in holes dug in the rocky ground. Many men had traded their coats to the guards for food during the summer, and were now freezing. Dysentery and smallpox spread. In early November, Belle Isle prisoners were dying at the rate of eight or ten a day, and as the weather worsened the death toll climbed. The bodies of the dead were burned, their ashes buried beneath planks bearing their names—until those boards were stolen by inmates desperate for firewood. "And thus ends the history of the unfortunate Belle Island prisoner," wrote an inmate named Roland Bowen. "Even the sacred spot of his burial is forever unknown."

Not all the captured enlisted men ended up on Belle Isle. Some were housed in tobacco warehouses on Cary Street. Robert Sneden of the 40th New York Volunteers was incarcerated with 600 other prisoners in the Pemberton warehouse across the street from Libby Prison. Freezing rain blew in Pemberton's windows, forming ice on the floor, and the prisoners tried to keep warm by sliding across it like skaters. Sneden kept a diary and described what he saw on Christmas Day of 1863. "All the guards and their officers were more or less drunk all day," he wrote. "Several fired their muskets right into the upper stories of Libby. I watched one fellow aim a dozen times before he fired. Some of our officers put an old hat on a stick, and three of the guards fired on it, thinking there might be a head behind it. . . . Two men died of smallpox last week, and the Rebels let the corpses lie on the floor nearly two days. And still not taking them out for burial, they were thrown out of the windows by their companions on the heads of the Rebel guard fifteen feet below on the sidewalk!"

Corpses flying out windows: It was a memorable Christmas on Cary Street.

T WO BLOCKS DOWN CARY STREET in Castle Thunder, conversations that Christmas buzzed with speculation about the fate of the prison's commandant. In early December, Captain Alexander was charged with "malpractice in office," accused of trading in greenbacks and accepting bribes from prisoners to ensure their release. He demanded his day in court and ultimately he was acquitted; but on December 19, Alexander was relieved of his position.

His replacement was a Confederate artillery officer named Lucien Richardson. Neither a pirate nor a playwright, Captain Richardson— no relation to Albert Richardson—was far less flamboyant than Captain Alexander but just as tough. Junius Browne called him "a much meaner man."

In the citizens' room, life continued much as it had under Alexander. The new commandant banned the exchange of money between inmates and guards, but somehow the residents of the citizens' room still managed to purchase food to augment their increasingly meager rations. And they remained relatively warm because the citizens' room, unlike most rooms in the prison, actually had glass windows that could close, and a functioning stove.

The punishment cell above the citizens' room had no such amenities, and the prisoners who occupied it were too cold to sleep at night so they paced back and forth, trying to keep warm. This would not have affected the sleep of the pampered residents of the citizens' room, except for one additional factor: Each of the pacing men wore a ball and chain.

"A thousand bowling alleys all in full blast could not make more noise than the ball-and-chain gang occupying the room above our heads," wrote Leonard Hendrick, one of the *Herald* reporters.

Smallpox swept through Castle Thunder that winter, and it did not spare the citizens' room. Several residents of the room contracted the highly contagious disease, which scared some inmates into shunning the stricken men. But Richardson and Browne tended the sick, helping to feed and wash them, and never fell ill. "We had no fear of it," Browne wrote. "Why should a man in a Rebel prison fear anything?" Always the grim fatalist, Browne joked that dying of smallpox was, after all, one sure way to avoid living in a Confederate prison.

In mid-January 1864, Leonard Hendrick and George Hart, the two *Herald* reporters captured in October, were released, sent north in exchange for two Richmond *Enquirer* reporters caught by the Union army. That trade infuriated Richardson and Browne. They'd been imprisoned for nearly nine months, the *Herald* reporters for only three. Obviously, the Confederates were again displaying their hatred of the *Tribune*—and their preference for the *Herald*, a Democratic paper that had denounced Lincoln and his cabinet as "ghouls, vultures, hyenas and other feeders upon carrion."

Of course the Rebels would prefer to release the *Herald* reporters, Richardson grumbled, but why did the United States government agree to it? Why didn't the army refuse to trade the *Enquirer* reporters unless the Rebels gave up the *Tribune* correspondents? It was only fair to demand the release of reporters who'd been imprisoned longest, wasn't it? Why didn't their government stand up for them? And why didn't Greeley and the *Tribune* do something? Didn't anybody care about them?

Richardson unleashed his anger in a long letter to Sydney Gay on February 1, 1864. "This thing of our government exchanging other citizens and other correspondents, who have been here but a short time, while we have been here nine months is unjust both to you and us," he wrote. "And I presume it only happens because no one is pressing our case properly. Unless proper influence is used on our behalf, I presume we may stay indefinitely."

He reminded Gay that Humphrey Marshall had failed to make their case. After that, Richardson said, he'd written directly to James Seddon, the Confederate secretary of war, enclosing his parole document from Vicksburg in the letter. Seddon never replied and didn't return the document. And now the Rebels were telling the *Tribune* reporters that they would be held as hostages for *all* Southern citizens held by the Union army. "Not for any designated persons, one for each of us, as usual in holding hostages, but for them *all!*"

Prison breeds paranoia, and Richardson began to suspect that the *Tribune* editors weren't working for their release because they figured Richardson and Browne were just getting what they deserved for taking foolish risks in their attempt to steam past Vicksburg. "I wonder if you consider our capture a piece of deserved punishment for mere foolhardiness?"

Richardson ended the letter by urging Gay to write to General Benjamin Butler, the Union army's new agent of prisoner exchanges, and demand that he work out a deal for their release. "I beg you to understand that we have not the slightest disposition to whimper or complain. We are in excellent health, unruffled spirits and can stay here just as long as the Confederates can keep us. We simply don't want our case to go *by default*, from lack of the use of proper influence on our behalf."

Gay did write to Butler, and Butler did try to convince Robert Ould to make a trade for the *Tribune* reporters. But Ould refused once again, so Richardson and Browne remained in Castle Thunder, feeling increasingly angry, bitter, and cynical.

"We grew skeptical of everyone, even our nearest friends, and doubted if we had any," Browne wrote. "We became cynical in spite of ourselves, and reached Schopenhauer's plane—hoping nothing, expecting nothing, caring for nothing. Few persons, unless they have had the experience, can determine how much a long captivity dries up the heart, narrows the mind, and withers all the freshness of existence."

★

ALTHOUGH BROWNE AND RICHARDSON and the other residents of the citizens' room avoided many of the worst aspects of life in Castle Thunder, they could not escape the repulsive smell of the place. The stench wafted in from the "condemned cell" next door, where prisoners were held while they awaited execution. The guards tormented the condemned men by neglecting to empty the tub they used as a toilet, and the smell permeated the building.

Only when the stench got bad enough to annoy the prison's management would guards remove the condemned men from their cell while workers—inevitably they were *black* workers—were sent in to empty the tub and clean the room. During several of these cleaning sessions, Browne and Richardson invited a condemned prisoner named Spencer Deaton into the citizens' room to warm himself by the fire. He was a tall, haggard man of 36 with a haunted look in his eyes.

Deaton had grown up in the mountains of East Tennessee, a hotbed of pro-Union sentiment. He was one of many prisoners who came to Castle Thunder from the Appalachian mountain region of the South, most of them accused of disloyalty to the Confederacy. The Appalachians seethed with disloyalty. The people there tended to be poor folks working small farms; most did not own slaves, and many were not particularly eager to fight for slavery and the rich lowland planters who profited from it. East Tennessee voted against secession in 1861, and when the state joined the Confederacy, many young men from the mountains enlisted in the Union army. Deaton was one of them, and he soon became a well-known "pilot"—traveling through East Tennessee, recruiting pro-Union men, and sneaking them through the Confederate lines into Kentucky, where they could join the Union army. In August 1863, he was captured by the Confederates and charged with recruiting behind their lines. Convicted and sentenced to death, he was locked in the "condemned cell" at Castle Thunder.

He was a young man with a wife and children back home, and the death sentence broke his spirit. He stopped eating. He barely spoke. He sat in a stupor and wasted away. When Richardson and Browne invited him into the citizens' room, he sat by the hot stove warming his frozen feet, but he said nothing. He just stared into the air.

"I have rarely witnessed a more melancholy spectacle," Browne wrote. "Haggard, emaciated, ragged, almost barefooted, bent as with a crushing weight, a strange light in his sunken eyes, he seemed more dead than alive."

When the prison officials noticed that Deaton was wasting away, they worried that he might die of starvation before they could hang him. Dr. Upshur, the prison physician, prescribed a potion for Deaton—a cocktail of whisky and laudanum—and told the *Examiner* that it kept the condemned man alive until his execution day.

On a bitter cold day in February, Deaton was taken from his cell and escorted to the gallows erected in Castle Thunder's exercise yard. Weak, frightened, and stupefied by Dr. Upshur's concoction, Deaton could barely stand, much less walk. John Caphart—the infamous Mr. Anti-Christ who served as the prison hangman—held Deaton up as he shuffled forward.

"Dressed in a dilapidated frock coat, red, dingy homespun britches and tall black felt hat such as Yankee officers usually wear," the *Examiner* reported, "the condemned was a vivid picture of abject yet speechless terror and despair in the presence of death."

Standing beneath the gallows, sweating profusely despite the freezing cold, Deaton listened as a Confederate captain read the bureaucratic verbiage of the death warrant, his eyes gazing blankly into the distance. A preacher stepped forward to say a prayer, and then Caphart held the prisoner up as he climbed the ladder to the gallows. Caphard tied Deaton's arms and feet, and pulled a white hood over his face.

"Oh, Lord, have mercy on my soul," Deaton mumbled through the hood. "I am innocent! Oh, Lord, save me, I am innocent!"

Caphart adjusted the noose around Deaton's neck, then hustled down the ladder to pull the bolt that would release the trap door beneath Deaton's feet. But Deaton collapsed in a faint, the rope around his neck holding him up in an awkward sitting posture. Caphart climbed back up the ladder, pulled Deaton to his feet, and ordered him to stand up like a man. But Deaton collapsed again.

"Oh, I cannot stand," he said. "You must hold me up."

Caphart and a guard named Wiley lifted Deaton to his feet. Wiley held him while Caphart descended the ladder again. He pulled the bolt, the trap door opened, and Deaton fell through it, dangling motionless in the frigid air.

After Deaton hung there for half an hour, Dr. Upshur pronounced him dead, and two Negroes carried him off and placed him in a simple pine coffin painted red.

"The intensely cold weather prevented a large attendance of spectators outside the enclosure," the *Examiner* reported, "but nevertheless the housetops, windows and other elevations affording a view of the execution were early peopled with men, women and children."

11

THE HEAVY BLOW

ONLY DEATH COULD SAVE SPENCER DEATON from the miseries of Castle Thunder, but Richardson and Browne were luckier. One night in February 1864, a guard told the reporters to pack up their things because they were leaving in the morning, heading to another prison, this one in Salisbury, North Carolina.

They stuffed their clothes and blankets into a box and gave away what didn't fit. At dawn the next morning, they were standing on Cary Street in a crowd of 70 or 80 ragged prisoners, most of them Rebel deserters, along with a few men deemed disloyal to the Confederacy and a handful of criminals forced to drag a ball and chain. Browne wasn't impressed with their fellow travelers: "We were the only Northerners in the Southern shipment and, I might say, the only persons, save a few straggling Tennessee and Virginia Unionists, who would not have picked their father's pocket, or sold their grandmother, for a sufficient pecuniary inducement."

Under the cold eyes of armed guards, they marched to the station and boarded a train for the short ride to Petersburg, where they were herded into the street to await the arrival of a train heading towards

North Carolina. It was the first time since May that Browne and Richardson enjoyed the simple human pleasure of standing on a city street and watching people walk by. But Browne couldn't savor the experience. He was mortified to be seen standing among a crowd of scraggily, stinking prisoners, and he blushed as he observed the looks of disgust and contempt on the faces of the well-dressed passersby. Junius Browne considered himself an educated gentleman, a student of history and philosophy, and a professional writer fluent in French and Latin, but he knew that all these people saw was another dirty, low-life criminal. "I had never fancied before the war," he groused, "that I should be a show and a spectacle in an American city—one of a crowd of ruffians and villains, from whom I could not be discriminated, passing from one prison to another—to be leered at by the vulgar."

If Richardson harbored similar feelings of shame, he didn't mention them—but he was never as finicky as Browne about preserving his status as a respectable gentleman.

They changed trains in Raleigh in the middle of the night and for a brief moment they saw a chance to slip away and escape into the darkness. But they were tired and tentative, and they failed to seize the moment—a missed opportunity they would soon come to regret.

Late the next afternoon they arrived in Salisbury, a prosperous provincial town of 2,400 in western North Carolina. From the station, it was a short walk to the prison. Surrounded by a wooden stockade twelve feet high, Salisbury Prison consisted of a large brick building—a former textile factory four stories tall, 100 feet long and 40 feet wide—and six smaller brick structures. When Browne and Richardson arrived, it housed about 600 prisoners—deserters from both armies, Confederate soldiers convicted of crimes, and about 150 Southern Unionists. Some were men the reporters recognized from Libby and Castle Thunder. After nine months in captivity, the *Tribune* correspondents had become involuntary experts on the Confederate prison archipelago.

That night, Richardson and Browne bedded down in a large, open room that filled an entire floor of the old factory building. The windows had bars but no glass, and two stoves pumped out little heat but plenty of blue smoke that caused water to leak from the eyes of the 150 men who lived there. The stench of latrines and unwashed humans pervaded the room, as did the inevitable legions of lice. Richardson, a former Massachusetts plow boy, joked that no self-respecting Yankee farmer would house his horse or ox in such a squalid place. Browne, an urban creature, issued a more genteel critique: "A gentleman seemed more out of place there than the Angel Gabriel would be in a prize-ring, or the Pope of Rome at a Five Points dance-house."

But Salisbury Prison had one redeeming feature that neither Libby nor Castle Thunder possessed—a lovely yard. The stockade enclosed four acres of grassy lawn shaded by towering oak trees. Richardson thought it looked like a college campus. The reporters had arrived during a mid-winter warm spell, and they reveled in their freedom to stroll beneath the blue sky and breathe fresh air after so many months cooped up in fetid urban warehouses.

"Here I am in the open air nearly all the time—to me after the active outdoor life of the last seven years an inestimable privilege," Richardson wrote to his brother's wife, Jennie, shortly after he arrived in Salisbury. "For the last few days, we have played baseball several hours daily—the only time I have done so, with one exception, since the days of boyhood. I enjoy it just as well as I did then, and after nine months confinement, it does me vastly more good."

A WEEK AFTER BROWNE AND RICHARDSON arrived in Salisbury, Colonel Thomas E. Rose of the 77th Pennsylvania Infantry squeezed into a hole in the cellar of Richmond's Libby Prison, crawled on his belly through a crudely dug 50-foot tunnel, and then cautiously eased his sweaty head into the cold night air on Canal Street behind the prison. When he saw that the sentry patrolling the street was walking away from him, Rose popped out of the hole, tiptoed into the shadows, and strolled down the street, past a warehouse that held 5,000 packages sent from the North to Union prisoners but never delivered.

A few minutes later, another officer slipped out of the tunnel, followed by another, and another. Guards patrolling the area spotted some of them hustling down the street, but they figured the men were fellow Rebel soldiers who'd broken into the warehouse to steal food and clothing out of the Union packages—a common occurrence in Richmond that winter.

Among those trying to escape from Libby was Richardson's friend, Abel Streight, the colonel who had led the ill-fated, mule-mounted invasion of Alabama and Georgia. Streight was a huge man, six-feet-two-inches tall and well over 200 pounds. When he reached the

thinnest part of the tunnel, where a boulder narrowed the passageway
to 16 inches in diameter, he couldn't squeeze through. Unable to move
forward, he tried to back up, but he couldn't do that either. He was
stuck. He wiggled and squirmed and finally managed to inch back-
wards into Libby's cellar. He stood up, shed his coat, vest, and shirt
and then tried again, dragging his clothes behind him. This time he
made it.

That night, 109 of Libby's 1,200 prisoners crept through the tunnel
before the approach of dawn ended the exodus. Traveling alone, or in
groups of two or three, most of them headed south, towards the Union
army lines near Williamsburg, about 100 miles away. A handful
walked to the homes of Union sympathizers in Richmond, including
Elizabeth Van Lew's. Tipped off by one of Libby's black workers, who
had ties to Van Lew's group, Streight and three other escapees went to
a house near the prison, where they met a black woman who led them
to the home of one of Van Lew's pro-Union friends on the outskirts of
Richmond.

The next morning, February 10, 1864, Libby's clerk, Erasmus
Ross—another member of Van Lew's network—presided over the daily
count of inmates and found that 109 were missing. Slowly, painstakingly, he took a second count, calling out each prisoner's name and me-
thodically noting which ones were missing. Somehow, he managed to
stretch this process out for nearly four hours. Then he reported to his
superiors that there had been a mass escape. Guards searched the
grounds and soon discovered the tunnel.

"EXTRAORDINARY ESCAPE FROM LIBBY PRISON," read
the headline in the next day's Richmond *Enquirer*, "ONE HUNDRED
OFFICERS HOMEWARD BOUND."

Five days after the breakout, 26 prisoners reached the Union lines
at Williamsburg, many of them telling stories of being fed and sheltered by slaves along the way. All told, 59 of the 109 escapees reached
Union lines, while 48 were recaptured and two drowned en route.

In Richmond, the newspapers lamented that one of the missing
was the hated Colonel Streight—"a notorious character," the *Dispatch*
called him, "charged with having raised a negro regiment." Searching
for Streight, Richmond detectives raided a dentist's office, firing shots
at fleeing suspects, who turned out to be gamblers roused from an il-
licit poker game. Meanwhile, Streight and his three companions lay
low in their hideout for eight days, then started walking towards

Washington. Traveling at night in the bitter cold, they were spotted south of the half-frozen Rappahannock River and pursued by hundreds of General Lee's soldiers. But slaves hid them in a cabin until the soldiers departed, then rowed them across the river. Nineteen days after squeezing through the tunnel, they reached Washington.

The great escape from Libby Prison was a sensation, and when the news reached Salisbury Prison, Browne and Richardson rejoiced at their old friends' breakout.

Naturally, the story of the escape inspired endless talk among the inmates about how they might tunnel out of Salisbury. Nobody thought it would be easy. Their main impediment was their favorite aspect of the prison—the yard. The prison buildings were surrounded by the spacious fields, so a tunnel would have to be very long. And even if they managed to tunnel under the fence and escape, they'd find themselves a long way from the nearest Union army, in Knoxville, Tennessee, 200 miles away and across the Blue Ridge and Appalachian mountains. Still, the prisoners never stopped discussing tunnels, planning tunnels, and debating various theories of tunnel engineering.

"We grew very familiar with the occult science of tunneling," Richardson reported.

"Tunnels were my thought by day and my dream by night," wrote Browne. "Freedom was in some way associated in my mind with a tunnel. I fancied Adam must have crawled into Paradise through a tunnel."

"**I DON'T KNOW IF IT WILL SOUND WILD** to you but everything else has been tried," Louise Richardson wrote to Sydney Gay on February 1, shortly before her husband left Castle Thunder. "Do you suppose it would be of any use for me to try for a special exchange, either by correspondence or personally? Others have done so, why might I not try? If there is any hope of success, I would brave anything to accomplish it—only I should need a good deal of advice as to how to begin to proceed."

What Gay wrote in reply is unknown, but Louise Richardson never made the trip from her father-in-law's farm in Franklin, Massachusetts, to Washington or Richmond to plead for her husband's freedom. On February 24, she wrote to Gay again.

"I have not heard from Mr. R. for three weeks," she reported, sounding worried. "In regard to his escape or liberation, my fears are more easily excited than my hopes. I have lived through nearly ten months of unceasing anxiety—and I hope to go through as bravely as he whatever is in store for us yet. . . . Just now I am suffering from the symptoms of measles, which is an interesting complaint. I expect to share it with three of my children in a few days. There has never been a year since my marriage that I have had so much sickness in my family as in the past 12 months."

The next letter Gay received from Franklin, Massachusetts, came not from Louise but from Richardson's brother Charles, and it included a check Gay had sent to Louise, part of her husband's salary:

Dear Sir,

I am greatly overwhelmed with grief in saying that my brother's wife, Mrs. A. D. Richardson, is lying at the point of death with no probability of living many hours. She was taken with measles a week since, and congestion of the brain has followed. As this state of affairs makes the face of the enclosed draft more, rather than less, needful, will you please send it payable to MY order instead of hers.

Yours respectfully.

C. A. Richardson

The next day, March 5, 1864, Charles Richardson wrote another letter to Gay: "Our worst fears are realized. My brother's wife has died most unexpectedly to us all, as she was in full strength ten days ago. She suffered very greatly during her sickness and was not fully rational at all from the time when the disease first assumed a serious look, so that she spoke no parting words to anyone, and could leave none for her husband."

Charles asked Gay to print the news of Louise's death in the *Tribune* so that Richardson's friends would learn of it. He ended his letter with this: "Sister has often expressed her warm obligation to you for your uniform kindness." In the envelope, Charles enclosed a clipping from that day's *Boston Journal*, the newspaper that had employed Richardson when he and Louise lived in Kansas while he covered the bloody battle over slavery:

SAD BEREAVEMENT

One of the most painful cases incident to the separation of families by the protracted confinement of Union prisoners at the South is that of Mr. A. D. Richardson, correspondent of the *N.Y. Tribune* and formerly the Kansas correspondent of the *Boston Journal*. Mrs. Richardson, who with her four children has lived with her husband's father in Franklin in this state, died on Friday, the 4th, of congestion of the brain, induced by the measles, after a sickness of only one week. Mr. Richardson, who has been a prisoner since May 1863, was moved from Castle Thunder to Salisbury, N.C., early in February, and the first intelligence he receives of the sickness of his wife will probably be accompanied by the crushing news of her sudden death. We deeply sympathize with him in his afflicting bereavement.

Richardson learned of Lou's death in a letter from Charles that he received in the filthy, noisy room he shared with 150 other prisoners. "Amid all that meanness and coarseness and desolation," Browne recalled, "the heavy blow fell upon, and almost crushed him."

In three years of war, Albert Richardson had seen hundreds of men die on battlefields and in prisons, but he wasn't there to witness the death of the woman who was closest to him. In his grief, he lacerated himself with guilt. He'd left Lou so many times to chase adventures, he thought, and when she needed him most, in her week of sickness and death, he wasn't there to comfort her or bid her farewell. And now, when his children needed him most, he wasn't there, and had no way to get there.

In prison there was nothing to take his mind off of Lou—no work to do, no place to go—so he brooded about her, remembering every time he'd treated her cruelly, every moment of anger and harshness, every instance when he'd been selfish and unkind to the woman he loved. How could he have been so callous?

And his children—what would become of them? He hadn't seen them in 14 months, since the winter before he was captured. Leander was now a boy of eight, Maude was four, Albert two. Would he even recognize them if he saw them? He certainly wouldn't recognize the baby, his six-month-old daughter Mary Louisa. He'd never seen her: She was born while he was in Libby Prison. The children were all safe, living with his family, but how would they get along with their mother dead and their father locked in this godforsaken prison?

"My thoughts are much with you all at home—& especially on my poor, motherless children—who have met, on the threshold of life, with the severest of all losses," he wrote to his brother Charles. "May they find, in those who guide their little feet, the best approximation possible to that perfect sympathy, that patient forbearance, that tender, untiring, undying affection, which God gives, in full measure, only to the mother's heart."

After receiving letters of condolence from friends in New York who had read of Lou's death in the *Tribune*, Richardson wrote to Gay, asking him to print a notice of her death in the *Tribune*'s weekly national edition to inform Lou's friends and relatives in the West. "She died in Franklin, Massachusetts, March 5 of congestion of the brain after an illness of one week. Four little children—the youngest an infant of six months—remain at my desolate home—which can never again be a home to me."

At night, Richardson lay awake, his memories tormenting him, and in the morning he arose in the wretched prison dormitory and walked to the bench outside the infirmary, where inmates who died during the night were laid out and covered by a sheet. He would lift the sheet to see who had died; he noticed that the dead seemed so calm, so peaceful, and he realized that he envied them. At 30 years old, the man who had embraced the adventure of life so enthusiastically since his teens now found himself longing for death.

"Hope—the one thing that buoys up the prisoner—was gone," he wrote. "That picture of home, which had looked before as heaven looks to the enthusiastic devotee, was forever darkened."

12

HEROES OF AMERICA

A NEW COMMANDANT TOOK OVER SALISBURY PRISON on May 1, 1864—Captain George Washington Alexander, the pirate, playwright, and songwriter who was fired at Castle Thunder after being accused of bribery. He lasted only five weeks at Salisbury—he was replaced on June 8—but it was long enough for Browne and Richardson to be moved from the big, noisy room in the prison's main building to more comfortable quarters on the top floor of one of the smaller buildings. A coincidence? Or perhaps the commandant and the correspondents had agreed to renew their previous financial arrangements.

"Our room is the entire third (upper) story of a small building," Richardson wrote to his sister-in-law Jennie, "and is about 14 feet by 25, well ventilated and, except for 2 or 3 hours on the hottest days, cool."

Richardson and Browne shared the room with three Union sailors who had been captured when Confederates seized their ship off the coast of Virginia. "All my room mates are pleasant companions," Richardson told Jennie, and one of the sailors was an excellent cook:

"I never saw a man who could accomplish so much with so little—or a woman either. Our rations are flour or cornmeal & bacon, salt & sugar and enough of each article. With no other ingredients, he makes quite good light biscuits & very passable griddle cakes."

Occasionally, they were able to buy some extra groceries from local residents—potatoes, eggs, lettuce, onions, chinaberries, and, once in a while, butter. "On the whole we are better situated and in better health than ever before since our capture," Richardson wrote. "The fare is not as good as when we got frequent boxes from the North, but free exercise in the air more than compensates."

After assuring Jennie that he was doing well, he begged her to take care of his children: "May God shield them and preserve to them a mother's love to guide their little feet."

In July, Richardson and Browne welcomed another reporter to the room they shared with the sailors. William E. Davis—a correspondent for the *Cincinnati Gazette* and former clerk of the Ohio Senate—arrived in Salisbury after being captured while covering General Sherman's invasion of Georgia. Browne and Richardson were delighted for the company of another Bohemian, particularly one bringing fresh stories of Sherman's army, which was inching towards Atlanta.

Located far from the front lines of the war, Salisbury Prison had a more relaxed policy on visitation than the prisons in beleaguered Richmond. Salisbury residents were permitted to drop by and chat with the inmates. Some came to sell food, or to trade food for Yankee souvenirs—the buttons from Union uniforms, or the rings and brooches that prisoners carved out of soup bones. Others came just for the chance to meet some Yankees. Always curious, Richardson enjoyed talking to the visitors, and he was surprised by how many of them found an opportunity to take him aside and whisper, confidentially, that they opposed secession and supported the Union.

One regular visitor was Luke Blackmer, a prosperous 39-year-old lawyer and businessman who lived a few blocks away. Born in upstate New York and educated at Union College in Schenectady, Blackmer had moved to Salisbury in the 1850s and become a prominent member of the Episcopal Church and the local Masonic Lodge. When the war began, he helped to create a hospital for wounded Confederate soldiers. He also served as a *pro bono* defense attorney for the hungry soldiers' wives arrested for stealing flour during a food riot in Salisbury in the spring of 1863. Blackmer frequently walked from his house to the prison, and he gave food and money to prisoners, including Browne and Richardson. He also loaned the reporters books from his extensive personal library, delivered to the prison by a little black boy who carried them in a basket propped on his head.

Blackmer's Northern roots and his kindness to Yankee prisoners raised suspicions in Salisbury, and some of the city's more zealous Confederates began spreading the rumor that he was a member of a pro-Union secret society called the "Heroes of America."

"A SECRET OATH-BOUND SOCIETY, of a treasonable character, exists in North Carolina," the *Raleigh Conservative* declared on July 2, 1864. "There can be no doubt of the fact. The proof has been gradually accumulating and is now overwhelming."

The treasonous society, named the Heroes of America, was, the *Conservative* charged, "a covert and cowardly means of affecting the subjugation and slavery of the Southern people."

Ten days after the *Conservative*'s shocking revelation, the *Salisbury Watchman* reported that a local man had confessed to being a member of the Heroes of America after two escaped Yankee prisoners appeared at his house expecting him to help them reach the North.

When the newspapers printed their breathless exposés, the Heroes of America had existed for three years, and had recruited perhaps 10,000 members, most of them in North Carolina and the mountain regions of Tennessee and Virginia. Many of the Heroes were poor farmers who owned no slaves; others were Quakers opposed to war and slavery. And some were simply men who'd fought for the United States in the Mexican War—or whose fathers and grandfathers had fought in the Revolution or the War of 1812—and retained a deep patriotic loyalty to the country they'd always believed was the hope of humanity.

The Heroes performed elaborate initiation ceremonies complete with secret passwords and secret handshakes and the kind of quasi-Masonic rituals popular in nineteenth-century America. Members learned to identify each other through a memorized dialogue:

"These are gloomy times," a Hero would say to a man he thought might be a member.

"Yes," the second man would reply if he was a Hero, "but we are looking for better."

The secret symbol of the Heroes was a red cord, a reference to the biblical Book of Joshua, in which Rahab hid Joshua's spies in Jericho and lowered them to safety on a "scarlet cord." Heroes identified themselves by wearing a red thread or by hanging a red cord on their windows, and they came to be known as the "Red Strings."

The Heroes of America was the best-organized component of an amorphous peace movement that arose in North Carolina as the war dragged on. The state had been the last to secede from the Union but later, in the summer of 1861, a wave of Confederate fervor swept North Carolina. Within a year, though, the romance of war began to fade and disillusionment grew. In 1862, the Confederate government instituted the first military draft in American history while providing exemptions for men who owned 20 slaves and men who could afford to hire substitutes. The law inspired an embittered saying in the Confederate army: "A rich man's war but a poor man's fight." In 1863, food prices soared in the South, causing some soldiers' wives to riot and many more to write to their husbands complaining that they couldn't feed the children. Many of the men who received those letters deserted and headed home to help their families. The Confederate defeats at Gettysburg and Vicksburg in July 1863 only added to the sense that the war was futile and the Confederacy doomed.

The Heroes of America and other peace activists organized more than 100 public meetings in North Carolina during the summer of 1863. Many of the meetings passed resolutions urging that North Carolina leave the Confederacy and negotiate a separate peace with the United States. The meetings received favorable coverage in the *Raleigh Standard*, whose editor, William W. Holden, advocated making an "honorable peace" with the U.S. government. On September 9, a mob of Confederate soldiers attacked the office of the *Standard*, battered down the door, smashed furniture, and splashed printer's ink across the walls and the floor. The next day, a mob of Holden's supporters retaliated by wrecking the offices of the pro-Confederate *State Journal*, which had denounced Holden as a traitor and "a desperate and despicable blackleg."

Two months later, in the election of November 1863, peace candidates won five of the ten seats in North Carolina's delegation to the Confederate Congress. Their success inspired Holden to run for governor against the Confederate incumbent, Zebulon Vance, in the election scheduled for August 4, 1864.

Many North Carolina politicians, including Vance, believed that Holden stood a strong chance of winning. If he did, and if he led North Carolina out of the Confederacy, the South would be shattered. In Richmond, the Confederate Congress voted to suspend the writ of habeas corpus for any person "advising or inciting others to abandon the Confederate cause." In North Carolina, the Confederate establishment went on the offensive, charging that Holden was a secret member of the Heroes of America. The accusation was probably false but widely believed. Meanwhile, Vance, a spellbinding orator, traveled to Virginia to campaign among his state's soldiers, then returned to stump across North Carolina, delivering dozens of fiery speeches.

"We all want peace," he told the crowds. But Holden's plan would not provide it. "Instead of getting your sons back to the plow and fireside, they would be drafted [into the Union army] to fight alongside of Negro troops in exterminating the white men, women and children of the South."

Vance's strategy worked. On Election Day, he crushed Holden, winning 80 percent of the vote. "I have beaten him worse than any man has ever been beaten in North Carolina," Vance crowed.

The governor had certainly won in a landslide, but Browne and Richardson, studying the results in newspapers, could find reason for hope. One out of five North Carolina voters had cast a ballot to end the war. And voting was restricted to white males. A third of the state's population was composed of black slaves, who loathed the Confederacy. Pondering those numbers, a Salisbury prisoner could reasonably conclude that he would find many sympathetic souls in North Carolina if only he could manage to sneak outside the stockade.

Inside the stockade, a Southerner imprisoned for disloyalty initiated William Davis into the Heroes of America. And Davis began signing up other members, including Browne and Richardson.

★

WHEN THE *TRIBUNE* REPORTERS learned that Edward A. Pollard had been captured, they rejoiced: This was a development that could win them their freedom.

Pollard was an editor of the *Richmond Examiner*, and the author of countless fire-breathing editorials attacking Abraham Lincoln, abolitionists, and the cowardly Yankees, as well as several ludicrous editorials insisting that the Confederates had won the battle of Gettysburg.

Son of a wealthy Virginia planter, Pollard was a lawyer, a former clerk for the United States Congress, and the author of a tract called *Black Diamonds Gathered in the Darkey Homes of the South*, which argued that slavery was "a great improving and progressive work of human civilization" because it elevated the Negro from "the condition of a nomad, a heathen, and a brute to that of a civilized and comfortable creature, and gives to him the priceless treasure of a saving religion." While writing *Examiner* editorials, Pollard established himself as one of the fastest historians in history. He published his history of the first year of the Civil War, titled *The First Year of the War*, in 1862, which was the second year of the war. He published his history of the second year of the war, *The Second Year of the War*, in 1863, which was the third year of the war. And, not surprisingly, he published *The Third Year of the War* in 1864, which was the fourth year of the war. He would no doubt have written *The Fourth Year of the War*, too, if he hadn't been captured by the Yankees.

He was sailing to England to meet with his British publisher in May 1864, when an American warship seized the Confederate ship he was traveling aboard. Pollard was arrested and imprisoned in Fort Warren in Boston.

Reading news of his capture, Browne and Richardson were thrilled: The Union now held a very prominent Rebel newspaperman. Pollard had many powerful friends in Richmond's ruling circles, and they would no doubt be eager to win his release—perhaps eager enough to trade a couple of previously-paroled Yankee reporters who'd already spent more than a year in captivity. Surely, the Union's agent of exchange would demand Richardson and Browne in trade for Pollard, the *Tribune* reporters figured, and surely the Rebels would agree to the deal.

They were wrong. On August 12, after three months in prison, Pollard was paroled, released to the custody of a relative who lived in Brooklyn. He was free to do as he pleased as long as he remained in Brooklyn and didn't commit hostile acts against the United States government.

"This news cut us like a knife," Richardson wrote. He and Browne were enraged: Here they were, locked in prison while that vitriolic Rebel propagandist was strolling the streets of Brooklyn, maybe heading for an elegant dinner party where he could entertain the guests with his witty and erudite defenses of slavery and treason. Richardson and Browne were so infuriated by the injustice that they finally agreed never to mention it again, just for the sake of their sanity. But Richardson still felt outraged and betrayed, and on August 27, he let off steam in a blistering letter to his brother Charles.

"Is this not infamous?" he wrote. "He is free in one of the pleasantest cities in the world; we shut up in a foul, loathsome prison! He about to be sent home after a month's nominal confinement; we entering upon our seventeenth month of captivity, with no prospect of release, after having suffered that which rather than endure again, *we would unhesitatingly choose immediate death.* Is it the indifference and neglect of our own friends, or the obstinacy and stupidity of the authorities that has caused this?"

Charles Richardson received that letter, and then sent it to Sydney Gay, but Richardson heard nothing from either man. This didn't surprise him. Neither he nor Browne had received any letters at all since the spring. He wrote home regularly, begging for news of his children, but he never heard a word.

"The North to us is like the grave," he wrote in one letter, "no voice ever comes back to us from it."

He didn't believe that his relatives had abandoned him. He figured the Rebels simply weren't delivering the letters—and he was correct. But the isolation from his family, along with the unrelenting idleness and boredom of prison life, began to take a toll. One day, Richardson looked into a mirror and saw the feral face of a hardened prisoner— "the disturbed, half-wild expression of the eye, the contraction of the wrinkled brow which indicates trouble at the heart."

Browne was just as despondent. When he arrived at Libby Prison in May 1863, he believed he couldn't possibly survive even three months in captivity. Now, 16 months later, he wondered why prison hadn't killed him—and why he hadn't killed himself. What kept him alive? Why did he cling to such a dull and pointless life? He concluded that it was philosophy—the teachings of the Stoics—that kept him going: "Man must be a brute or a philosopher to bear up under all the trial of confinement."

During the summer of 1864, Luke Blackmer—the sympathetic attorney who lent them books and gave them money—traveled to Richmond to lobby for their release, but he found no grounds for hope. When he returned, he told Richardson and Browne that the only way they'd get out before the end of the war was to escape.

They'd already reached the same conclusion. Every day they devised escape plots; and every night, as they lay in their blankets in their airless little garret, they discussed their schemes in hushed whispers. But all the plans had drawbacks, and Browne, a pessimist by nature, would enumerate the reasons why each couldn't possibly succeed. Still, they were so desperate that they persisted, promising each other that they would break out or die trying.

Late in the summer, they settled on a plan. They'd cultivated a friendly guard who was willing—out of sympathy or bribery or both—to slip them out of the stockade one night at precisely midnight. Before their quarters were locked for the night, the three Bohemians—Browne, Richardson, and Davis—tiptoed out of the building. Browne and Richardson hid under an infirmary, which was built on stilts. They lay there, waiting for Davis, who was waiting for a messenger who was supposed to bring $400 from a friend outside the prison, probably Blackmer. But the messenger got drunk and didn't arrive with the money until after midnight. The *Tribune* reporters could have escaped without Davis and the money, but they declined. They figured they could try again the following night. They were wrong. The next day, by sheer coincidence, the friendly guard was shipped north to help General Lee defend Richmond from the Yankee hordes.

They were devastated. Once more, they'd botched an escape opportunity. It seemed as if the fates were mocking them. The Bohemians sank into a depression so deep that Browne finally decided that he needed to do something to cheer them up. He snuck off and secretly shaved his beard and his head and then reappeared, announcing to his friends that he wasn't Junius Henri Browne of the *New York Tribune*, he was an ancient and venerable Chinese sage named "No Go."

That got them laughing, at least for a while.

13

THE DEAD CART

HE WANDERED IN A DAZE through a three-story brick building, looking for a way out. He tried doors, but he couldn't open them. He tried windows, but they didn't open either. He was hungry and he saw great mountains of bread outside, but he couldn't get to them. Then he spotted an open door and walked through it. Free at last, he suddenly felt very thirsty. He saw a stream and he threw himself upon the ground and plunged his head into the water and drank and drank until the stream was dry.

And then drums sounded and Benjamin Booth awoke from his dream to find that his unit, the 22nd Iowa Infantry, was under attack. The Iowans scrambled from their blankets and picked up their rifles, but the Rebels were already upon them, yelling "Surrender!" Booth and many others were captured. It was dawn on October 19, 1864, at Cedar Creek in Virginia's Shenandoah Valley, and the Confederate surprise attack forced General Phil Sheridan's Union army into retreat. Before the day was out, Sheridan would rally his troops and win the battle, but not soon enough to rescue Booth and 1,300 other Yankees captured early in the fighting.

The Rebels confiscated the captives' guns, blankets, and can-teens—and sometimes their boots—then stuffed them into boxcars and shipped them south.

Late one afternoon, the train arrived in Salisbury and the Yankees plodded through a cold rain into the prison. The yard once used for baseball games was packed with thousands of men, some living in tents, others in holes in the ground.

Hungry, wet, and shivering, Booth wrapped a piece of tenting material around his shoulders, leaned against a tree, and fell asleep. He woke up when somebody tried to steal the tenting off his body. He hollered and kicked and drove the thief away, saving his possessions, including the pencil stub and paper he would later use to record the horrors he witnessed in Salisbury Prison.

BENJAMIN BOOTH WAS ONE OF nearly 10,000 men sent to Salis-bury in the fall of 1864. With Grant's army threatening Rich-mond, the Confederates decided to move their prisoners. Thousands went to the newly constructed prison near Andersonville, Georgia, which soon held 33,000 men in horrendous conditions. Thousands more were shipped to Salisbury.

Earlier that summer, Salisbury Prison had housed about 800 men, all of them living indoors in relative comfort. By mid-October the buildings were full, and nearly 9,000 newcomers were camped in the once bucolic yard. The prison authorities provided some tents, but not enough to house even half the men. The rest, including Booth, dug holes in the ground and covered them with pieces of cloth or branches hacked off the yard's oak trees. It was a cold, rainy autumn and the yard turned to thick mud, which sometimes froze at night.

"Imagine nine or ten thousand scantily clad, emaciated, woebegone soldiers in an enclosure of five or six acres, half of them without other shelter than the holes they had dug in the earth or under the small buildings employed as hospitals," wrote Junius Browne. "The weather is cold; perhaps a chilly rain is falling or the ground is covered with snow. There are soldiers—hundreds of them with naked feet, and only light blouses or shirts, hungry, feeble, despairing of the Present and hopeless of the Future."

The Confederates divided the prisoners into squads of 100 and dis-tributed food once a day to each squad. On a good day, a man got a loaf of cornbread and a cup of thin soup. More frequently, he received a serving of raw cornmeal and had to cook it himself. The men stirred water into the cornmeal and heated it like soup over campfires, or wrapped it in a homemade clay container and placed it in the coals, where it baked into something approximating bread. When the prison guards dined on beef, they would sometimes dump a wheelbarrow full of raw cow offal on the ground—heads, hooves, guts—and then watch the hungry prisoners fight for it.

"We got the hearts, livers, lungs and heads, etc." Booth wrote in his diary on November 18. "My friend Connely got one eye of a beef for his share."

"Charley Bowen caught a mouse this morning," Booth wrote two days later, noting that Bowen boiled the critter to make mouse soup, "which he pronounced one of the most delicious dishes he had ever eaten since becoming a guest of Jeff Davis at his Hotel de Salisbury."

Starving, the desperate prisoners traded whatever they owned for food. Guards would give a sweet potato for a button from a Union uniform, and several loaves of bread for a jacket or a pair of boots. As the weeks wore on, the grim diet whittled the men down to skin and bone; they looked, Browne said, "like skeletons in rags."

Sanitation was primitive. There was water to drink but little for washing, and the thousands of men in the yard shared a few open-pit latrines set up along one wall of the stockade. The stench could be smelled three miles away.

"I don't know why you all smell so," a guard told Booth. "Why, you Yanks smell worse than niggers!"

Eating wretched food and sleeping in the wet cold, the prisoners fell prey to disease. Diarrhea and pneumonia were epidemic, and so were typhoid, smallpox, and dengue fever, which the prisoners called "breaky-bone fever" because it made a man's joints swell, causing excruciating pain. The death toll soared, rising from one or two a day in early October to 20 or 30 a day by mid-November.

Disease wasn't the only killer: The guards were also deadly. Patrolling atop the stockade wall with muskets, they shot anyone who crossed the "dead line"—a four-foot-wide ditch dug along the fence. Sometimes they fired at men who only came *near* the dead line, including a lieutenant from New York who was shot dead while hanging his shirt on a tree to dry. With most local men of fighting age away on battlefields, Salisbury's guards tended to be men older than 50 and boys in their early teens. The prisoners considered the young guards particularly trigger happy, but both groups shot prisoners often enough to fuel the false rumor that they earned a furlough for killing a Yankee.

Whatever the cause of death, the resulting corpses were carried to a small brick building called the "dead house," where they were stripped of their clothes and loaded naked on a horse-drawn wagon— the "dead cart." The wagon carried eight corpses at a time. Most days, it made several trips.

"The last scene of all," Richardson wrote, "was the dead cart with its rigid forms piled upon each other like logs—the arms swaying, the white ghastly faces staring with dropped jaws and stony eyes."

Not all the ghastly faces were white. Some belonged to black soldiers. One day, as the wagon carried a load of corpses, a prisoner noticed that a dead black man had been loaded atop the dead white men. Irate at this racial affront, the prisoner protested, loudly and profanely, attracting a crowd of angry inmates. Eager to avoid a riot, the guard leading the cart dragged the black corpse off the wagon, dropped it on the ground, and drove away.

On another day, the dead cart got stuck in thick mud. The driver attempted to prod his horse forward with a jab of his bayonet and accidentally fired his rifle, killing the animal. The prisoners watched with delight. "We thought now was our opportunity to get some fresh meat, and we united in asking the prison authorities permission to dress the dead horse, but they denied the request," Booth wrote in his diary. "One man asked the officer why he would not let us have the horse. His answer was: 'I do not want you 'uns to go home and tell the folks up thar that we'uns fed you 'uns on dead horse.'"

The dead cart's destination was a field outside the prison, where inmates had dug trenches four feet deep, six feet wide and 60 yards long. The guards pulled the corpses off the dead wagon, one man grabbing the arms, another taking the legs, and then they swung the naked bodies into a trench, piling them three or four deep. The prison chaplain, a kindly man named A. W. Mangum, would gather leaves so he could cover the faces of the dead men before the guards shoveled dirt on them.

The horror of life and death in Salisbury drove some prisoners to madness. "Two poor fellows have gone totally insane," Booth wrote. "They run around the ground crying, *'Bread! . . . Bread! . . . Bread!'*

This one word they scream at the top of their voice. Their eyes are glassy, their walk unsteady."

Other prisoners simply gave up and committed suicide by deliberately crossing the dead line so the guards would shoot them.

But there was an easier way out: An inmate could exit the prison simply by joining the Confederate army. Recruiters periodically entered the yard, stood atop a box, and delivered a speech, promising the prisoners good food, new clothes, a $100 signing bonus and $20 a month. Frequently, a Catholic priest accompanied the recruiter and made a special appeal to the Irish prisoners. Sometimes, recruiters would promise to send the Yankees to Confederate forts in Florida, or some other warm place far from the front lines. It was a difficult offer for a starving, freezing man to resist, and between October 1864 and February 1865, more than 1,500 Salisbury prisoners took the deal, most of them swearing that they'd desert at the first opportunity.

"I cannot blame them," Browne wrote. "Who could demand that they should await certain destruction in the form of disease and cold and hunger when relief was offered them?"

Sometimes prisoners approached Browne and Richardson with tears in their eyes, begging for advice: Should they stay here and die slowly or save their lives by joining the Rebel army?

"I always answered," Richardson recalled, "that they owed no obligation to God or man to remain and starve to death."

RICHARDSON AND **B**ROWNE observed the horrors of Salisbury Prison up close, but they did not suffer the worst of them. They weren't living in a hole in the ground or struggling to survive on a cup of uncooked cornmeal a day. They still occupied a room on the third floor of one of the prison's smaller buildings, and they were frequently able to supplement the meager prison rations by purchasing food with money that Luke Blackmer and other sympathetic outsiders smuggled in. Neither their food nor their quarters were luxurious, but compared to the cold, starving men they saw every day, they were living like pashas, and that knowledge filled them with guilt. But what could they do—invite 9,000 men to sleep in their room or share their extra potato or slice of bacon?

Browne, Richardson, and Davis volunteered to work in the prison hospitals, and the overworked head surgeon, Dr. Richard Currey, eagerly accepted their offer. The "hospitals" were merely a series of rooms in several buildings where sick men could get out of the elements and sleep inside, on floors carpeted with dirty straw. Six hundred men packed the hospitals' floors, many of them too weak to get up and hobble to a latrine. The smell was horrendous and the air reverberated with the constant staccato cacophony of hacking and coughing.

Richardson became the hospital clerk, interviewing every new patient and recording his name, regiment, hometown, and diagnosis. He also recorded the daily death toll, and he was given the gruesome task of distributing the dead men's clothing to prisoners desperate for any garment, no matter how foul.

Davis, the *Cincinnati Gazette* reporter, became the "general superintendent" of the hospitals, distributing supplies and helping Currey take care of the patients. Assisting him was Thomas E. Wolfe, a Connecticut sea captain, who'd been captured by the Rebel navy.

Browne became a kind of visiting nurse, taking water and medicine to the "outdoor patients"—the thousands of sick prisoners who couldn't fit into the hospitals, or refused to enter them because nobody ever seemed to come out alive. Every day, he wandered the yard, asking prisoners to lead him to their sick friends, then crawling into crude tents and muddy holes to tend to them. He had only two medicines—one for diarrhea and one for coughs, neither very effective—so he couldn't do much for the men. But he gave them water and medicine and he talked to them and tried to leave them with a little bit of hope.

The prisoners appreciated Browne's efforts and called him "Doctor." When they asked what kind of doctor he was, he identified himself, in his usual droll fashion, as an "amateur physician," and the phrase quickly spread through the prison grapevine. One day, a prisoner asked Richardson what kind of college an "amateur physician" attended— they seemed to know a lot more than the average doctor.

That was a rare moment of levity in a grim autumn. The faces of dead and dying men haunted Richardson and Browne, and they were tormented by their inability to save the sick from a future in the burial trenches.

"Suffering everywhere and no power to relieve it," Browne wrote. "In every tent and hole in the ground, wherever you tread or turn, gaunt and ghastly men, perishing by inches, glare on you like accusing specters, until you find yourself forced to exclaim, 'Thank God, I am not responsible for this!'"

At night, after a long day of work, they returned to their room to eat a meager meal that seemed sinfully extravagant when compared with the other prisoners' fare. Gaunt and despondent, Richardson told Browne that he was certain the horrors they witnessed every day must somehow be part of God's great plan.

"If anything could shake my faith in the Love and Wisdom that rule the universe, my faith would be shaken here," he said. "You are skeptical, I know, but be sure it will all come right in the end. Everything happens for the best, and is guided by some all-pervading spirit of Love."

Perhaps he was attempting to comfort his agnostic friend, or maybe he was trying to convince himself. Both men fought despair by getting up every morning and wading into the vast sea of misery, hoping to do some tangible good for somebody. They were too reticent to write much about their own work among the sick at Salisbury, but each praised the other's compassion and kindness.

"Brave men often sent for Richardson when they knew their end was approaching," Browne wrote, "that he might bear some final message to wife or mother, sweetheart or sister, and that they might die clasping his friendly hand."

"Mr. Browne did far more than I," Richardson told the relative of a dead prisoner. "He has far more of the tendency so seldom found in men—always found in women—to self-sacrifice than any man I ever met."

Although the two reporters agonized over their inability to save the dying, at least one prisoner believed that Richardson had saved his life. Henry Mann was the youngest inmate at Salisbury, captured at the age of 16. He was sick and scrawny and nearly ready for the burial trenches when Richardson spotted him in the yard and brought him up to the reporters' room to convalesce in comparative comfort. Decades later, Mann read Benjamin Booth's diary, which was published in 1897, and he wrote a letter to Booth about his experiences in Salisbury. "I would have gone to the trenches, but for the kindness of a civilian prisoner, Mr. Albert D. Richardson, correspondent of the New York Tribune, who noticed my youth and emaciated condition, and took me to his quarters."

In 1901, Robert L. Drummond, a former Salisbury prisoner who had become a prominent New York lawyer, saluted Richardson and Browne in a speech to Hamilton College students about his prison experiences. "I have crawled out of one of those holes in the ground in order to let Browne pass in, there being insufficient room for us both in addition to the sick inmates," Drummond said. "And I have stood and witnessed Richardson distribute clothing to a crowd of ragged skeletons. He was a man of highly sensitive and sympathetic nature and upon those occasions, he had the saddest face that I ever saw."

ON NOVEMBER 17, 1864, when the prisoners learned that Abraham Lincoln had been reelected, some of them responded by singing "The Star-Spangled Banner." A guard ordered them to stop; when they didn't, he fired at them, wounding a sergeant.

Richardson did not mention either the election or the shooting in the letter he wrote to his brother Charles that day. His letters had become perfunctory because he hadn't received mail in six months and wasn't confident that his own letters were arriving in Massachusetts. "With little expectation of them reaching you, I still go through the form of sending occasional letters," he told Charles. "Junius, Davis and myself all keep busily employed in the hospitals, accomplishing the double purpose of occupation and trying to do a little good to the suffering. The field is great and the laborers are few."

Several days later, he received a handful of letters from home, some recent, some dating back to August. The news they contained was grim. His daughter, Mary Louisa, born while he was in Libby Prison, had died in August, just shy of her first birthday. He had never met her and now he never would. Also, his eight-year-old son Leander, was no longer living with the Richardsons, instead staying with another family for reasons the letters did not quite explain.

Richardson quickly scribbled out a reply, begging for more information about the baby and Leander and his other children, Maude and Albert. "I have had no particulars whatever of the baby's sickness and death. How is Maude? Remember that I have not had a word of her or Le for six months. . . . I trust that Le, even though among strangers, is where special attention is paid to his advancement in study, but above all where he receives sympathy and affection. I want *particulars* about him."

Two days later, on November 23, Richardson wrote another letter to Charles: "Your vague statements about Le only tantalize me. I want you and Jennie to write me in *detail* concerning him. I want the person who now has charge of him to do the same. You can write as often as you please, you know."

On the day Richardson wrote those words, Benjamin Booth noted in his diary that the prisoners had received no food "since the day before yesterday." A Rebel recruiter had come through the yard promising three bushels of sweet potatoes to any man willing to join the Confederate army. "This is a strong temptation to men who are starving to death," Booth wrote, but few prisoners took the deal. "It is wonderful to see with what determination and scorn these slowly-murdered men reject the alternative. Death anytime and in any way! Treason and disloyalty, never!"

The next day, November 24, hungry men gathered in groups around the yard, talking about fighting back. They'd learned that the Junior Reserves—the young teenage guards—would be shipped to Virginia the next day to join General Lee's army. Once they left, only the old men of the Senior Reserves would remain to guard the prison, and it seemed an opportune moment for an uprising.

"There is considerable whispering going on among the prisoners about making a concerted rush for one of the gates, breaking it down and gaining our liberty if we can, or dying if we must," Booth wrote in his diary. "If it must be death by starvation or by the bullet, the latter is our first choice. Hence, preparation and plans are being seriously and carefully made for an outbreak."

14

INSURRECTION

THE PLAN WAS TO OVERPOWER the guards as they arrived inside the prison, grab their weapons, charge the main gate and break out, then head for the nearby Salisbury arsenal, steal guns and ammunition, and march off to join General Sherman's army, which was out there somewhere, tearing up the Confederacy.

It was a bold, desperate, foolhardy plan that depended on quick, concerted action by a large number of prisoners, so the plotters spread the word to their friends, telling them to be ready to move at the sound of the battle cry, "Strike for Liberty!" But the plotters also feared that somebody would tip off the guards—a few days earlier, a hungry prisoner had revealed the location of a tunnel in return for a couple loaves of bread—so they tried to keep the plan quiet. Consequently, only about 1,000 of the prisoners—maybe a sixth of the men living in the yard—knew of the plan and were prepared to fight.

The morning of Friday, November 25, 1864, was clear and cold. The "young bloods" marched to the train station, which was adjacent to the prison, and waited for the troop train to arrive, some of them wearing scraps of blanket or canvas tied to their feet because they had no shoes. Inside the stockade, the guards began the long, slow process of distributing the day's rations—four ounces of bread and some soup—to one squad of 100 men after another. Early in the afternoon, the troop train arrived, blowing its whistle. The plotters were delighted to hear it, figuring the young bloods were leaving town.

At two o'clock, a group of 16 guards walked into the yard to relieve the sentries guarding the buildings inside the stockade. As they passed through the hordes of hungry, dirty men, somebody called out the signal—"Strike for Liberty!"—and the prisoners attacked, mobbing the guards, grabbing their guns. One guard fought back and was stabbed with his own bayonet. Another raised his musket to fire and was shot in the head, his brains splattered on the wall behind him.

Screaming battle cries, hundreds of prisoners charged towards the main gate, some now armed with muskets, the rest carrying sticks and stones. Between the mob and the gate stood a crowd of men waiting for their rations. These hungry prisoners knew nothing about the uprising. When they saw hundreds of screaming men heading towards them, they figured they'd come to steal their food. When the two groups met, fistfights broke out—some men fighting to escape, others fighting to defend their meager rations.

The insurgents shoved their way to the main gate. Those with muskets fired at the guards patrolling on a parapet atop the stockade fence. The other men threw rocks. A few of the guards panicked, dropped their guns, and fled, but others fired down into the mob. During the fight, a group of prisoners managed to break out of the gate, only to find themselves facing a charge of Confederate soldiers. The troop train had not yet left the station, and when the "young bloods" heard the shooting, they rushed back to the prison, eager to kill Yankees. They shot some of the escapees and drove the rest back into the stockade. Then they climbed onto the parapet and began firing.

Two cannons were mounted atop the stockade. The guards loaded them with small chunks of metal and fired into the yard. The shrapnel tore a swath through the crowd, ripping into the prisoners' flesh. Amid the screams, frightened inmates dove into holes for cover.

The uprising was over, crushed in a matter of minutes.

Eventually the yard fell silent, the inmates hiding in tents or burrowing into holes or crouching behind trees. The guards paced the top of the stockade, ready to fire at anything that moved. Salisbury residents arrived, carrying muskets, pistols, and shotguns. The locals had long feared a revolt by the prisoners—who outnumbered Salisbury citizens nearly four to one. For half an hour, the guards and the local citizens stood atop the stockade taking potshots at the tents and holes in the yard.

Richardson and Browne watched the insurrection from their little apartment in a building located several hundred yards from the skirmish at the front gate. When the cannons had cleared the yard, the reporters hunkered down on the floor, listening to bullets thudding into the log walls of the building, and worrying that a stray shot might fly through one of the spaces between the logs and kill them.

The doomed insurrection was a brief and bloody failure. Major John Gee, the prison commandant, reported that three guards were killed and ten wounded. Richardson, the official hospital clerk, reported that 16 prisoners were killed and 60 wounded, most of them men who had nothing to do with the uprising.

Freezing rain fell all night, and in the morning the corpses piled outside the dead house glistened with a thin coating of ice.

"YOU HAVE HEARD OF THE ATTEMPT by some of the prisoners to overpower the Confederate guards on the 25th," Junius Browne wrote to Sydney Gay a week later. "The garrison, regarding the insurrection as general, fired indiscriminately on the prisoners until the officers ordered them to desist. It was a most unfortunate and ill-managed affair for no one escaped."

Browne assured Gay that he and Richardson were healthy and "trying to do what little we can" to help the hundreds of sick prisoners. "You are aware no doubt that early in October some 9,000 of our enlisted men were sent here from Richmond. Since their coming, there has been a great deal of sickness and suffering among the prisoners. About 1,000 have died and mortality is on the increase. At the present rate of death, next August will find none of us alive. But then we will be free. Dante, with all the gloom and horror of his 'Inferno,' did not dream of that."

Browne's glum letter reflected the despair that pervaded the prison after the failed revolt. Roughly 30 inmates died every day and the rest were wasting away. They wondered why their government wasn't doing anything to help them—except sending packages of clothing that were usually stolen by the Confederates. Why didn't the army arrange to exchange them for Rebel prisoners held in the North?

"Is it possible," Benjamin Booth wrote in his diary on the day of the insurrection, "that our friends in the North, and especially the government at Washington, have forgotten us?"

The government hadn't forgotten the prisoners, and neither had the public. Northern newspapers published many vivid descriptions of the Confederate prisons, particularly Andersonville, and the articles were frequently illustrated with woodcuts of emaciated inmates. An editorial published in an Atlanta newspaper in August 1864 was widely quoted in Northern papers: "During one of the intensely hot days of the last week more than 300 sick and wounded Yankees died at Andersonville. We thank Heaven for such blessings."

Lincoln's secretary of war, Edwin Stanton, denounced the Confederates for their "deliberate system of savage and barbarous treatment"—a statement that fueled rumors that the Rebels were intentionally starving Union prisoners. That wasn't quite true. Union prisoners were certainly starving, but for the most part, starvation was not the result of a coldly calculated plan. The Confederates were simply running out of food. They could barely feed their own army, much less tens of thousands of Yankee prisoners. When General Grant dispatched an army into the Shenandoah Valley with orders to turn that Confederate breadbasket into a "barren waste," he was destroying not only the South's ability to feed its soldiers but also its ability to feed its prisoners.

Northern newspapers protested that Rebels held in federal prisons were eating better in captivity than they ate in the Confederate army, which was mostly true. In May 1864, Stanton responded by announcing that he was reducing the prison rations to the same level as the Confederate army issued to its soldiers. By then, though, few Rebel soldiers were actually receiving the Confederate army's official rate of rations, so the prisoners were probably *still* eating better than their friends in Lee's army. Rebel inmates in Northern prisons were also housed in conditions far better than those of the prisoners in Salisbury or Andersonville. Most lived in crude barracks, some in tents, none in holes in the ground. But thousands died anyway, succumbing to disease and exposure to the bitter Northern winters.

The two sides arranged some small, informal exchanges of prisoners in 1864, but there had been no major exchanges since the summer of 1863, when the process had broken down over the question of race. The Rebels refused to exchange black prisoners and President Lincoln refused to agree to whites-only exchanges. During his reelection campaign in 1864, Lincoln came under intense pressure to change that policy. Republican Party bosses told Lincoln that he would lose votes if people perceived that his sympathy for Negroes was keeping white men incarcerated in Southern hellholes. But Lincoln insisted that all Union prisoners be treated equally, regardless of race. General Grant agreed, ordering that "no distinction whatever will be made in the exchange between white and colored prisoners."

Grant was suspicious of *all* prisoner exchanges. When he conquered Vicksburg in July 1863, he captured 30,000 Confederate soldiers and promptly paroled them, requiring only that they promise not to fight again until they had been exchanged for Union prisoners. No such exchange ever took place, but thousands of the parolees rejoined the Confederate army. When Grant captured some of them a second time four months later at the battle of Chattanooga, he was irate, and not inclined to view exchanges favorably.

Since Grant had far more soldiers than the Confederates, he knew that the Rebels were therefore eager to exchange prisoners. He also believed that most Confederates housed in Northern prisons were healthy and ready to fight as soon as they were exchanged, while most Yankees in Southern prisons were too sick to return to the battlefield. "It is hard on our men held in Southern prisons not to exchange them, but it is humanity to those left in our ranks to fight our battles," Grant wrote to Union exchange agent Benjamin Butler in August 1864. "Every man we hold, when released on parole or otherwise, becomes an active soldier against us at once either directly or indirectly. If we commence a system of exchange which liberates all prisoners taken, we will have to fight on until the whole South is exterminated."

That sounded cold-blooded, but Grant was amenable to some exchanges. In October 1864, General Lee sent Grant a letter proposing an exchange of prisoners seized in the recent fighting around Petersburg, Virginia. Grant agreed, but reminded Lee that the prisoners included "a number of colored troops" and asked whether Lee was proposing to exchange "these men the same as white soldiers." When

Lee replied that his offer did not apply to "negroes belonging to our citizens," Grant rejected the deal.

Of course, the Union prisoners suffering in Salisbury knew nothing of these backstage machinations. They simply wanted their government to bring them home before they starved to death.

"TAKE A SEAT, MR. POLLARD," said General Benjamin Butler. Then he offered his guest a Havana cigar.

Pollard took the seat but declined the cigar, explaining that smoking was bad for his nerves.

Edward Pollard was the fiery Rebel editor of the *Richmond Examiner* who was captured by Union sailors and then paroled to Brooklyn, much to the disgust of Browne and Richardson. He'd been transferred to Fortress Monroe, the Union base in Virginia that served as a transfer point for exchanges of mail and, occasionally, prisoners. Two days later, on December 3, he was summoned to the office of General Butler, the Union exchange agent. Pollard was nervous about meeting Butler. An ugly man with a drooping left eyelid that gave his face a frightening, lopsided look, Butler was detested in the South. Early in the war, he angered Confederates by refusing to return runaway slaves to their masters, an act that inspired thousands of slaves to flee to the Union lines. Later, while serving as military governor of occupied New Orleans, Butler responded to an incident in which a woman dumped her chamber pot on Admiral Farragut's head by issuing General Order Number 28, which declared that any female insulting a federal officer would be "treated as a woman of the town plying her avocation." Southern gentlemen expressed great outrage over this insult to Southern womanhood and dubbed Butler "The Beast." Now, though, the Beast was treating Pollard with disarming courtesy.

"Perhaps you would like to look over the Richmond morning papers," Butler said, pushing a pile of newspapers towards the prisoner, and apologizing that he didn't have the *Examiner*.

Butler permitted his guest to peruse the papers for a while, then he revealed why he'd summoned him: He was planning to exchange Pollard for Albert Richardson. It would take some time to make arrangements, Butler said, but in the meantime, he would allow Pollard to roam freely around the 63 acres of Fortress Monroe if Pollard would promise not to reveal anything he saw at the fort to anyone when he returned to Richmond.

Of course, Pollard quickly agreed.

At that point, several Union officers arrived and Butler asked Pollard to step outside for a moment. Pollard waited on the general's porch until a black servant led him inside to a dining room where a table held two dinner plates, each surrounded by elegant silverware and garnished with a bright white napkin.

"Mr. Pollard," Butler said, smiling, "you will get no dinner unless you take some with me."

Surprised at Butler's hospitality, Pollard sat down to a delicious dinner of soup, roast beef, and apple sauce, followed by a dessert of apple pie, cheese, almonds, and English walnuts. "The table was attended by two Negro waiters, whose appearance of cringing obsequiousness," Pollard later recalled, "surpassed anything I had ever seen of such behavior in the presence of a Southern master."

After dinner, Butler fired up a Havana cigar and the two men chatted long into the night. The general reminded Pollard that he'd been a Democratic politician in Boston before the war. In fact, he'd voted for Jefferson Davis for president on 57 consecutive ballots at the 1860 Democratic convention.

"I think he has made a poor return for old times in calling me a beast," he joked.

Butler had heard that Davis was considering using slaves to fight in the Confederate army. He thought it was a fine idea: Let your black soldiers fight our black soldiers, he said. It would be an interesting experiment.

He told Pollard that 60,000 slaves had fled to the protection of his army, and most of the men among them had eagerly enlisted as soldiers. "They do so for two reasons," he said. "It improves their social status, and the soldier's life is attractive to the Negro. Though there are in it some hours and days of tremendous exertion, there is plenty of stagnant leisure in which the Negro indulges his disposition to laziness."

When the convivial evening ended, Pollard concluded that Butler was not as beastly as he'd been portrayed, certainly not nearly as despicable as the "cold, snakish" Sherman, who was then marching through Georgia, destroying everything in his path.

Butler wrote to Robert Ould, the Confederate agent of exchange, proposing to trade Pollard for Richardson. But again Ould refused, preferring to keep Richardson as a bargaining chip for future negotiations.

"I have had dozens of offers from the enemy to exchange Richardson. I have refused all," Ould wrote in a letter to Confederate General Braxton Bragg. "As Richardson is so dear to his Yankee friends, ought he not be kept as a 'persuader' to them to come to some terms on the question of the arrest and detention of non-combatants?"

"**I** HAVE SEEN A GOOD DEAL OF wretchedness & death before, but I never lived with it & walked with it, or was environed with it, daily & nightly, as I am here," Albert Richardson wrote to his brother on December 14. "It is so constantly familiar to us & near us, that it does not impress us as one might suppose; but viewed through time & distance it would appall us beyond expression and description."

He inquired about his children, as always, but spent much of the letter detailing exactly how much money the *Tribune* owed him— $333.43 in expenses incurred before his capture, plus $25 a week in salary owed him since he was captured, minus whatever the *Tribune* had sent to him or to Lou while he was in prison. "I only send you this for reference or guidance," he explained, "in case I should never have the opportunity to settle the account myself."

He was worried about dying. He remained fairly healthy, having recovered from a nasty case of pneumonia, or something like it, earlier in the fall, but life in Salisbury had become increasingly precarious. Since the insurrection, the guards patrolling atop the stockade fence had taken to amusing themselves by shooting prisoners at random. On December 8, a guard saw three black soldiers standing in the yard and fired at them. He missed and killed a white soldier instead. When one of the prison doctors went to headquarters to ask what happened, he was informed that when the guard saw three black men together he figured that he'd probably never get such a good opportunity again so he shot at them, killing the wrong man by accident. The Rebels thought it was hilarious.

With human life that cheap, Richardson and Browne were desperate to escape. So were the other prisoners, and they began furiously digging tunnels. Nearly everybody seemed to be tunneling. Richardson heard rumors of at least 15 tunnels under construction. Browne, whose job required him to crawl into holes to bring sick men medicine, was invited to crawl into countless tunnels, too. Frequently, the diggers invited him to escape with them as soon as they had finished the tunnel. But somehow the tunnels never seemed to be completed on schedule, always taking far longer than anticipated.

"Tunnels linger longer than rich relatives whom expectant heirs are waiting to bury," Browne mused.

In early December, one group of prisoners managed to dig past the stockade fence, only to watch the tunnel collapse because the ground was soaked with melting snow. On another occasion, somebody tipped off the reporters that guards had discovered a nearly completed tunnel and planned to shoot the prisoners when they emerged from it. The reporters, who had hoped to be among the escapees, sent a warning to the tunnellers, probably saving their lives.

The frenzy of tunneling troubled the prison commandant. He responded by creating a second line of guards, who patrolled outside the prison, about 100 feet past the stockade wall. That made escape by tunnel nearly impossible.

Always the droll pessimist, Browne pointed out that even if they managed the near-impossible feat of tunneling out, they would be faced with the near-impossible feat of walking at least 200 miles through enemy territory to reach the nearest Union army, which was in Knoxville, Tennessee.

"To walk the same distance in Ohio or Massachusetts, where we could travel by daylight upon public thoroughfares, stop at each village for rest and refreshments, and sleep in warm beds every night, we would consider a severe hardship," Browne said. "Think of this terrible tramp of 200 miles, by night, in mid-winter, over two ranges of mountains, creeping stealthily through the enemy's country, weak, hungry, shelterless. Can any of us live to accomplish it?"

Unable to refute that logic, Richardson began to despair of ever escaping. But then he met Lieutenant John R. Welborn, a Confederate officer who had joined the prison staff in November. Welborn said he was a member of the Heroes of America, and he knew all the passwords and handshakes. He also said he was a member of a related group called the Sons of America, which helped Yankee prisoners escape. He told Richardson that it *was* possible to get out, and that the mountains teemed with sympathetic men who would help them reach the Union lines.

Young, bold, and optimistic, Welborn told Richardson exactly what he wanted to hear: "You shall be out very soon."

15

SWEET GODDESS OF LIBERTY

WELBORN CAME FROM **W**ILKES **C**OUNTY, North Carolina, a pro-Union bastion in the Blue Ridge Mountains, one of only three counties won by William Holden, the antiwar candidate, in the election for governor four months earlier. Welborn told Richardson and Browne that he had plenty of kin living in the mountains and they were all loyal to the United States. They'd be happy to feed and shelter escaped prisoners, and to introduce them to other loyal men who'd help them get across the mountains to Knoxville.

But Wilkes County was 50 miles north of Salisbury, and escaped prisoners had to traverse a lot of Confederate territory to get there. The Rebels patrolled the roads, sometimes with bloodhounds, searching for escapees. The only way to make it was to travel at night and stay off the main roads. Slaves would hide a Union man during the day, and give him something to eat, according to the prison grapevine, but you had to find the field slaves because the house slaves were more cozy with their masters and might turn you in.

The odds of an escapee reaching the Union lines were dismal. Seventy prisoners had escaped during the ten months Richardson and

Browne had spent in Salisbury, and as far as they knew, only five had reached Knoxville. The rest had either been captured and hauled back to prison or shot dead somewhere in the mountains. But the reporters no longer worried about the odds. They just wanted to get out. Browne said he fully expected to be shot along the way, but at least he'd have the satisfaction of knowing that he died trying to win his freedom—a fate more befitting an American citizen, he said, than passively wasting away in captivity.

The other reporters agreed. They abandoned hope of tunneling out and decided to simply walk out instead. In this goal, they had an advantage: Their hospital jobs gave them some freedom of movement. Browne and Davis had passes that enabled them to walk through a gate in the stockade and enter a smaller enclosure outside, which held several buildings, including one in which hospital supplies were stored. Thomas E. Wolfe, the Connecticut sea captain who worked with them in the hospitals, also had a pass. Browne, Davis, and Wolfe sometimes went in and out of the enclosure several times a day, carrying supplies. Since the enclosure didn't house prisoners, and consequently was less rigorously guarded than the stockade, the conspirators figured they might be able to slip out of a gate in the dim light of dusk by posing as prison employees heading home after work. Welborn helped by keeping them informed about the movements of the guards, and Luke Blackmer, the lawyer who lived a few blocks away, agreed to hide them until they could sneak out of town.

But there was a problem: Richardson didn't have a pass to enter the enclosure. He requested one, and fully expected to get it, but he hadn't received it by Saturday, December 17, when the Bohemians learned that a new commandant was due to take over the prison on Monday. Figuring that the new man might crack down on their freedom of movement, they decided they'd better make their escape on Sunday.

Browne spent Saturday night trying to create a perfectly forged pass for Richardson, who spent Saturday night, and much of Sunday, painstakingly copying the names and regiment numbers of every man who'd died in the prison hospitals since October. He was determined to smuggle the list out of Salisbury as evidence of the horrific conditions in the prison—and to inform relatives of the men's fate. When he finished, he'd copied more than 1,200 names—and that didn't include prisoners who died in the yard, and thus had not passed through the hospital before their corpses were tossed into the burial trenches.

After completing the list, Richardson returned to the reporters' little apartment, took off his pants and shirt, and put on a second undershirt and underpants over the ones he was wearing. If he managed to steal out of the prison, he'd need all the clothes he could get, and he couldn't very well walk out carrying a suitcase. He also had two Yankee $100 bills sewn into the cuffs of his pants, and two more hidden in the lining of his coat. And he stuffed one of his pockets with a commodity that was rare in the Confederacy—a bag of tea.

As they prepared to leave, the conspirators made one final change of plans: Instead of using the pass that Browne had forged, which might not withstand a close inspection, Richardson would carry Browne's authentic pass, while Browne, whose face was well known to the guards, would attempt to stroll past the sentry without being asked to show his papers.

They were forbidden to enter the enclosure after dark, so they made their move about half an hour before dusk. One by one, feigning nonchalance, Browne, Davis, and Wolfe approached the gate. It was cold and raining, and the guard, who recognized them, waved them into the enclosure without asking to see their passes. They entered the storehouse and waited for Richardson. If he made it into the enclosure, they would all try to escape. If he didn't, they'd go without him.

A few minutes later, Richardson walked towards the gate, carrying a prop—a big wooden box filled with empty medicine bottles—and trying to affect the arrogant air of a man who has every right to go wherever he wants. It didn't work. The guard looked at him, failed to recognize his face, and stopped him.

"Have you a pass, sir?"

"Certainly I have a pass," Richardson responded, pretending to be peeved at this foolish request on such a nasty night. "Have you not seen it often enough to know by this time?"

"Probably I have," the guard said. "But they are very strict with us, and I was not quite sure."

Richardson put down his box of bottles and pulled the pass—Browne's pass—out of his pocket and handed it to the guard.

Headquarters, Confederate States Military Prison, Salisbury, N.C.

December 5, 1864,

Junius H. Browne, Citizen, has permission to pass the inner gate of the Prison, to assist in carrying medicines to the Military Prison hospitals, until further orders.

J. A. Fuqua,
Captain and Assistant Commandant of Post

The guard inspected the pass, read it slowly, and studied the captain's signature. Then he handed it back. "Go on, sir."

Richardson strolled into the enclosure. Since he had no right to be there, he looked for a place where he could hide before somebody recognized him. But he hadn't walked ten yards when he saw a Confederate lieutenant who knew him well. The lieutenant was walking straight towards him. It was a terrible stroke of luck and Richardson figured his escape was about to end. He couldn't avoid the lieutenant, so his only chance was to bluff his way through this encounter. He greeted the officer with a cheery hello, and then, as his heart pounded with fear, he spent a few minutes casually chatting about the weather. When the lieutenant moved on, Albert stashed his box of medicine bottles and ducked into an outhouse to wait for dark.

Browne, Davis, and Wolfe watched all this from the building where hospital supplies were stored. When night fell, Browne walked to the outhouse where Richardson was hiding and told him it was time to go.

One by one, over the next half-hour, the four men strolled casually to a side gate—Welborn had probably suggested which one would be safest—and walked out of the prison and into the street.

It was amazing—and a bit absurd: After ten months in the prison, and countless nights of struggling to concoct the perfect escape plan, they had simply *strolled out the gate*. Now they were free—and, of course, subject to being shot without warning.

Separately, they each made their way to the place where they'd agreed to meet—in the corner of a field about half a mile away. When all four had arrived, they crouched in the weeds and conferred in hushed whispers, deciding to send Davis off to find Luke Blackmer's house. While the other three waited for Davis to return, they heard somebody walking towards them in the darkness. They lay on their bellies on the wet ground, holding their breath and hoping the stranger didn't see them. He swept past so close that his long overcoat brushed Richardson's cheek, but the man kept going and disappeared into the darkness.

A few minutes later, Davis returned and led them through dripping bushes and down a street. There, leaning against a tree, was Blackmer.

"Thank God, you are out at last!" he said. "I wish I could extend to you the hospitalities of my house, but it is full of visitors and they are all Rebels."

He led them instead to his barn, and showed them the best way to stay hidden in it. He said he had to leave town on an overnight train in half an hour but his cousin would come by the next day to help them. Then he shook their hands, wished them luck, and walked back to his house and his Rebel guests.

The four escapees—Browne, Richardson, Davis, and Wolfe— climbed into the loft of the barn and burrowed deep into the fodder. Drenched in sweat and rain, they lay there, luxuriating in the sweet, musty, pungent odor of hay, straw, and cornhusks, which seemed like the incense of heaven after months of working in hospitals that reeked of filthy bodies and human waste.

It was Sunday, December 18, 1864, and after 19 months and 14 days of captivity, Albert Richardson and Junius Browne were free— yet still so close to the prison that they could hear the guards announcing the passing of every hour.

"Ten o'clock and all's well!"

"Eleven o'clock and all's well!"

They drifted into slumber once or twice, but they were too excited to sleep for long. The weary despondency of prison life had disappeared and their hearts pumped with an unfamiliar glee. The euphoria of freedom was strong enough to overpower even the perennial sardonic pessimism of Junius Henri Browne. Two hundred miles to Knoxville? It didn't seem so impossible to him now.

I could walk to the ends of the earth, Browne thought, if that's what it takes to reach the sweet goddess of liberty.

PART 3:
FLIGHT

16

GOD BLESS THE NEGROES

THE NEXT MORNING, they heard the beating of drums that began each day at the prison, and they listened to stray wisps of conversation floating from a house a few yards from the barn. Children, some white, some black, scampered into the barn and bounded up the steps to the loft. The escapees burrowed deeper into the fodder and stilled their breath while the kids ran and jumped in the hay around them, giggling merrily.

The day was sunny and warmer, but they couldn't go outside to enjoy it. Their plan was to remain in the barn until nightfall, then return to the field where they'd first gathered after their escape. There, they would meet John Welborn, who had promised to bring a guide to lead them to his family's home in Wilkes County. They waited all day, lying in the hay with nothing to eat or drink, worrying that soldiers might appear at any moment and drag them back to the prison, which was still visible to them if they peered through the cracks between the boards of the barn.

At dusk, Luke Blackmer's cousin arrived. He gave them a canteen full of water and apologized that he hadn't been able to bring any food.

His wife kept it locked up to prevent the Negro servants from stealing it, he said, and she was too loyal a Rebel to trust with the knowledge that he was helping Yankee prisoners. The cousin was a Confederate captain bearing the magnificent name Elon God Blackmer. He had fought in many battles in Virginia, and had lost an eye fighting at Frayser's Farm in 1862, but now he cursed the Confederacy and told the Yankee escapees that he longed for the day when it would burn in the flames of Hell.

They drank his water and shook his hand as he wished them good luck, and then they slipped off into the darkness. They found Welborn waiting in the appointed spot, accompanied by a man wearing a Confederate uniform. But the man wasn't the guide Welborn had promised to bring. He was a Yankee prisoner named Charles W. Thurston, a 25-year-old sergeant in the 6th New Hampshire Volunteer Infantry, who'd been captured outside Petersburg on September 30, and shipped to Salisbury, where he worked in the prison bakery. With help from Welborn, he'd escaped the previous night by donning the Confederate uniform and calmly strolling out of the gate behind a couple of departing soldiers.

The escapees now numbered five—Richardson, Browne, Davis, Wolfe, and Thurston. They waited a couple of hours for the guide to arrive but he never showed up. Welborn wrote directions to his sister's house, and then the five men bade him farewell and headed off into the night.

They walked down a dark dirt road, slogging through mud so thick that it sucked the shoes off their feet. It was Monday night, December 19. They hadn't eaten since Sunday afternoon, nor had they slept more than a few fleeting moments since Saturday night. They trudged for three miles until they reached the railroad tracks that led out of town, which they followed west, towards Statesville, until they saw a campfire blazing nearby. Fearing that Rebel soldiers might be huddled around the fire, they gave it a wide berth, veering off into the woods, where they tripped over logs, splashed through puddles, ripped their clothes on thorns, and banged their faces on branches they couldn't see in the darkness. It could have been funny, a slapstick farce, but they were too scared, hungry, and tired to laugh at anything.

After circling the campfire, they found their way back to the railroad tracks. Richardson, who had fought off pneumonia earlier in the fall, was gasping for air, and he felt so weak that he leaned on Browne's shoulder as he walked. Around midnight, he had to lie down for nearly an hour before he managed to rise to his feet again and plod on.

By three in the morning, they'd covered about 12 miles and decided to quit for the night. They left the railroad tracks and searched for a hiding place. Undergrowth was scarce because it was winter and every place seemed naked and exposed. Finally, they settled on a stand of pine trees and they lay down on the cold, wet ground and tried to sleep.

ROOSTERS CROWED AT DAWN and the bedraggled escapees looked around and realized that their hiding place, which they had thought was safely secluded, was quite close to a road and a farm. They were shivering, chilled to the marrow, but they didn't dare light a fire, certain that it would quickly be spotted. Instead, they lay hidden in the pines all day, watching the road, hoping in vain that they'd see a Negro pass by unaccompanied by a white man. But nobody passed by.

When night fell, they set off again, their stomachs groaning for food, as a cold, hard rain began to fall. Stumbling through the dark, they found a plantation and located the slave quarters. They hid nearby and sent Charles Thurston, in his soggy Confederate uniform, to knock on the door.

Thurston encountered two middle-aged slaves, a man and a woman. He told them he was one of five Yankee prisoners who'd escaped from Salisbury and hadn't eaten since Sunday. They gave him a loaf of corn bread and directed him to a nearby barn. They were cooking for a dinner party hosted by their master, and promised to bring food to the barn when their work was finished.

Sometime that night, the black man entered the barn carrying cornbread and bacon, and the fugitives wolfed it down, ravenous after more than 48 hours without a meal. After midnight, the slave returned and led them back to the railroad and told them where they could find another sympathetic slave on a farm several miles away.

All night, they slogged down the railroad tracks, pounded by torrents of cold rain. Their soaked clothes hung heavy on them and chaffed their wet skin. The railroad ties were slippery and difficult to negotiate in the dark. Wolfe twisted his ankle, and had to lean on his friends as he hobbled along.

As Browne plodded down the tracks, water sloshing in his boots, lines from *King Lear* drifted through his mind:

> *Poor naked wretches, whereso'er you are,*
> *That bide the pelting of this pitiless storm,*
> *How shall your homeless heads and unfed sides,*
> *Your loop'd and window'd raggedness, defend you*
> *From seasons such as these?*

Browne wondered if even Lear himself, in all his deranged wanderings, had ever encountered a rougher and drearier night.

It was almost dawn when they located the slave cabin. The slaves inside said the area wasn't safe—several white men were nearby—and led them to a barn down the road. It was filled with damp cornhusks and the Yankees burrowed into them, seeking warmth and sleep. They found little of either, but remained there until dark, when they emerged, their muscles sore, their joints aching, their skin itching from the husks. They shook out their wet clothes and made a few feeble attempts to comb their hair and beards. Browne realized that he'd lost his hat somewhere among the husks, but there was no time to look for it. They needed to set out in search of someone who might feed them.

Ten minutes later, they came upon another slave cabin. When the old man who lived there heard they were Yankees, he said he'd be happy to feed them. He invited them into the cabin, and introduced them to his wife and daughter. Then he went outside and killed two chickens. He stayed outside, on guard, while the women cooked the birds and the Yankees huddled near the fire, their wet clothes steaming.

Looking around the little cabin, Richardson realized that it was the first private house he'd entered in 20 months. It was crude and cramped, but it had a dinner table with plates and utensils and beds with white sheets—civilized amenities that made him long for his own home and family.

When the Yankees had devoured the chicken and hot cornbread, Richardson took out the bag of tea he'd smuggled out of prison. The women had never seen tea before, so he showed them how to brew it, and then the slaves and the escaped prisoners sat down to an odd little tea party.

Revived by the food and the tea, the Yankees thanked their host and hostesses and got up to leave.

"May God bless you," the old woman said with tears in her eyes.

Her husband noticed that Browne had no hat to wear on the long, cold journey, so he pulled off his own and handed it to Junius. The hat was humble—an ancient, shapeless, sweat-soaked woolen sock—but the gesture was grand. Here was a man who owned almost nothing—he did not even own himself—but he was willing to give his hat to a stranger he'd probably never see again. Browne thanked him, pulled the hat over his naked pate, and the fugitives headed off into the night.

BACK IN SALISBURY, news of the Bohemians' escape slowly made its way through the prison grapevine, a rare bit of good news to cheer up the inmates.

"It is wonderful how ready the prisoners are to appreciate and make merry over a good joke, notwithstanding their extreme suffering," Benjamin Booth wrote in his diary on December 20.

> A good one has just come to our knowledge, and is causing many smiling faces, and much sharp, but pleasant bantering between the guards and ourselves. A correspondent for one of the New York papers, named Richardson, has been in the pen for some time, but has also been busily engaged in maturing a plan for his escape. Day before yesterday he carried his plans into execution by assuming the role of a hospital physician, and as such, he boldly walked up to one of the gates and passed out, the guard showing him all the respect due one of their own physicians. His plans succeeded admirably and he is now breathing free air, while he is making all speed towards the Federal lines, followed by our earnest prayers that he may succeed in escaping the Rebels and their bloodhounds. His absence was not discovered until late today. We are joking with the guards over this exhibition of Yankee ingenuity, deceiving their authorities and throwing even the bloodhounds off the trail. They wince under it, but have to admit it.

★

THE ESCAPEES WERE NOT feeling quite so cheerful. By one o'clock in the morning on Thursday, December 22, the five fugitives had reached no farther than the outskirts of Statesville, barely 20 miles from Salisbury. There, they left the railroad tracks and headed north, searching for the road to Wilkes County.

The landmark they were looking for was Allison's Mill, but they got lost and walked in circles for miles. The rain had stopped but the night was cold and a bitter wind whipped out of the north, freezing their faces and squeezing tears from their eyes. As dawn approached, they searched for a slave cabin, and after what seemed like hours they finally found one.

Richardson knocked on the door and a slave called out from his warm bed, asking who was there. Yankee prisoners escaped from Salisbury, Richardson answered. Then he asked if the man could help them hide.

"I reckon so," the slave said. His master was a Confederate officer who wouldn't hesitate to kill him for helping a Union soldier, he said. "But I kept a sick Yankee captain here last summer for five days, and then he went on. Go to the barn and hide, and I will see you when I come to fodder the horses."

The barn was constructed of logs with gaps between them to facilitate the drying of fodder, and the cold wind whistled through them. The fugitives buried themselves in hay, but it offered little warmth. Shivering, their lips blue, Richardson and Browne huddled side by side, then wrapped their arms around each other and snuggled like lovers, but still they couldn't get warm. Finally, they gave up, crawled out of the hay, and jogged around in the barn, trying to get their sluggish blood flowing.

Before noon, the slave appeared, bringing a basket of bacon and cornbread and some apple brandy he said he'd lifted from his owner's storehouse. After dark, he returned and led them to his cabin. There, they warmed their chilled bones around the fire and ate another meal. A dozen slaves came to the cabin, eager to meet the Yankees. Some were adults, some teenagers, and one was a good-looking woman of about 25, obviously of mixed race, who was the wife of a slave and the unwilling mistress of their owner, whom she spoke of with bitter loathing. They all wanted to hear about the war and the North and the Yankees. They repeated the stories their master had told them about how the Yankees would whip them and make the men fight in the Union army and leave the women and children to starve. They said they didn't believe those stories, but they seemed to want reassurance that they weren't true. Most of all, they wanted to know what would happen to them when the war ended.

Richardson was happy to inform them that the Union was winning the war and the Confederacy was crumbling. President Lincoln had proclaimed the end of slavery, Richardson said, and soon no person would ever again be permitted to own another. Then they would be free to go where they pleased and to work for themselves instead of their master.

They talked for more than an hour and then one of the slaves led them off into the darkness to the road that headed north, towards Wilkes County and the mountains.

So far, despite the rain and the cold, the fugitives had been lucky: For three nights and days, they'd been confident that when they found a black man they had found an ally. Their survival hinged on the kindness of slaves, and the slaves had never let them down, feeding and sheltering these strangers and leading them to safety, risking a beating—or worse—if they were caught. It was, the Bohemians realized, the story of the Underground Railroad with the colors reversed: Escaping white people heading north towards freedom, and sympathetic black people risking punishment to help them.

"By this time, we had learned that every black face was a friendly face," Richardson recalled. "They were always ready to help anybody opposed to the Rebels."

"God bless the Negroes!" Browne wrote. "They were ever our firm, brave, unflinching friends. We never made an appeal to them they did not answer. They never hesitated to do us a service at the risk even of life, and under the most trying circumstances revealed a devotion and self-sacrifice that were heroic. The magic word 'Yankee' opened all their hearts, and elicited the loftiest virtues. They were ignorant, oppressed, enslaved, but they always cherished a simple and beautiful faith in the cause of the Union and its ultimate triumph, and never abandoned or turned aside from a man who sought food or shelter on his way to Freedom."

Now, though, the fugitives were heading into the mountains, where farms were small and few farmers owned slaves. Up there, it would no longer be possible to tell friend from foe by the color of his skin. In the mountains the conflict had no armies or borders or battle lines. It was a bitter guerrilla war of bushwhackers and ambushes and secret killings in secluded forests.

17

WAR IN THE MOUNTAINS

IN THE DIM LIGHT OF THE COLD DAWN, a line of men shuffled through the snow. Some of them carried guns. They were Confederate soldiers, members of the 64th North Carolina Regiment. The others were prisoners, 13 pro-Union guerrillas captured two days earlier, after a skirmish in which eight men had been killed. The soldiers were marching the prisoners off to jail and then to trial—or so they said.

The column halted near an icy creek in a meadow surrounded by hills. The soldiers pulled five prisoners out of line and shoved them to their knees in the snow. The prisoners looked up and watched their captors form a firing squad.

"For God's sake, men," said one prisoner, a 60-year-old grandfather named Joe Wood, "you're not going to *shoot* us."

Nobody replied.

Wood understood what that silence meant. "At least give us time to pray," he said.

"You promised us a trial," another prisoner muttered.

Lieutenant Colonel James Keith, the Confederate commander, drew his sword and raised it. Several of his soldiers balked, stammering out a protest against being used as executioners.

"Fire or you will take their place," Keith ordered.

The soldiers fired. The sound of their shots echoed off the hills as the kneeling prisoners slumped to the ground, their blood staining the snow. Four of them lay dead, but the fifth flailed and writhed in the snow, clutching his bleeding gut, screaming and begging for mercy.

A soldier responded by stepping forward and shooting him in the head. Other soldiers dragged five more prisoners into the bloody snow and shoved them down to their knees. One of them was a 13-year-old boy named David Shelton.

"You have killed my father and brothers," Shelton said. "You have shot my father in the face. Do not shoot me in the face."

The soldiers fired. Again, four of the prisoners died quickly but one survived. David Shelton, shot in both arms, crawled towards the firing squad, pleading for his life. "You've killed my old father and my three brothers," the boy said. "You've shot me in both arms. I can forgive you all this. I can get well. Let me go home to my mother and sisters."

The soldiers fired again, finishing Shelton off. Then they executed the last three prisoners.

The killing completed, the soldiers dug a mass grave, hacking at the hard, frozen ground beneath the snow. When they had scraped away enough of the rocky earth to make a shallow trench, they threw the bodies into it and covered them with a thin layer of dirt and snow.

One of the soldiers, perhaps crazed by what he had seen and done, began clapping out an old minstrel tune, "Juba, Juba," and dancing on the grave, shouting, "I'll dance the damn scoundrels down to Hell!"

It was January 18, 1863, in Shelton Laurel, a pro-Union section of Madison County in the mountains of western North Carolina, not far from the Tennessee border. When Governor Zebulon Vance heard about the Shelton Laurel massacre, he was outraged, but he wasn't surprised. Vance was born in the mountains and he knew that the war fought there was unusually vicious—"conducted on both sides without any regard whatever to the rules of civilized war or the dictates of humanity," he wrote. "The murder of prisoners and non-combatants in cold blood has, I learn, become quite common."

In the mountains of North Carolina and Tennessee, the Civil War was not fought by huge armies but by small groups skirmishing in secluded woods, sometimes killing men they'd known since boyhood. One reason for this was geographical: The mountains were too remote and too rugged for the movement of large armies. Another reason was sociological: The people of the Appalachians were unlike other Southerners.

In the South's vast flatlands, society was dominated by rich men who owned large plantations and many slaves, and who considered themselves aristocrats. In the mountains, where the land was unsuited for plantation agriculture, few people owned slaves and most families scratched out a living growing corn, raising hogs, and shooting deer. The flatland aristocrats controlled the state governments and mocked the mountaineers as ignorant, uncultured hillbillies. Proud and a bit prickly, the mountaineers detested the aristocrats as haughty, greedy, and arrogant. William G. "Parson" Brownlow, the acid-tongued Methodist preacher who edited the *Knoxville Whig*, summed up the mountaineers' attitude: "We have always despised, in our heart of hearts, a hateful aristocracy in this country, based on the ownership of a few ashy Negroes, and arrogating to themselves all the decency, all the talents, and all the respectability of the social circle."

The flatland aristocrats reacted to Abraham Lincoln's election by demanding that their states secede from the Union, but most mountaineers didn't see Lincoln as a threat to their way of life. In the wave of secession conventions in 1861, most delegates from mountain counties in Georgia, Alabama, Virginia, North Carolina, and Tennessee voted against secession. In the referendum in North Carolina, the mountain counties voted overwhelmingly against secession. In Tennessee's referendum, voters in the mountains of East Tennessee opposed secession by a ratio of more than 2 to 1. Virginia's mountain counties also voted against secession, and when Virginia seceded from the United States, they in turn seceded from Virginia, forming the state of West Virginia.

When their states joined the Confederacy and the war began, thousands of mountaineers volunteered to join the Confederate army and fought valiantly for their new nation. But thousands of others did not. Whether they felt loyal to the Union or were simply uninterested in fighting for the Confederacy, these men stayed home and tried to ignore the war. A year later, however, the Confederacy passed a conscription law—the first in American history—and began drafting the men who hadn't volunteered. In the mountains, the law was extremely unpopular, and thousands of men dodged the draft, many hiding in the hills, sometimes in secret bunkers they dug in hillsides. This activity was known as "lying out" and the men who did it were called "outliers." Using secret signals—a certain quilt hung out on a line, for instance—their wives let the outliers know when it was safe to return home.

When Confederate conscription agents came to round them up, some of the outliers responded by firing at the agents from hiding places. These bushwhackers were also known to ambush tax collectors who attempted to enforce the Confederate government's "tax in kind" law demanding that farmers turn over 10 percent of their crops for the war effort.

Confederate officials responded to these acts of rebellion by dispatching soldiers—or the local militia, known as the Home Guard—to chase the draft dodgers. The wives of the outliers usually knew where their husbands were hiding, so the Home Guard sometimes beat or tortured the women until they revealed that information. A few days before the Shelton Laurel massacre, for instance, Confederate soldiers tied a young mother to a tree during a snowstorm, set her baby on the frozen ground just out of reach, and told her she could bring the crying infant inside as soon as she revealed where the local Unionist guerrillas were hiding—an incident depicted 13 decades later in the novel and film *Cold Mountain*.

As the war dragged on, many disillusioned Confederate soldiers deserted from General Lee's army and fled to the mountains of North Carolina. In some places—Wilkes County, among others—deserters and draft dodgers gathered in remote camps and formed guerrilla bands that ambushed the Home Guard and raided the houses of affluent Confederates, stealing food, money, and horses.

"Deserters now leave the Army with arms and ammunition in hand," George W. Lay, a Confederate conscription agent in western North Carolina reported in a letter to his boss in September 1863. "Arriving in their selected localities of refuge, they organize in bands variously estimated at from fifty up to hundreds at various points, . . . In Wilkes County, they are organized, drilling regularly, and entrenched in a camp to the number of 500. . . . These men are not only determined to kill in avoiding apprehension (having put to death yet another of our enrolling officers), but their *esprit de corps* extends to killing in revenge as well."

By December 1864, when Browne and Richardson escaped from Salisbury Prison, the mountains of western North Carolina and eastern Tennessee teemed with bands of armed men—Confederate soldiers, Home Guard militiamen, Union guerrillas, Rebel partisans, and gangs of freelance bushwhackers, cutthroats, and thieves. Many of these men were colorful characters who flaunted their eccentricities.

Thomas's Highland Legion, a Confederate militia composed of Cherokee Indians, performed elaborate war dances before heading into battle, and sometimes they scalped their victims—the wounded as well as the dead. A brutal gang of Union guerrillas, led by a mountaineer named Jack Vance, specialized in plundering the homes of rich Confederates. The gang included one man who wore a turban decorated with eagle feathers, and another who wrapped himself in the fur of a huge bear and pulled the beast's skinned head over his face like a cowl. He accessorized this grisly outfit with a rattlesnake skin tied around his neck in a bow.

A husband-and-wife team of Union guerrillas, Keith and Malinda Blalock, became legendary in the Appalachians. When Keith Blalock joined the Confederate army in 1862, Malinda, his teenage bride, went with him, posing as his younger brother. Although the two were permitted to share a tent, Keith didn't enjoy army life. He contrived to get out of it by rolling naked in a patch of poison oak. He showed the resulting rash to a regimental doctor, who feared it might be a communicable disease and gave Keith a medical discharge. At that point, Malinda revealed her secret and she, too, was discharged. They returned to their home near North Carolina's Grandfather Mountain and lived peacefully until conscription agents came looking for Keith. He met them with a volley of gunfire and then the couple took to the hills, waging a guerrilla war against their Confederate neighbors.

Perhaps the most vicious of the mountain guerrillas was Champ Ferguson, a Rebel sociopath infamous for his habit of executing pro-Union mountaineers in cold blood, sometimes while their wives watched. Rumors spread that Ferguson had been driven mad when Union soldiers sexually abused his wife and teenage daughter. But Ferguson denied the rumor and protested that he needed no such excuse to kill Union men. After the war, he was arrested, charged with

53 counts of murder, convicted, and sentenced to hang. On the gallows, he stood waiting while the hangman read his long list of his crimes. Halfway through the recitation, Ferguson lost his patience.

"I could tell it better than that," he muttered.

T RAMPING UP THE DIRT road that led into Wilkes County, Richardson and Browne were well aware of the anarchy and barbarity that awaited them in the mountains. In Castle Thunder and Salisbury, they'd met scores of inmates imprisoned for disloyalty to the Confederacy, most of them from the mountains of Virginia, North Carolina, and Tennessee. The mountaineers, many of them poor and barely literate, told stories about the horrors of the war in the mountains. They emphasized the atrocities of the Confederates, of course, but many also gleefully recounted grisly tales of their own adventures in bushwhacking and brutality. They were hard, tough men who swore that if they ever managed to get back home, they would quickly begin killing their enemies. Richardson and Browne were impressed by their tenacious loyalty to the Union, but a bit frightened by their vehemence and violence.

The mountaineers assured the Bohemians that they would find plenty of pro-Union friends in the mountains, but warned that they'd find plenty of Confederates there, too—and it was impossible to tell the two groups apart unless you knew the individuals. They did offer one piece of advice: Generally speaking, the richer the man, the more likely that he was a Confederate. So a Union fugitive had a better chance of finding a friend in a humble log cabin than in a more affluent house. But there were many exceptions, of course, and one mistake could result in a quick, violent death.

The war in the mountains was frightening, but Browne and Richardson and their fellow fugitives had more immediate problems on their minds as they marched north into Wilkes County on Thursday, December 22, 1864. The night was bitter cold, the dirt road was frozen solid, and they were exhausted and footsore and ready to collapse. Wolfe limped on his painfully sprained ankle. Davis, who'd complained of an aching back for months, looked haggard, his eyes bloodshot and weary. Richardson struggled to suck air into his sick lungs. Browne was weak, and his heavy boots, which had shrunk after getting soaked in streams and puddles, scraped his feet and ankles bloody. Only

Thurston was still strong. Since he was younger than the others, and hadn't been imprisoned for nearly as long, he took the lead, walking ahead in his Confederate uniform, keeping an eye out for danger.

They walked "Indian style"—single file, with each escapee staying far behind the man in front of him. They communicated by subtle sounds: A soft hiss meant danger, a cough was a sign of recognition, a low whistle meant it was time to gather together. Moving forward in the darkness, their ears were alert for suspicious sounds—the snap of a twig, the rustle of a branch or, worst of all, the barking of a dog. Dogs were their enemies. Farmers' dogs alerted their owners that somebody was passing by. And, as they'd learned from earlier escapees who'd been recaptured and returned to prison, the Rebels tracked fugitives with bloodhounds and coon-hunting dogs.

Shortly before dawn, they came to a stream. It was wide and full, roaring with icy water, and they were exhausted, so they decided to build a fire and wait for daylight before crossing. When it was light enough to look around, they saw a log that bridged the creek. It was too slick with ice to walk across, so they had to crawl on their hands and knees, praying they wouldn't slip into the freezing water.

They pushed on, and as the sun rose, they wondered where they would stop for the day when it became too light to travel inconspicuously. And then they came to a fork in the road. Which way should they go? They had no idea. A farmhouse stood nearby, so Charley Thurston went to ask for directions.

While his four friends hid, Thurston knocked on the door, wearing his Confederate uniform and posing as a Rebel soldier on furlough, traveling to his home near Jonesville to spend Christmas with his family. An elderly farmer answered and pointed out the right road. Thurston thanked him and set off, the others following, discretely hidden until they passed out of sight of the farmhouse. When the fugitives regrouped, Thurston told them that he thought the old farmer was probably a Rebel.

They kept walking until it was too light to continue, then they stopped in a secluded stand of trees and prepared to rest until nightfall. But they heard a twig snap behind them. They swiveled their heads to look and spotted the farmer who'd given Thurston directions. He was stalking them, skulking in the bushes. When Thurston called to him, he darted away. Thurston chased after him, but the farmer scooted off, disappearing into the woods.

Obviously, the old farmer now knew that Thurston's story was a lie and that five Yankees were heading north towards Jonesville. They figured he would soon gather a posse of men and dogs and chase after them, so they left the road and bolted into the woods as fast as they could run. They'd been walking all night and were exhausted, but fear is a powerful engine and it propelled them on. They ran five miles through woods and fields before they finally collapsed in a stand of pine trees at about nine in the morning.

They knew that lighting a fire during daytime might give away their location, but they were freezing so they did it anyway, trying to burn only dry branches that wouldn't smoke much. They huddled around the blaze all day, warming their frozen feet, too scared to sleep for more than a few minutes at a time, constantly peering around for signs that somebody was chasing them.

W HEN NIGHT FELL, they hobbled out of their little sanctuary, their sore muscles tight and cramped after lying on the frozen ground for hours. They headed in the direction they hoped was north, figuring they were about 15 miles from the place where Welborn had promised they would be welcomed by his relatives. With a little luck, they hoped to get there by dawn.

Browne began the night's trek in high spirits, but soon he began to fade. Cold, hungry, sleepless, and weary, he could barely lift his feet. His strength was gone, his boots felt like anchors, and his legs trembled. Breathing hard, he leaned on Richardson, just as Albert had leaned on him during their first night out. Richardson felt his friend's head and found it burning with fever. He'd nursed Browne through a bout of typhoid fever in St. Louis two years earlier, and he suspected that this was the start of another. Browne disagreed, insisting that he was merely exhausted. In a weak voice, he said they should go on without him because he was slowing the group down. Richardson refused, vowing that he would never abandon his best friend by the side of the road.

They kept going.

Around eight o'clock, they came upon a ramshackle country tavern. Thurston, their designated Confederate, went inside while the other four hid. He ordered food and drink and chatted with another customer. The man flashed him the secret greeting of the Heroes of America. Thurston gave the countersign. The two men stepped outside to talk. The Hero told Thurston that he could lead the group to the home of his brother, who was another loyal Union man. Not only that, the Hero had a few mules with him. He went to the tavern stable and returned with the mules. He put Browne on one mule and Wolfe, with his sprained ankle, on another, and they all traipsed off.

They crossed a field, then headed down another road. Browne was relieved to be off his feet but there was no saddle on the mule and its backbone was a jagged ridge of sharp spikes that felt as if they were slicing through his buttocks. He squirmed into different positions, but none was comfortable. The mule bounced along as Browne winced in pain.

After a few miles, they came to a cabin, the home of the Hero's brother. He welcomed them and let them warm themselves by the fire. He fed them and passed around jugs of apple brandy and corn whiskey. Richardson was amused to see that Davis, a dedicated temperance advocate, was swigging from the jugs. Browne wasn't much of a whiskey drinker but he figured maybe this moonshine would make him feel better. He took a swig for medicinal purposes. It burned his throat and warmed his belly. A mellow glow began to spread over his sick body. He felt better, so he took another swig. And another.

The Hero's brother owned some mules, so they all rode off towards the place where Welborn had said they'd find sympathetic souls. Browne's mule swayed from side to side as it lumbered along, shaking up the corn whiskey in Browne's belly. He began to feel queasy, then queasier. He vomited, then vomited again, and again. Always the classicist, he couldn't help seeing himself as an erupting Vesuvius. Unable to ride any more, he slid off the mule and stumbled along, drunk, sick, and utterly miserable.

When the group neared its destination, the two brothers left, taking their mules with them—but not before they had instructed the fugitives never to tell anybody, even people who swore they were Unionists, that they'd provided this assistance. Helping escaped prisoners was a hanging offense.

The fugitives walked on, Browne again leaning on Richardson's shoulder. When they found what seemed to be the house they were looking for, everybody hid in the bushes. Richardson lowered Browne to the ground and walked to the cabin.

It was five o'clock on the morning of December 24—Christmas Eve. Richardson rapped on the door.

18

CHRISTMAS

"**C**OME IN."

Richardson opened the door and stepped into the house. It was a one-room log cabin. The woman who'd called him in was doing her morning chores. Her husband and children were still in bed.

"Can you direct me to the widow Welborn?" Richardson asked.

"There are two widow Welborns in this neighborhood," the woman said. "What is your name?"

Richardson ignored her question. He didn't want to reveal his name until he knew he'd found the right house. "The lady I mean has a son who is an officer in the army," he said.

"They both have sons who are officers in the army," she said. "Don't be afraid. You are among friends."

Friends—it was a welcome word but in this context it could mean a friend of either Confederates or Unionists, but probably not both.

"The officer is a lieutenant," Richardson said, "and his name is John."

"Well, they are both lieutenants, and John is the name of both."

The conversation had turned into farce, neither participant willing to reveal information to a stranger.

"He is in the second regiment of the Senior Reserves," Richardson said, "and is now on duty at Salisbury."

"Oh," she said, "that is my brother!"

Richardson relaxed. He was in the right place, and he'd found John Welborn's sister. He introduced himself, and told her he was one of five Yankee prisoners who'd escaped from Salisbury Prison, and that her brother had promised that they would find help here.

"If you are Yankees," she said, "all I have to say is that you have come to exactly the right place."

She offered him a seat, and some food, and then she scampered nervously around the room, feeding the fire, waking her husband and children, and then reaching under a bed and pulling out the mountaineer's symbol of hospitality—a jug of apple brandy. Later, when she had calmed down a bit, she told him that she'd never seen a Yankee before but the minute she looked at his clothes she figured he must be one. "I wanted to throw my arms about your neck and kiss you."

Richardson went outside to fetch his friends and returned carrying Browne. Inside the house, he helped Junius out of his wet clothes and laid him down in a soft, warm bed. Browne sank into it and fell into a deep sleep.

Soon, the cabin was crowded with people, most of them Welborn relatives, all of them Unionists. They'd heard through the Heroes of America grapevine that the fugitives were coming and they peppered them with questions until the men were too tired to talk anymore. Then the escapees climbed into their hosts' beds and passed out for a few hours.

Around noon, Richardson woke Browne to serve him a cup of rye coffee and a plate of fritters. Browne ate and drank with gusto and said he felt fine. Then he sank back into sleep. Richardson was relieved to see Browne eat so eagerly. Maybe he didn't have typhoid fever after all. Maybe he'd merely been exhausted.

After dark, their hosts lent them quilts and led them to the barn where they would sleep that night, warning them that the woman who lived in the house nearby was an avid Confederate, so they should keep out of sight.

Snug in the hayloft, they slept like dead men and woke the next morning when they heard the barn door open and stealthy footsteps on the wooden floor. A soft voice said, "Friends, are you there?"

They crawled out of the hay and peered down from the loft to see one of their hosts, who'd come to wake them for breakfast.

It was Christmas Day. The fugitives spent the day meeting the dozens of Welborn relatives and friends who came to greet the escaped prisoners. Some brought their children, who wanted to see what a Yankee looked like. They also brought gifts of food for the fugitives, and volunteered to shelter them or help guide them to the Union lines.

"Had we been their own sons or brothers, they could not have treated us more tenderly," Richardson wrote. "This Christmas may have witnessed more brilliant gatherings than ours, but none, I am sure, warmed by a more self-sacrificing friendship."

THE MAN WHO OWNED the barn they'd slept in was Maberry Welborn, a white-haired patriarch who was the grandfather, father, uncle or in-law of most of the Welborns in the area around New Castle in Wilkes County. Approaching 70 years of age, he'd fought in the War of 1812—or as he called it, more accurately, "the war of '12 to '14." Maberry was still loyal to the flag he'd fought under, and he had no sympathy for the Rebels. Chatting with the fugitives on Christmas Day, he offered blunt opinions about the war between the Home Guard and the outliers in Wilkes County.

"The Home Guard are usually pretty civil," he said. "Occasionally, they shoot at some of the boys who are hiding. But pretty soon afterward, one of them is found in the woods some morning with a hole in his head."

He estimated that there were a thousand young men "lying out" in Wilkes County. "I have always urged them to fight the Guards, and have helped to supply them with ammunition," he said. "Two or three times regiments from Lee's army have been sent here to hunt conscripts and deserters, and then the boys have to run. I have a son among them. I asked him the other day, 'Won't you kill some of them before you are ever captured?' 'Well, father,' says he, 'I'll be found a-tryin'. I reckon he will, too, for he has never gone without his rifle these two years, and he can bring down a squirrel every time."

One of the Christmas visitors was a fat man who'd worked as a guard at Salisbury Prison. Browne and Richardson knew him well. He used to lumber up the stairs to their room and then sit down, huffing and puffing from the climb. He'd look around, make sure no other guards were there, and then tell them how much he hated the damn Confederates.

He explained why he was no longer working at the prison. In the fall, he had been among the soldiers scheduled to go to Lee's army in Virginia. Of course, he had no desire to fight the Yankees, so he told the doctors he was suffering from an attack of rheumatism and managed to postpone his trip to the battlefield for six weeks. The day before he was finally supposed to travel to Richmond, he asked the doctor for a pass to go into downtown Salisbury. He got the pass and walked towards town, hobbling on his crutches, groaning audibly. When he turned a corner and got out of sight, he threw down his crutches and darted off into the woods. Then he walked back home to Wilkes County, traveling at night, just like the Yankee fugitives.

He laughed when he told that story, and then he gave Richardson a very valuable Christmas present for a man planning to walk across the mountains—a new pair of boots.

The holiday ended abruptly that night when the Welborns heard a rumor that the Home Guard had learned about the arrival of the Yankees and might soon raid the place. Quickly, the fugitives gathered their things and exchanged the warmth of the fire for the cold of the night, following one of the Welborn men towards the house of a relative several miles away.

★

THEY MARCHED THROUGH THE dark forest, careful to tread lightly so they wouldn't snap a twig and reveal their position to anyone who might be listening. After an hour and a half, they arrived at their destination—a log cabin occupied by Lieutenant Welborn's wife and daughters, all of them wearing simple dresses made from homespun cloth. It was a large cabin, divided into three rooms, with white curtains on the windows and pictures cut from newspapers decorating the walls. The girls gave up their beds so the visitors could sleep in comfort.

In the morning, Mrs. Welborn made breakfast while her two youngest daughters, aged four and six, stood guard outside, watching for anybody coming up the road that passed by the cabin. When a local woman of dubious loyalties wandered up the road, Mrs. Welborn and one of her daughters casually stood in the doorway, blocking the view into the cabin while the Yankees scrambled to hide.

After breakfast, the girls reported that a squad of Confederate cavalry was riding up the road. Mrs. Welborn motioned to her visitors to hide under the beds. Then she walked out to the porch and casually bantered with the horsemen for several minutes, feigning nonchalance, until they rode off.

"All is safe, boys," she announced.

The fugitives crawled out from under the beds. A few minutes later, the young lookouts spotted a couple more strangers coming up the road. The Yankees dove back under the beds and lay there, still and silent and nervous, until Mrs. Welborn told them the strangers were gone.

The war in the mountains had turned ancient roles upside-down, Browne thought: Men were no longer protecting women and children; now women and children were protecting the men. And they did it, he thought, with a silent and unconscious heroism that made it all the more beautiful.

With so many people passing by, the fugitives decided to hide in the loft above the cabin, where corn was stored. Up there, they passed the time by performing the same chore they'd done every day in prison—stripping down and searching their clothing and bodies for lice. They were engaged in this daily "skirmishing" when a neighbor driving an ox cart arrived at the cabin to collect a bushel of corn that Mrs. Welborn owed him. Unfortunately, her corn was located in the corn loft alongside the Yankee visitors. She needed to buy time to hide the fugitives.

"You know my husband is away," she told the neighbor. "I have no fuel. Won't you go and haul me a load of wood, as a Christmas present?"

The neighbor couldn't resist an appeal for help from the long-suffering wife of a Confederate soldier. While he went off to fetch firewood, she told her visitors to get back under the beds.

Browne was buck naked, deep into his skirmishing project. He scrambled into his underwear and scooted down the ladder, carrying the rest of his clothes. The fugitives hustled into the back room and slid under the beds. The neighbor returned with the firewood and came inside to collect his corn. He loaded it into the ox cart and then stood on the porch, chatting with Mrs. Welborn.

When the neighbor finally left, the fugitives crawled out from under the beds. Browne was still half-naked and clutching his clothes, like a lover caught *in flagrante delicto* by a jealous husband. His friends found this much funnier than he did.

Mrs. Welborn swore she had more visitors that day then she'd seen in the previous month. They believed her but they decided that the house wasn't safe enough for comfort. After dinner, they left, slogging back through the dark woods to the barn where they'd spent Christmas Eve.

BACK IN THE BARN, the fugitives learned that two other escapees from Salisbury Prison had arrived during their absence—William Boothby, a sailor from Philadelphia, and John Mercer, a North Carolina Unionist. They'd escaped from Salisbury two nights after the Bohemians, paying guards $800 in Confederate money to help them slip out.

The fugitives huddled together to plan their trip to Knoxville. It would be a long, hard trek—more than 200 miles, and across two mountain ranges, both of them likely to be covered with snow and infested with Rebels. They figured that small groups would attract less attention and be easier for sympathizers to hide, so they decided to divide into two bands. The first, composed of Boothby, Mercer, and Charles Thurston, would leave that night, guided by one of the Welborns. The second group—Richardson, Browne, Davis, and Wolfe—would wait until the following night before heading west with another guide.

Richardson pulled out his list of 1,200 prisoners who'd died in the Salisbury Prison hospitals that fall, and the fugitives all made a solemn vow: Any man who managed to reach the Union lines alive would do everything in his power to convince the government to save the Salisbury prisoners before they all perished.

After dark, more hard rain fell and the fugitives left the barn and walked to the cabins of various Welborn relatives to sleep in the comfort of real beds. Browne was eating supper in one cabin when his hostesses—a mother and her teenage daughter Lucy—heard a distinctive whistle from outside, a signal that meant somebody was approaching. Alarmed, they told Browne to run. He bolted out the door, half expecting to be shot by the Home Guard. But there was no gunfire, just the torrential rain. Browne slipped silently into the bushes, and then he felt somebody take hold of his arm and whisper, "Come this way."

It was Lucy, the dark-haired, dark-eyed girl of 16 or 17 he'd been dining with a few minutes earlier.

"What are you doing here?" Browne whispered. "Why don't you go in out of the storm and let me take care of myself."

"I want to stay with you," she said. "Do come with me. I will show you where to hide."

She led him off, still clinging to his arm, and without thinking, he swung his other arm around her waist, pulled her close to him, and kissed her. She kissed him back and for a moment they stood there, smooching, as the downpour drenched them.

Soon, they heard the signal that meant they were safe and they returned to the cabin. The stranger whose arrival had caused the alarm was a young Rebel deserter who was smitten with Lucy and had come to visit her. When he left, she explained to Browne that the deserter was not her boyfriend, but she liked him because he'd shot two Home Guards.

Lucy was the first woman Browne had kissed in more than two years. He was shocked that he'd done it, but pleased, too: "Her voice and manner had touched even my worn-out heart."

He dreamed about Lucy that night. She was a beautiful princess who commanded her black-robed royal magician to conjure up a winged dragon. Browne and Lucy climbed on the dragon's back and flew away to New York City, where they dined on sumptuous delicacies at Maison Doree, the city's most opulent French restaurant.

But when Browne awoke the next morning, he was back in the one-room cabin in the mountains of North Carolina, and Lucy was cooking breakfast in the fireplace. She handed him a piece of cornbread.

IT WAS WEDNESDAY, December 28, 1864—the fugitives' tenth day of freedom. After spending five days with the Welborns, eating and resting and basking in the warmth of human kindness, they felt rejuvenated and ready to head across the mountains.

That night, the Welborns and their friends gathered in Maberry's barn to say goodbye to Browne, Richardson, Davis, and Wolfe. The men shook their hands and wished them luck. The women hugged them and promised to pray for them. Children climbed into their laps.

"They bade us adieu with embraces and tears," Richardson recalled.

"More kindness, affection and devotion, I have never seen," Browne wrote. "Those noble-hearted people—for the most part poor—gave me a higher idea of humanity."

19

NO ONE EVER REACHES THERE

GUIDED BY ONE OF THE WELBORN MEN, the fugitives hiked west through the darkness. After a few hours, they happened upon a camp of Confederate cavalry. They could hear horses snorting and neighing, and sentries making their rounds in the cold night air. Nervous as rabbits, the fugitives tiptoed through the woods, their ears alert for every sound, and they managed to slip past the Rebels undetected.

A few miles down the road, their guide told them to hide in the bushes while he visited the cabin of a friend who was a deserter from the Confederate army. The cabin door opened and the guide stepped inside. A few minutes later, he called the fugitives in, and they met the deserter, his young wife, and their baby, who was sleeping in a cradle made from a hollowed log. The deserter said he'd been lying out, hiding in the woods, but the Home Guard hadn't come snooping around lately so he figured he could risk spending a night at home. He pulled on his clothes and agreed to lead them to a secluded path a few miles away. As they left, his wife shook each fugitive's hand and wished him luck.

"There is great danger," she said, "and you must be powerful cautious."

The deserter took them to the home of a free black man, who agreed to lead them to a house where a Unionist farmer would put them up. Following their third guide of the night, the fugitives traipsed more than ten miles over hard, frozen hills before they reached a lonely house sitting beside a roaring stream in a deep valley. They banged on the door but got no answer for a long while. Finally the farmer awoke and opened the door. He said his barn was already full of escaped Yankee prisoners, who turned out to be the group that included Charley Thurston. The farmer directed the newcomers to a neighbor who lived half a mile away.

They woke the neighbor, who fanned the embers of his fire into flames so they could thaw their frozen bones while he cooked some pork and cornbread. When they had finished eating, he took them to a barn hidden in the woods.

"Climb up on that scaffolding," he said. "Among the husks you will find two or three quilts. They belong to my son, who is lying out. Tonight he is sleeping with some friends in the woods."

The fugitives lay down in the corn husks, trying to burrow deep enough to escape the wind. It was nearly dawn and they were exhausted from their long, nerve-wracking hike, and they soon fell asleep.

A FTER DARK, THEIR HOST SERVED them a meal and some apple brandy to wash it down, and then they started walking again, guided by a neighbor who did not seem eager for the task. He set a brisk pace over the steep, rocky hills. As the fugitives scrambled to keep up with him in the darkness, they tripped over rocks and roots, stumbling like drunks and occasionally falling on their faces. Although the wind was cold, they were moving so fast that they dripped with sweat.

Sometime after midnight they came to Wilkesboro, the county seat, which signaled its presence with a cacophony of barking dogs. To avoid the Home Guard, they skirted the town, and in the process their guide led them down the wrong road. Wolfe, the sea captain, studied the sky and pointed out that the North Star was on the wrong side of them. They turned around and retraced their steps until they found the right road.

By then it was nearly dawn, and they were cold and weary and footsore. They hiked into a thick patch of pines, found a ravine that shielded them from sight, and built a fire. They lay down around the fire and tried to sleep—without much success—on the frozen ground. When the sun came up, they moved on, hoping to cross the Yadkin River and find the home of a man named Ben Hanby, who was reputed to be a Unionist who would give them shelter.

They reached the river just in time to watch a canoe arrive from the opposite shore, paddled by a young woman with a round, ruddy face that reminded Richardson of a big red apple. She was taking a pail of butter to Wilkesboro to sell in the market.

The fugitives asked if she knew where Ben Hanby lived.

"Just beyond the hill there, across the river," she said, eyeing the strangers suspiciously.

"How far is it to his house?"

"I don't know," she said.

"More than a mile?"

"No, I reckon not."

"Is he probably home?"

"No, he is not." She studied her questioners closely. "Are you Home Guard?"

No, we are Union men, they told her, Yankees escaped from Salisbury Prison and trying to get home.

She looked them over again, and noticed that none of them carried a gun. The Home Guard never ventured into these hills without plenty of firepower. She concluded that these strangers were telling the truth, and figured she could do the same.

"Ben Hanby is my husband," she said. "He is lying out."

She informed the fugitives that her children had stood on a hilltop and watched them approaching for the last hour. Her husband figured they were Home Guard and he grabbed his rifle and headed out to join the other men who were lying out in the woods. By now, she said, every Union man in the area had heard the news that the Home Guard was coming and they had gathered in the woods with their guns, ready to fight.

She ferried the fugitives across the river in her canoe, gave them directions to her house, and then continued on her journey to Wilkesboro. The Yankees followed a path through the woods to a little cabin and found it occupied by three Hanby children and their grandmother.

The fugitives told the old lady that they were Yankee prisoners escaped from Salisbury, but she didn't believe them. For an hour, they attempted to convince her but failed. It was frustrating and a bit ridiculous: How do you prove that you are a Yankee to someone who has never met a Yankee? The old woman believed they were Home Guards traveling incognito and trying to trick her into revealing secrets. To every question they asked, no matter how innocuous, she replied that she didn't know. She was, Browne reflected ruefully, "utterly destitute of information of any kind on any subject."

Finally, after a long, absurd conversation, something they said must have convinced her that they were telling the truth. She cooked them a breakfast of fat pork, cornbread, and buttermilk. When they had finished eating, she instructed one of her grandchildren to take them to a secluded hillside in the woods where they could rest in a patch of warm sunshine.

Wait there, she told them, and somebody will come to see you.

AFTER DUSK, A BAND OF ARMED MEN emerged from the shadows of the forest and greeted the fugitives. They each carried a rifle, a revolver or two, and a big Bowie knife, as well as a knapsack and a canteen. They were Union men, and friendly enough, but Richardson noticed a certain fierce look in their eyes that he remembered seeing in the faces of guerrillas back in Bleeding Kansas—the haunted look of hunted men.

They were bushwhackers, a class of humanity that the fugitives regarded with horror—men who killed their enemies from ambush like common murderers. But these men did not seem depraved or uncivilized. They were polite, soft-spoken fellows with honest faces, and one of them had brought his children with him. As he stood talking, he playfully tossed his baby into the air while his little daughter stood at his side, clutching his shirt.

The bushwhackers invited the fugitives to dinner, and of course the Yankees accepted. They walked to a nearby house and sat down to supper while the bushwhackers took turns standing guard outside. As they ate, the men told stories about their lives. Some of them were draft dodgers, some were deserters from the Rebel army, and two were Union soldiers who'd recently snuck back home while on furlough. All were lying out—hiding from the Home Guard, living in caves and crude shelters in the mountains.

"At night we sleep in the bush," one man said. "When we go home by day, our children stand out on picket. They and our wives bring food to us in the woods."

They were living this way because they didn't want to fight against the United States, they explained. When the war began, they hoped to stay out of it and keep working their farms as they'd always done. But then the Confederates passed the Conscription Act and sent the Home Guard out to capture them and force them into the army. Some of them were drafted and then deserted. The rest took to hiding in the hills. Some of them had been lying out for two years.

"When the Rebels let us alone, we leave them alone," one bushwhacker said. "When they come out to hunt us, we hunt them."

Sometimes, a contingent of Home Guards or a band of Confederate cavalry would come chasing them. News of the Rebels' approach would spread quickly through the area, and soon 20 or 30 outliers would gather together, choose a good spot and ambush them. If you pick the right place to fight, the bushwhackers told their guests, a dozen men can defeat 70 or 100 soldiers. They'd done it often enough that the Rebels generally refrained from trying to round up large groups of outliers. Now, they just tried to catch one man at a time, usually when he went home to sleep with his wife. They'd raid a cabin looking for draft-age men. If they didn't catch any, they'd search the place, tearing it apart, and then, as often as not, steal anything that caught their fancy. It was a bitter war in the hills, the bushwhackers said, and any outlier unlucky enough to be captured by the Rebels was likely to be hanged—or simply executed quickly with a bullet to the head.

The bushwhackers' stories were fascinating, but the fugitives had a more pressing problem on their minds—getting across the mountains to Knoxville. They asked the bushwhackers for advice and received an answer they didn't want to hear: *Don't go.*

Deep snow covered the mountains, which meant that it would be extremely difficult to cross them on foot—and extremely easy for Rebels on horseback to follow their tracks. And of course they now knew what they could expect if the Confederates captured them.

"It is 200 miles to Knoxville," said one of the bushwhackers, "and no one ever reaches there. All who try it are murdered on the way."

That statement was so matter-of-factly grim that Browne burst out laughing when he heard it.

The Yankees told the bushwhackers that they were willing to risk the danger and asked if anybody in the room would serve as their guide. No one volunteered. They offered to pay good money for the service, but still nobody volunteered. It was a frightening realization: If even these grizzled bushwhackers were too scared to cross the mountains in winter, then the mountains must be a truly terrifying place.

"Stay with us till the snow is gone," one of the bushwhackers suggested. He said they would feed and shelter the Yankees until spring, then guide them to Knoxville.

So the fugitives faced a choice: Should they become bushwhackers for a few months, or take their chances crossing the mountains now?

20

ANYTHING FOR FREEDOM

THEY DECIDED TO GO. They wanted to keep moving, not to spend two or three months hiding in the woods. Besides, the Blue Ridge was still 20 miles to the west and they figured they ought to get a closer look at it before making any decision about whether it was safe to cross.

They left that night, guided by one of the bushwhackers, who agreed to lead them to the home of a Union man seven miles away. Seven fugitives were now traveling together—Browne, Richardson, Davis, and Captain Wolfe, plus the second group consisting of Thurston, Boothby, and Mercer. When they reached the home of the Union man, he told them his house was too close to the road to be safe from the Home Guard and directed them to his barn.

"You will find two Rebel deserters sleeping there," he said.

The deserters panicked when the fugitives entered the barn. They figured they'd been caught and now they'd be executed for the crime of desertion. When the fugitives explained that they were Yankees escaped from Salisbury, the deserters calmed down enough to tell their story. One was from Alabama, the other from Florida, and they'd both snuck away from Lee's army outside Petersburg three months earlier. They had walked more than 200 miles since then, dependent on the kindness of slaves and sympathetic white folks all the way. Now they were filthy, ragged, emaciated, and exhausted.

The next morning, their host moved the fugitives into a storehouse, which was less secluded, and thus less safe, but much warmer. It was Saturday, December 31, 1864—the last day of a terrible year for Richardson and Browne, who had spent all but 13 days of it in Rebel prisons and the rest slogging across cold mountains, worrying that they might be shot at any moment. That night, the fugitives split up again: Thurston, Boothby, Mercer, and the two Confederate deserters headed west towards the Blue Ridge while the three reporters and Wolfe stayed behind for another day.

They spent that day—New Year's Day—dozing in the storehouse, wrapped in quilts, while their hostess mended the worst of the many tears in their tattered clothes. Browne traded the Union Army cape he'd been wearing in lieu of an overcoat for one of the woman's quilts. He wrapped it around his shoulders, just below his scraggy beard and the filthy, floppy wool hat that a slave had given him ten days earlier. Richardson looked at his old friend's outfit and couldn't resist teasing him, saying that he looked like a cross between a bushwhacker and a mad genius.

After supper, they headed west, guided by their hosts' 11-year-old son. The boy took them about five miles, to the home of a Unionist friend, who greeted them without leaving his bed, and gave them detailed instructions about the trail ahead. It was a steep, rugged path that crossed a roaring stream two dozen times in the next 12 miles. The fugitives forded the stream by navigating carefully across icy logs. They each slipped into the water several times, soaking their pants. At one crossing, there was no log big enough to use as a bridge, so they stripped off their boots and pants and held them over their heads while they sprinted through waist-deep water speckled with chunks of ice.

Shivering, they knocked at the door of a cabin at the foot of the Blue Ridge, not knowing if they'd find a friend or foe, but desperate for some warmth.

"Come in," said a woman inside.

They stepped into the house and started to introduce themselves, but the woman interrupted.

"Oh, I know all about you," she said. "You are Yankee prisoners. Your friends who passed last evening told us you were coming, and I have been sitting up all night for you. Come to the fire and dry your clothes."

They slept in a barn that day, then ate dinner and warmed their bellies with the remains of Richardson's tea and their hostess's apple brandy. Fortified, they headed back out, led by the man who'd guided Thurston's party the night before. He rode a horse while they followed on a long, tough climb through several inches of snow to the top of the Blue Ridge. They stood on the summit as the sun came up, gazing out at the breathtaking view, but they were too cold, exhausted, and frightened to appreciate it.

Their guide warned them that the descent would be harder than the climb, and he was right. As they headed downhill, tripping and slipping in the snow, rain began to fall. They understood that rain was good for them—at least theoretically—because it washed away the snow that revealed their footprints to anybody who might be chasing them. But this rain was cold; it soaked through their clothes and left them shivering and miserable. As they trudged on, they started grumbling, complaining half-jokingly that they should never have left Salisbury Prison.

★

"THIS HAS BEEN A DISMAL, gloomy day to the prisoners in this stockade," Benjamin Booth wrote in his diary on New Year's Day in the Salisbury Prison yard. "Groups of starving men, reduced to mere skeletons, may be seen huddled together talking of what they would have to eat today if they were at home."

The next day, Booth wrote that a dead body had been discovered in the prison's huge pit latrine. "From the appearance of the body, it must have been buried in the depths of the awful filth for a week or more." The poor man had probably fallen into the latrine and drowned. He certainly hadn't been thrown in after he died—he was still wearing clothes and no prisoner would have let any clothes go to waste in wintertime. The prison authorities brought in a couple of black men, who carried a rope equipped with a large hook on the end. The men hooked the corpse, dragged it out to the burial ground, and threw it into one of the mass graves. Then the authorities announced that they were withholding the day's rations to punish the prisoners for failing to remove the corpse sooner.

On January 3, Booth noted that a recently constructed chimney in one of the hospital buildings had collapsed, killing ten sick prisoners who were lying in its path when it fell. "It can scarcely be called a disaster," he wrote. "Rather let it be called a kind act of providence by which poor, suffering men are released from their misery."

A ROUND MIDNIGHT on January 3, the fugitives reached the New River in the northwest corner of North Carolina. Unlike most American rivers, the New flows north, and the homesick Yankees considered that a good omen. They celebrated by kneeling reverently on its banks and drinking from it. This river is our Jordan, Richardson thought, flowing towards the promised land.

One by one, they hopped on the back of their guide's horse and rode to the western side of the river. From there, they labored through the snow for another couple of hours until they reached the home of one the guide's Unionist friends. A hulking man, he stepped out of his house to meet the wet, weary escapees hiding outside.

"Gentlemen, there are, unfortunately, at my house tonight two wayfarers who are Rebels and traitors," he said, speaking in the deep voice and grandiloquent diction of a melodramatic actor. "If they knew of your presence, it would be my inevitable and eternal ruin. Therefore, unable to extend to you such hospitalities as I could wish, I bid you welcome to all which *can* be furnished by so poor a man as I. I will place you in my barn, which is warm and filled with fodder. In the morning, when these infernal scoundrels are gone, I will entertain you under my family roof."

After such a bizarrely grandiose oration, the fugitives began to think that the man was comically pompous—until he told them the story of his family. "I had three sons," he said. "One died in a Rebel hospital. One was killed at the Battle of the Wilderness, fighting against his will for the Southern cause. The third, thank God, is in the Union lines."

At nine the next morning, their host entered the barn to wake them up. "Gentlemen, I trust you have slept well," he said in his portentous voice. "The enemy has gone and breakfast awaits. I call you early because I want to take you out of North Carolina into Tennessee, where I will show you a place of refuge infinitely safer than this."

They left after breakfast on one of the first daytime journeys they'd made since their escape. They were happy to travel in sunlight for a change, but their guide led them on a brutal march up steep hills that left them doubled over, gasping for breath. Ten inches of snow covered the mountains, and they plodded through groves of laurel so thick they seemed impenetrable. Going up the mountains, they grabbed branches and pulled themselves forward; going down, they slid and tripped over logs and rocks hidden by the snow. And as soon as they reached the bottom of one steep hill, they found themselves facing another that seemed even steeper.

Late that afternoon, they crossed the border into Tennessee. That milestone felt like a triumph, and they finally allowed themselves to think that their escape might succeed. They kept going for another couple miles before reaching a small log cabin occupied by a friend of their guide's—a large, matronly woman with a genial smile.

"I am very glad to see you," she said. "I thought you must be Yankees when I heard of your approach."

"How did you hear?"

"A good many young men are lying out in this neighborhood and my son is one of them," she said. "Nobody can approach this settlement, day or night, without being seen by some of the young men. The Guard have come in twice, at midnight, as fast as they could ride, but the news traveled before them and they found the birds flown. When you appeared in sight, the boys took you for Rebels. My son and two others, lying behind logs, had their rifles drawn on you not more than 300 yards away."

Her boy and his friends had been ready to shoot until they noticed that the strangers weren't carrying guns. The fugitives had come awfully close to death.

Hearing that, Browne grumbled that if he had to be killed, he preferred to be shot by an authentic Rebel, not a Union bushwhacker making a lethal blunder.

But now they were safe in a hamlet populated by pro-Union Tennesseans, who invited them to stay as long as they wanted. Hungry as hogs after their trek over the mountains, they ate ravenously, then lumbered off to a barn, burrowed under the fodder, and passed out.

They woke the next morning and decided to spend another day in the friendly village. While their hostesses mended their torn clothes and ripped boots, the fugitives listened to stories of wartime life in the mountains. The woman mending Richardson's clothes told him that her husband was off fighting in the Union army. Richardson asked how she managed to support her daughter without him.

"Very easily," she said. "Last year, I did all my own housework, and weaving, and spinning and knitting and raised over a hundred bushels of corn with no assistance whatever, except from this little girl, eleven years old. The hogs run wild in the woods during the summer, so we are in no danger of starving."

Later that day, Richardson and Browne met a woman who knew Lafayette Jones, an inmate they'd encountered in Castle Thunder. Jones was one of many pro-Union mountaineers in the prison. He'd been arrested by the Home Guard for helping men travel to Kentucky to join the Union army. That was a hanging offense, but Jones managed to get out of prison by volunteering to join the Confederate army. As soon as he got the chance, he deserted and made his way home. When he arrived in Tennessee, the woman said, he went to the home of a rich Rebel named William Waugh—the leader of the Confederates who had arrested and beaten him—and shot Waugh dead. Then he went off and joined the Union army. Now he was a captain in the 9th Tennessee Cavalry.

The woman told another story, too: A local Rebel leader who was feared and hated by the Unionists had disappeared sometime in early November. Nobody seemed to know where he was until a few days earlier, she said, when his rotting corpse was found in the woods with 21 bullet holes in his clothes. His money and his watch were still in his pocket. Apparently, whoever killed him wanted people to know that they did it for revenge, not for profit.

While the reporters chatted with their hosts that afternoon, Charley Thurston and his traveling companions arrived in the settlement, reuniting the Salisbury fugitives once again. For safety, the two groups of travelers spent much of the day hidden in a barn. Local bushwhackers visited them there, eager to tell stories of their adventures. One of them was a man Browne and Richardson had met at Castle Thunder named, improbably, Canada Guy. He was one of three sons of a pro-Union mountaineer named Levi Guy, who had been captured by Home Guards in 1863 and hanged from a chestnut tree in his own yard. Canada was arrested in a separate incident and sent to Castle Thunder. Like Lafayette Jones, he escaped the prison by joining the Confederate army, then deserted and returned home. Now he was a bushwhacker armed with a 16-shot rifle, a revolver, and a reputation for bloodthirstiness.

Guy was a wanted man, hunted by the Home Guard, but he didn't seem to mind. Noisy and blustery, he bragged that he'd killed seven Rebels, and he promised that he'd kill plenty more. He also boasted that he enjoyed robbing local Confederates, saying traitors had no right to their property. Browne listened to the man and concluded that his thirst for revenge had driven him mad.

When Guy left that afternoon with another bushwhacker, they didn't slip silently into the woods like other outliers. They walked off yelling and singing and firing their guns, as if daring the Home Guard to come after them.

"Guy always goes through the country that way," said the woman who had told Richardson about Lafayette Jones. "He is very reckless and fearless. The Rebels know it, and give him a wide field. He has killed a good many of them, and no doubt they will murder him sooner or later, as they did his father."

She was right. A month later, in February of 1865, the Home Guard captured Guy and a teenage boy named Jacob May, and proceeded to hang both of them.

★

JUST AS THE FUGITIVES SETTLED into a hayloft that night and began drifting off to sleep, a man burst into the barn, yelling that they should get up, fast. "Five Rebel cavalry are reported approaching this neighborhood, with three hundred more behind them, coming over the mountains from North Carolina."

The reporters were skeptical—they'd heard many false alarms about approaching Rebels—but they crawled out of their nests and scrambled out of the barn because, as Browne put it, "extreme prudence is the best policy of unarmed men." Outside, a bright moon illuminated a snow-covered landscape. Following their guide, the fugitives set out, walking single file, careful to step in the footprints of the man ahead of them so their tracks would appear to be the trail of a solitary woodsman instead of a fleeing group. After two hours, they reached a barn that their guide declared to be safe. They climbed into the hayloft.

Browne lay shivering all night long, too uncomfortable to sleep, contemplating this miserable life of long, cold marches and sneaking from barn to barn. They'd been on the road for 17 days, but it felt like months. Salisbury prison seemed like a place he'd passed through decades ago. The carefree days of Bohemian pillow fights in Jefferson City in 1861 seemed like memories from childhood. Would they *ever* reach safety? Would they *ever* see the North again? And would they ever eat anything other than pork and cornbread? Browne was sick of pork and cornbread. Richardson sometimes defended the diet, even calling it "the ambrosia of the immortal gods." He said that whenever he'd seen strong men performing hard labor—Colorado gold miners or New Orleans stevedores—they always fueled themselves with pork and cornbread. But Browne didn't care. He'd eaten enough to last a lifetime. He longed for a gourmet meal in an elegant restaurant, preferably with a beautiful woman.

At dawn, Browne gave up trying to sleep. He hobbled outside on his cold, stiff legs. In the dim light, he took out his notebook. Two days earlier he'd jotted down a thought: "How I long for the snowy sheets and soft pillows—shall I say the softer snowy arms?—I have known in the beloved and blessed North!" Now, he scribbled another philosophical rumination: "This experience will be pleasant some day to look back upon, and talk about; but it is difficult to undergo, requiring all the patience and philosophy I can muster."

Then he added a more defiant phrase: "Anything for freedom!"

THEY SET OUT AGAIN AT THREE that afternoon—seven Yankee escapees and two Rebel deserters led by a local guide who promised to take them to a place called Carter's Depot. They climbed Stony Mountain, which was covered with a foot of snow. At the summit, they caught their breath and gazed out at the territory ahead. It was beautiful but daunting—wave after wave of mountains, bristling with green pines and sliced by silver streams.

Their guide announced that he had to turn back. He said his wife was pregnant and sick, and he must return to her. Stunned, the fugitives offered him money to keep going. He refused. He said farewell and headed back. The fugitives kept moving forward, apprehensive about traveling without a guide through enemy territory.

That night, they came upon an isolated cabin and found it occupied by an old man and his wife. Luckily, they were Union supporters willing to feed hungry fugitives. The old man warned them that there was a settlement a few miles away that the locals called Little Richmond because it was the home of a band of Rebel guerrillas. After supper, the old man offered to lead them past Little Richmond, which made his wife very nervous. As they left, she clutched Richardson's hands and looked him in the eye.

"May God carry you safely to those you love," she said. "But you must be very cautious. Less than six weeks ago, my two brothers started for the north by the same route, and when they reached Crab Orchard, the Rebel guerrillas captured them and murdered them in cold blood."

A couple miles down the trail, the old man stopped. He gathered the fugitives around him and whispered instructions. "We are approaching the worst place. Let no man speak a word. Step lightly as possible, while I keep as far ahead as you can see me. If you hear any noise, dart out of sight at once."

They tiptoed for the next two miles, barely daring to breathe. Then the old man stopped again, and told them that they'd passed the most dangerous area. He gave them directions to the home of a friend a few miles ahead, then bid them farewell.

"My health is broken and I shall not live long," he told them. "But it is a great consolation to know that I have been able to help some men who love the Union made by our fathers."

They reached the home of the old man's friend at about three in the morning. He fed them and directed them to a pro-Union settlement, where they were amazed to see three men wearing United States Army uniforms. They were Union soldiers home on furlough, and they felt so confident of their safety that they didn't even bother to remove their uniforms. The soldiers led the fugitives to a secluded farmhouse, hidden between high hills and a swollen stream. The next day, they built a fire and boiled their filthy, louse-infested clothes in a kettle while they bathed their stinking bodies. Scrubbed clean, they slept that night in the glorious luxury of feather beds.

They were safe, the locals assured them, but they were still more than a hundred miles from the Union lines near Knoxville, and there were plenty of Rebels roaming those miles. What the fugitives needed to do, they said, was find the Old Red Fox.

The Old Red Fox was Dan Ellis, the so-called "Union pilot" famous for guiding packs of men through the mountains to join the Union army. Ellis was a legendary character in the Appalachians, and the fugitives had already heard many stories about him. The Rebels detested him, and had put a price on his head, but they couldn't catch him. Every time they had him cornered in some remote forest, he disappeared, fading into the hills like a wisp of fog. The mountain Unionists talked about Ellis as if he were some kind of superman, a cross between Davy Crockett, Robin Hood, and Moses.

"If you can only find Dan Ellis, and do just as he tells you," they told the fugitives, "you will be certain to get through."

21

CHASING THE OLD RED FOX

HE RIPPED HIS PANTS and he had no needle to make repairs, so Dan Ellis decided to visit the cabin of a woman he knew. It was an autumn afternoon in November 1864. Ellis knew that the Confederates were chasing him, so he hunkered down on the ridge above the woman's house and watched it for a while. He saw no sign of Rebels, so he walked down the hill and knocked on her door. While she fetched a needle and thread, he glanced nervously out the door and saw a squad of Home Guard galloping towards the cabin.

"Get in the cellar and we can hide you," the woman said, but Ellis dashed out the door and sprinted for the ridge. The Rebels chased him, firing their pistols. As he bounded over a fence, a bullet hit the top rail, spraying splinters in his face.

He kept running. He dropped the gunbelt that held his two Colt navy revolvers, but held on to his 16-shot Henry rifle as he scampered up the hill.

"Halt!" the Rebels hollered, but Ellis knew that if he stopped they would kill him. He kept running.

"Shoot him! Shoot him!"

He scrambled up the hill, pulling himself up by grabbing bushes and stumps. The Rebels kept firing, their bullets slamming into the dirt at his feet, slicing through leaves over his head.

When the terrain became too rough for horses, the Rebels dismounted and chased him on foot. Gasping for air, he kept running, zigzagging up the ridge, dodging and weaving and trying to stay hidden behind trees. Exhausted, he ducked behind some rocks and prepared to fight to the death, hoping to dispatch as many Rebels as he could before they killed him.

But the Confederates lost his trail and gave up, firing one final volley in his general direction, then trudging back downhill, frustrated that the Old Red Fox had slipped away again. He lay on the ground, panting so hard that he thought his pounding heart would explode in his chest. He slowly caught his breath, then opened his canteen and took a few swigs of apple brandy. He inspected himself and found that a bullet had sliced across the back of his shirt, and another had cut through one of his boots. But he was alive and unhurt and he'd escaped again—further proof that God was on his side.

"A kind and beneficent Providence had protected me from injury from their bullets," he later wrote in his memoir. "It seemed that my work was not yet done."

His work was spiriting Union men out of Confederate territory, and he made about two dozen trips during the war, guiding thousands of what he called "*stampeders*"—caravans of pro-Union mountaineers, Confederate deserters, runaway slaves, escaped prisoners, and other refugees—to safety in the Union lines.

Tall and gaunt, with dark hair, deep-set eyes, and a scraggily beard that drooped to his chest, Dan Ellis detested Confederates— "wicked wretches," he called them, traitors who had taken arms against "the best form of government which has ever been devised by the wisdom of man." He was born in the mountains of East Tennessee in 1827. One of nine children of a poor farmer, he learned to read and write in a one-room schoolhouse. After serving in the Mexican War, he had returned home, married a woman named Martha May, and supported his family working as a wagon maker.

When Tennessee seceded in 1861, Ellis joined a pro-Union militia. That fall, the Unionists plotted to burn bridges on the railroad line that connected Richmond with Memphis and Atlanta. On the night of November 8, 1861, they attacked, raiding nine railroad bridges simultaneously. Ellis and his men burned their target—the bridge over the Holston River—while other raiders destroyed four other bridges. The Confederate government reacted by dispatching 10,000 troops to East Tennessee. Judah Benjamin, the secretary of war, ordered his soldiers to capture and hang the bridge-burners and make a spectacle of them by "leaving their bodies hanging in the vicinity of the burned bridges." The soldiers obeyed, hanging four men so close to the railroad tracks that passengers could whack the dangling corpses with their walking sticks as the train rattled past.

Over the next few months, the Confederates arrested more than 1,000 East Tennessee Unionists, including William G. "Parson" Brownlow, the Methodist preacher and master of vituperation who edited the *Knoxville Whig* and printed fiery editorials denouncing Confederates as "God-forsaken scoundrels, hell-deserving villains and black-hearted assassins," among other choice epithets. The soldiers briefly captured Ellis, too, but he managed to escape by sprinting into the woods, shedding his bearskin coat as he fled. That was his first miraculous escape, and it convinced him that he was "a special object of the care of divine Providence."

A wanted man, Ellis became one of the first outliers, hiding in the woods for months. Occasionally, he'd slip home to visit his wife and kids, and on one visit he fathered his sixth child, christened Joseph Hooker Ellis in honor of the Union general known as "Fighting Joe." In 1862, Ellis began guiding groups of pro-Union mountaineers through the Confederate lines to Kentucky, where they could enlist in the Union army. In the fall of 1863, after federal troops seized Knoxville, Ellis changed his route, guiding refugees from North Carolina and East Tennessee to Union army camps near Knoxville. Both routes required long, tough marches through rugged mountains swarming with Confederate soldiers, Home Guards, and Rebel guerrillas. Ellis's modus operandi was simple in theory but exceedingly difficult in practice: He traveled at night, took the most arduous trails over the roughest terrain, and moved as fast as possible. He was a stern pilot, pushing his stampeders to their physical limit, but they loved the Old Red Fox because he got them to their destination alive.

After delivering a group of mountaineers to the Union army, Ellis would make the return trip carrying a fat knapsack full of letters from federal soldiers to their relatives in the mountains. The letters frequently contained money desperately needed by their wives and families, who quickly spent it in local towns. But these sudden influxes of greenbacks did not go unnoticed by Confederate officials, who dispatched the Home Guard to search the cabins of Unionists and steal their money. These quasi-official looting sprees enraged Ellis. "A desire for revenge crept into my heart," he wrote, "and I determined to give to some of these thieving villains who were plundering the houses of destitute women a taste of lead from my trusty gun."

He became a bushwhacker, ambushing Confederates and stealing their horses and mules. In the fall of 1864, Ellis and a group of ten Unionists ambushed a Home Guard posse led by a particularly brutal Rebel named Bill Parker. Ellis later claimed that he planned to capture Parker and deliver him to federal authorities. But Ellis's men shot Parker as soon as they spotted him. The wounded Rebel stumbled into the woods, where his corpse was discovered weeks later, the knees of his pants worn away as he crawled towards the home of a friend.

In December 1864, Ellis and his heavily armed lieutenants left a group of stampeders camped on a mountain and hid in the woods along a nearby road, waiting to ambush the posse of Home Guard that was chasing them.

"I saw the Rebels coming up the path to meet us," he later wrote. "We all jumped behind trees and as they come in we gave them a full volley and as they wheeled to run, they dropped their overcoats, hats and some of their guns. We charged them and kept firing into them until they got out of reach. . . . I don't think I ever saw men run so in my life. They never tried to fight us. We pored it to them as they went down the road and then went back and gathered up guns and coats and hats. We carried them up the mountain where a lot of men were gathered to go through the lines with me."

A few weeks after that incident, Richardson, Browne, and their traveling companions waited at a secluded spot in East Tennessee where they'd been told they could meet Ellis as he guided another group of stampeders towards Knoxville.

IT WAS AFTER DARK ON SUNDAY, January 8, 1865, when Ellis arrived. He was on horseback, leading about 70 men, 30 of them riding horses or mules, the rest on foot. Roughly 20 carried rifles. Some were Ellis's lieutenants, others were Rebel deserters or Union soldiers returning to the army after spending a furlough with their families.

Ellis stopped long enough to learn that the men who were waiting for his arrival had escaped from Salisbury Prison and plodded over the mountains for three weeks.

"Boys," Ellis announced to his men, "here are some gentlemen who have escaped from Salisbury, and are almost dead from the journey. They are our people. They have suffered in our cause. They are going to their homes in our lines. We can't ride and let these men walk. Get down off your horses and let them up."

A few minutes later, Richardson, Browne, and Davis were perched on mules, using sacks of corn for saddles, riding towards Knoxville, more than 100 miles away. Browne, who remembered the painful mule ride back in Wilkes County, found this beast equally uncomfortable. After a mile or so, he dismounted and joined the walkers who hustled to keep up with Ellis's punishing pace.

Richardson fared better. He rode with Ellis at the head of the long column, interviewing the legendary pilot. Usually taciturn, Ellis was happy to entertain a newspaper reporter with stories of his adventures. He said he made the trips about once a month, guiding groups ranging from 40 to 500 people. He charged no fee for his services, financing the excursions by stealing horses from the Rebels and selling them to the United States Army when he reached Knoxville. He introduced Richardson to his trusted sidekick, Elbert Treadaway, and bragged that the two of them had once fought off 14 Rebels who'd caught them by surprise. He owed his life to his 16-shot Henry rifle, he said, and he swore he never let it get out of his reach.

"That old gun has saved me a dozen times, and if the Rebels ever kill me, that carbine will be the last thing I will hold on earth," he said. "Why, it's my best friend. I'd as soon think of giving up my wife as that old blazer. Without that, I'd have been under the sod long ago."

They rode on through the cold night, Richardson struggling to stay upright atop the corn-sack saddle on the lumbering mule. He stopped at a creek, hopped off the beast, and paused for a drink of water and a bit of rest. Then he readjusted the corn sack and tried to climb back on the mule. But he was stiff and sore and slow and the mule kept stepping away from him, apparently uninterested in further labor. By the time Richardson managed to get back on the beast, the column of stampeders had disappeared into the darkness.

The mule plodded along and Richardson assumed the animal would instinctively follow the trail of the caravan. But after ten minutes of riding, he could neither see nor hear the stampeders. He dismounted and studied the trail, searching for hoof marks or foot-prints in the half-frozen mud, but he saw nothing. He stood still and listened for a long moment. He heard nothing.

He was lost.

What now? It was the middle of the night and he was exhausted and disoriented. He had no idea where he was, or what path might lead him back to the caravan, or whether the people who lived nearby were likely to be Rebels or Unionists. He *did* know that if the Home Guard caught him, they would probably shoot him.

He returned to the creek where he'd stopped for water. He tied the mule to a tree and sat down on a log to think. He silently cursed the damn mule and remembered that it was the stubbornness of a slow-moving mule that had gotten Davis captured by the Rebels in Georgia the previous spring. Now this stubborn creature might get *him* cap-tured, too. He tried to calm down and come up with a plan. He figured that Ellis might send somebody out to search for him, so he decided to lay down with his ear to the ground so he could hear the hoof beats of anybody riding nearby.

He lay there—still, quiet, listening.

And then he fell asleep.

★

THE COLD AWOKE HIM. He stood up and looked at his watch. It was three o'clock in the morning. Freezing, he ran back and forth until he warmed up.

When dawn lightened the forest, he walked along the creek until he spotted a small log cabin. He remembered the lesson he'd learned weeks earlier: The more humble the house, the more likely that the oc-cupant is a Unionist. As he approached the cabin, he saw an old man walk out, carrying a sack of corn on his shoulder.

Albert stared into the man's eyes, searching for some sign of his loyalties. "Are you a Union man or a secessionist?" he asked.

"I don't know who *you* are," the man said, "but I am a Union man, and always have been."

"I am a stranger, and in trouble," Richardson said. He blurted out his story and said he'd gotten separated from Dan Ellis's column dur-ing the night.

"I know Dan Ellis as well as my own brother," the old man said. He directed Richardson to the nearby ford where he expected Ellis would have crossed the Nolichucky River.

Richardson mounted his mule, raced to the ford, and crossed the river. On the other side, he saw Ellis and Treadaway riding towards him.

"Aha!" Ellis said. "We were looking for you."

The stampeders had stopped a few miles away to eat breakfast and rest for a while before heading off again.

"Today," Ellis announced, "we must cross the Big Butte."

"How far is that?" Albert asked.

"It is generally called ten miles," Ellis said, "but I suspect it is about fifteen, and a rather hard road at that."

They left about eleven in the morning, crossed a cold creek, and then began climbing a steep mountain covered in ten inches of snow. Ellis led the way, followed by the men riding horses and mules, with the walkers straggling behind. Browne was among the pedestrians, his feet aching in his boots, which had split and shrunk and stiffened. He limped along, breathing hard, struggling to keep up with Ellis's grueling pace. *Why do they have to go so fast?* Of course, he knew the answer: They traveled fast to avoid getting caught. But that didn't make the marching any easier. Browne kept moving, worried that he'd fall so far behind that he would lose their trail and be left alone in this strange land. That would mean forfeiting all hope of freedom, he thought, and probably all hope of living through this endless ordeal.

The stampeders struggled to the summit, paused to catch their breath, then headed down the other side. Rain fell as they trudged downhill, stumbling along a path that had been washed into a gully. It was dark when they reached the bottom. Ellis said he knew of an abandoned house where they could spend the night, but when they reached it, they discovered that it had collapsed into a heap of broken timbers topped by a leaky roof.

Working in a downpour, Ellis and his men propped a section of roof atop some timbers. They stretched out on the ground beneath it, clutching their rifles close to them, and promptly fell asleep. Richardson, Browne, and Davis thought the jerry-rigged shelter looked dangerously precarious, so they set off in search of a cabin that might be occupied by somebody sympathetic to their plight. They found one, and were invited to sleep in a nearby barn.

The Bohemians rose before dawn, ate a quick breakfast, and returned to the tumbledown house. The men who'd spent the night there looked wet, cold, tired, and troubled. During the night, Ellis had learned from local supporters that a sizable contingent of Confederate soldiers was bivouacked 10 or 15 miles ahead. That news frightened some of the stampeders so much that they decided to give up and head back to North Carolina. Among them were three Union soldiers.

"It is useless to go on," one soldier said. "The party will never get through. Not a single man of it will reach Knoxville unless he waits till the road is clear."

Ellis and Treadaway ignored the naysayers. They were determined to press forward on a route they thought would avoid the Rebel encampment. The Bohemians decided to stick with Ellis. One of the men who were turning back offered to sell his horse to the highest bidder. It was a tired old nag, but Richardson, feeling at least as tired as the horse, bought it for $50 in U.S. greenbacks.

Late in the morning, the rain let up and Ellis led the soggy stampeders on another grueling march, taking secluded paths through thick woods. Sometime in the afternoon, Ellis visited the cabin of a friend and learned that eight Rebel guerrillas had passed by only an hour earlier. Always eager to fight Confederates, Ellis gathered eight or ten armed men and galloped off after the Rebels.

With Ellis on the warpath, Treadaway led the rest of the stampeders on. Around dusk they stopped near a place called Kelly's Gap and made camp in an old orchard. A deserted farmhouse stood nearby. One of Ellis's men told Richardson that a Union man had lived there until the Rebels caught him and hanged him from one of his apple trees. The Rebels cut him down before he died, but the farmer got the message and fled for his life.

The stampeders built fires and cooked corn. After dark, Ellis and his men returned with a deserter they'd captured while chasing the guerrillas. While Ellis rode off to ask local Unionists about Rebel troop movements in the area, his underlings stayed behind to guard the prisoner. He was in his early 20s, with a heavy, expressionless face. He swore he wasn't a guerrilla, insisting that he'd deserted the Confederate army and traveled to Knoxville, where he'd sworn an oath of allegiance to the United States government. Now, he said, he just wanted to live in peace. Ellis's men thought the prisoner was lying and debated what to do with him. Some suggested that they take him to Knoxville and turn him over to the proper authorities. Others, who seemed to be in the majority, said they ought to take the damned Rebel out into the woods and shoot him.

Richardson watched this debate, marveling at how calm the prisoner remained while he listened to armed men arguing over his fate.

"Well, sir," one man asked the captive, "what have you to say for yourself?"

"I am in your hands," he replied. "You can kill me if you want to, but I have kept the oath of allegiance and I am innocent."

The debate continued. "He may deserve death, and he probably does," said a Union officer from East Tennessee. "But we are not murderers and he shall not be shot. I will use my own revolver on anybody who attempts it. Let us hear no more of these taunts. No brave man will insult a prisoner."

That settled the matter: The captive would be taken to Knoxville. He listened to this news in silence, his face showing no emotion.

AROUND MIDNIGHT, Ellis returned bearing frightening news: Some 70 or 80 Rebels were camped about two miles away. A force that large could easily ambush and massacre the entire caravan of Unionists. Ellis decided to divide the stampeders into two groups. He would lead the riders in one direction, traveling as fast as possible, while Treadaway would guide the walkers on another, more obscure, path. The idea was to lure the Rebels into chasing after the riders while the slower walkers slipped away unnoticed. If that didn't work, at least the Rebels were unlikely to attack *both* groups, so half the stampeders might escape unharmed.

Terrified, everybody scrambled to gather their possessions and move out. Richardson saddled his newly purchased horse while Davis climbed on a mule. Ellis offered Browne a mule, too, but it had no saddle, and Junius, wary of mules, declined the offer, opting to go with the walkers. The Bohemians figured they would meet again in a few hours, so Browne lent Davis the quilt he'd been using as a coat, which could serve Davis as a saddle blanket.

The riders galloped off. In the confusion of the abrupt change of plans, the prisoner whose fate had been hotly debated the previous night simply slipped off into the woods.

Treadaway called the walkers together and revealed his plan. They would cross a mountain, then descend into a ravine and camp there until the following night, when they would move out under cover of darkness. By then, the Rebels would be far away, chasing Ellis's horsemen.

"But where are we to meet the other party?" Browne asked.

"Oh, we won't see them again until we reach Knoxville," Treadaway replied. Then he added a bit of gallows humor: "*If* we have the good luck to get there."

That news stunned Browne. Knoxville was nearly a hundred miles away. He and Richardson had vowed to stick together until they reached freedom or died trying. They'd taken care of each other for 21 months, surviving three horrific prisons, several bouts of illness, and this endless march over frozen mountains. But now Richardson was riding off with Davis, and Browne was left behind. Worse, he was freezing because he'd given away his quilt, and penniless because Richardson was carrying the Bohemians' money.

Prone to pessimism even in good times, Browne now sank into gloom. All he could see in his future was death or a dungeon. They're going to freedom and I'm left behind, he thought. I'll die in these mountains and nobody will ever know what happened to me.

"I have no more hope now of getting through," he wrote in his notebook. "I am resolved never to give up. Still, I am most worn, weary, and wretched; and all my dark views of Human Life and Experience come up mentally darker and grimmer than before."

22

MELVINA

ELLIS LED THE RIDERS through the darkness at his usual breakneck pace, avoiding roads and galloping over hills, across streams, and through swampy ravines. Richardson, mounted on his newly purchased horse, bounced along in the middle of the pack while Davis rode up near the front. After a few miles, Davis hung back to let Richardson catch up to him.

"That young lady rides very well," Davis said.

"What young lady?" Richardson asked.

"The young lady who is piloting us."

Albert thought Ellis was guiding the group, but Davis told him that a teenage girl was leading the column—a beautiful girl of about 16 or 17 who rode as hard and fast as any man.

Richardson galloped off to see for himself. He spotted the young woman but couldn't get a good look at her in the darkness. He asked Ellis why she was there. Earlier that night, Ellis said, he had ridden off to ask a local friend about Rebels in the area, only to be told that Confederate cavalrymen were camped a couple miles away. Ellis decided to split up his group into riders and walkers, and lead the riders

off as quickly as possible. Their fastest getaway route crossed the Nolichucky River at Carter's Bridge, about seven miles away, but Ellis
worried that the Rebels might be waiting there to ambush him. He
needed somebody who would not draw suspicion to ride over the bridge
and see if it was safe to cross. His friend was too old for the task but a
teenage relative volunteered to do it. Her name was Melvina Stephens.
She had previously carried messages between local Unionists and
earned a reputation for courage. The Rebel soldiers in the area knew
her, too, and were smitten with her beauty. They frequently found ex-
cuses to drop by her house to visit, which helped her Unionist family
keep track of their movements.

So it was Melvina who was leading Ellis's column, riding hard over
obscure trails through the woods, careful to avoid the homes of Rebel
sympathizers. She stopped at a secluded spot overlooking the river
and told Ellis to wait there with the other riders. Then she rode slowly
across the bridge. She saw no sign of Rebels, and she proceeded to the
house of local Unionists, who told her they'd spotted no Rebels that
night. She rode back across the bridge and informed Ellis that it was
safe to cross. Then she trotted slowly past the waiting stampeders. By
now, they'd all heard that a beautiful girl was guiding them, and they
were eager to cheer for her. But she held a finger across her lips, signaling the need for silence, so they merely stood and saluted as she
rode by.

★

TREADAWAY LED THE WALKERS to a remote ravine in the woods
where they could build a bonfire without being seen. Despite the
fire, Browne was too cold to sleep so he paced around, trying to stay
warm, and brooded about his separation from his friends. There was
one positive aspect to the situation, he thought: It decreased the
chances that the Rebels would kill both *Tribune* reporters. If they
killed him, maybe Richardson would make it home. If they killed
Richardson, maybe he would live to tell their story.

Dawn arrived but the stampeders, who hadn't eaten in 24 hours,
had nothing to cook for breakfast. Around noon, a lookout spotted a
squad of Rebel cavalry approaching and everyone panicked, scram-
bling into the woods in all directions. Browne sprinted up a hill. After
running a few hundred yards, he stopped and looked around to see if
anybody was chasing him. Seeing no one, he tiptoed back to a spot

where he could see the bonfire. It was still burning, surrounded by blankets and knapsacks abandoned by the stampeders when they hurtled into the woods. Apparently, the Rebels never noticed they were there.

That afternoon, Treadaway managed to obtain some food from local Unionists and the stampeders wolfed it down before moving on. Treadaway was on horseback and, as usual, he set a grueling pace for the footsloggers behind him. Rushing along, Browne slipped and fell, smashing his knee into a tree root. It hurt so much he thought he'd shattered the kneecap. But he had to keep going, limping along as best he could, his mood growing bleaker with every step.

Shortly before dusk, Treadaway paused on a ridge overlooking a house in a valley. It was the home of Melvina Stephens. The previous night, she'd promised Ellis that she'd guide Treadaway's walkers across the same bridge she'd reconnoitered for Ellis and the riders. She had arranged to meet Treadaway at a certain secluded place in the valley after dark. As the stampeders waited for darkness, they watched a dozen Rebel cavalrymen ride up to her house and knock on the door. A few minutes later, they rode away. *What was happening? Did they know what she'd done the previous night? Had they come to arrest her? Or were they simply young men dropping by to visit a pretty girl?*

Cautiously, Treadaway led the walkers down into the valley to the place where Melvina had promised to meet him, wondering all the while if she would be there. She was. She sat on her horse, smiling calmly, as the walkers gathered around her—18 dirty, ragged, malodorous men, some in tattered civilian clothing, others in ragged Union or Confederate uniforms, all of them exhausted, nervous, and desperate. Junius Browne, who fancied himself as a discerning and unsentimental judge of female beauty, maneuvered himself close enough to study this young lady in the glow of the moonlight. He concluded that she was fair, graceful, intelligent, and comely, "with the warm blood of youth flushing in her cheek."

Speaking in a soft but commanding voice, she gave them directions to the bridge and instructed them to follow her at a distance. If she stopped, they should lie down out of sight. When it was safe to move on, she would cough. If she saw danger, she would sneeze.

After finishing her instructions, she rode off. Like Ellis and Treadaway, she set a punishing pace. Browne had to trot to keep up. If this is what it's like to follow a woman's lead, he grumbled to himself, I want no more of it. He managed to catch up with her for a moment, and gasped out a single sentence: "Do go a little slower."

She pulled back on the reins and slowed down. When she reached the hill overlooking the bridge, she stopped. She told the stampeders to wait there and silently watch her as she rode across the bridge. If she saw any sign of danger, they would see her stop. If she kept going, they should follow.

They crouched on the frozen ground and watched as she rode across the bridge, her horse's hooves clattering against the wooden planks. They saw her reach the other side and ride calmly on, disappearing into the darkness.

Confident that the bridge was safe, Treadaway led the pedestrians across the river. On the other side, he abandoned the road and set out over the countryside, leading the weary stampeders on a grueling 17-mile march, much of it uphill. He finally stopped around two in the morning near the top of an icy mountain, where the men could build a fire and settle down to sleep. Browne, who'd lent his quilt to Davis, might have frozen that night, but one of his fellow travelers permitted him to crawl under his blanket and the two bone-chilled men kept each other a little bit warmer.

"WHEN SHALL WE JOIN THE FOOTMEN?" Richardson asked Ellis.

"After we reach Knoxville," the Red Fox replied.

That news surprised Richardson as much as it had shocked Browne earlier. Like Browne, Richardson had assumed that the two groups would meet up again a few hours after they separated. He felt guilty about leaving Browne, and tried to reassure himself that Treadaway was Ellis's trusted lieutenant, and that he would lead the walkers on obscure trails that the Rebel cavalry couldn't follow. Browne was probably safer walking than he and Davis were riding.

The riding was rough. Ellis led the group across country so rugged that they regularly had to dismount and walk their horses. In the bitter cold, the frost-covered mud on the trails was so deep that the horses sank down to their fetlocks. Worried that the Rebels would catch up, Ellis pushed the tired men and their exhausted animals so hard that several horses died or came so close to death that they were simply abandoned. Their riders proceeded on foot or doubled up on healthier animals.

During the ride, Ellis's men encountered an old man perched on a fine horse. One of the stampeders, now without a horse, saw an opportunity.

"What are you, Southerner or Union?" he asked, holding his rifle menacingly.

"Well," said the old man, looking very nervous, "I have kept out of the war from the beginning. I have not helped either side."

"Come! Come! That will never do," said the stampeder. "You don't take me for a fool, do you? You never could have lived in this country without being either one thing or the other. Are you Union or Secession?"

The poor man had to guess, immediately, who these strangers might be. He could see that they were scraggy and dirty, wearing ragged, muddy, slept-in clothes that included pieces from the uniforms of both armies. They looked like Rebels.

"I voted for secession," he said.

"Tell the entire truth," his interrogator insisted.

"Well, sir, I do. I have two sons in Johnston's army. I was an original secessionist, and I am as good a Southern man as you can find in the state of Tennessee."

That statement delighted the horse-less stampeder holding the rifle. "All right, my old friend," he said. "Just slide down off that horse."

"What do you mean?"

"I mean that you are just the man I have been looking for in walking a hundred miles—a good Southerner with a good horse. I am a Yankee. We are all Yankees. So slide down and be quick about it."

The old man had no choice but to obey. He dismounted and watched as the man with the rifle climbed into his saddle and rode off on his horse.

TRUDGING ALONG on another nocturnal trek over cold, dark mountain trails, Browne and the other walkers followed Treadaway as he led them to a house owned by the father-in-law of a prominent Rebel guerrilla. Treadaway had heard a rumor that the guerrilla was holed up in the house, so he told the stampeders to surround the place while he pounded on the door, screaming for the "damned scoundrel" to come out or he'd blow his brains out.

The door opened. An elderly couple peeked out, obviously terrified. They swore their son-in-law wasn't there. Treadaway did not demand to search the house. He was more interested in the guerrilla's horses than in the fighter himself.

"Where are that damned traitor's horses?" Treadaway bellowed.

The old man came out of the house and led Treadaway to his stable, which sheltered two horses. Treadaway's friends saddled them up and rode off.

Browne hustled to follow his guide, but he was enraged at what he'd just seen. He felt sorry for the old couple, and guilty that he'd been a part of the mob that terrified them. If a man is a Rebel guerrilla, then he deserves to have his horses confiscated, Junius thought, but the incident he'd just witnessed looked more like simple horse theft.

I escaped from Salisbury to obtain liberty, not horses, he thought. He promised himself that if Treadaway and his cronies stole any more horses, he'd leave the group and walk to Knoxville by himself, whatever the danger.

ELLIS LED THE RIDERS past the town of Russellville, and then stopped for the night, making camp in deep woods. They built fires of pine, which crackled and spit sparks into the frosty air. They roasted some corn and then bedded down around the fires. The next morning, Ellis took them to the home of Treadaway's sister, who cooked a breakfast that included coffee, sugar, and butter—three luxuries they hadn't tasted in weeks, maybe months.

They were getting close to the Union army, encamped at Strawberry Plains, about 15 miles east of Knoxville. It was now safe to ride in daylight, and they had covered about 25 miles before stopping to camp in the woods.

Richardson and Davis were sick of sleeping on cold ground and no longer afraid of encountering Rebel soldiers, so they rode off in search of indoor accommodations. At the first cabin they tried, two women turned them away, clearly disgusted at the prospect of helping escaped Yankees. At the second cabin, an old woman listened to their plea for food and shelter, a skeptical look on her face. "What are you, anyway?" she asked.

"Union men—Yankees escaped from the Salisbury Prison."

"Why didn't you say so before?" she asked. "Of course, I can give you supper. Come in."

They ate well and slept soundly, and headed off the next morning, eager to reach Strawberry Plains. Along the way, Richardson's horse—the nag he had paid $50 for a few days earlier—looked about ready to drop dead. Richardson took pity on the animal, dismounted, and walked the horse. The beast had served him well, carrying him across nearly a hundred miles of rugged mountains, but now it was exhausted. It would be cruel to force him to keep going, Richardson thought, but he didn't want to simply abandon him. He saw a man standing by the road and asked, "Would you like a horse?"

"Certainly," the man said.

"Very well, take this one," Richardson said, handing the bridle to the stunned stranger.

As they closed in on the Union lines, now barely seven miles away, their heavy, tired feet grew light. At about ten in the morning, Richardson saw the Stars and Stripes rippling in the breeze. He and the others walked into an encampment of the United States Army, tears spilling from their eyes.

It was January 13, 1865—620 days since Confederate soldiers had dragged Richardson and Browne from the Mississippi River, 27 days since they had slipped out of Salisbury Prison, more than 300 miles across the mountains.

Richardson was exhausted, aching, filthy, and cold, but he had the presence of mind—and the journalistic flair—to send the *Tribune* a telegram guaranteed to be quotable:

> *Knoxville, Tennessee, January 13, 1865.*
> *Out of the jaws of Death; out of the mouth of Hell.*
> *—Albert D. Richardson*

SOMEWHERE OUTSIDE RUSSELLVILLE, Treadaway's walkers first heard a rumor that Ellis's group had made it safely to Strawberry Plains. Treadaway told them they'd spend only one more night camping before they, too, reached the Union lines. He guided them to the East Tennessee and Virginia Railroad and told them to follow the tracks west. Then he rode off, heading home.

The walkers breakfasted on parched corn, then marched down the tracks all day long. After dark, some of the men stopped for the night. Others, including Browne, kept going. Browne's feet ached, his muscles throbbed, and he was ready to drop from exhaustion, but he couldn't stop. Not now. Not after coming this far. Not with sanctuary so close. He felt a strange wave of energy surging through his body. His blood tingled and he felt as if he was glowing, as if a fire was burning inside him. He wondered if he'd gone mad, but he didn't worry about it. He just kept walking.

The night grew cold and a bitter wind whipped out of the north, but somehow it no longer bothered Browne. He fought the cold by walking faster. Periodically, groups of his companions quit, stopping to eat and rest for the night. But Browne kept on. After midnight, it was just him and another man, a tall, muscular fellow, and the two of them vowed not to stop until they reached Strawberry Plains.

They kept marching, bounding down the tracks as fast as they could go. Shortly before dawn they spotted a glow near the horizon. As they got closer, they realized that it was the campfire of sentinels guarding the periphery of the Union camp.

"Who comes there?" yelled one of the sentinels.

"Friends without the countersign," Browne answered. "Escaped prisoners from Salisbury."

The sentinel studied the two men who stood before him. They'd been walking as fast as they could for nearly 24 hours and they were sweating, panting, exhausted, and exhilarated.

"All right, boys," he said. "Glad to see you."

23

LIFE, LIGHT, AND LIBERTY

O N JANUARY 12, 1865, the day before Albert Richardson reached the Union army camp in Strawberry Plains, another prisoner of war arrived home.

Edward A. Pollard—editor of the *Richmond Examiner* and author of the pro-slavery polemic *Black Diamonds Gathered in the Darkey Homes of the South*—had been summoned to Union General Benjamin Butler's office in early January.

"I believe, Mr. Pollard, I promised to send you to Richmond."

"You did, General Butler."

"By God, sir, you shall go," Butler said. "I would send you through my lines tomorrow, but I sent a flag-of-truce down the road the other day, and some of your people fired upon it. They must have been damned drunk."

The general assured the prisoner that when flag-of-truce boats resumed operation, Pollard would be sent to Richmond. "I always keep my word," he said. He asked only one favor—that when Pollard arrived in Richmond, he attempt to arrange for the release of Albert Richardson. Pollard promised to try.

On January 12, Pollard boarded a flag-of-truce boat at Fortress Monroe and sailed up the James River to Richmond. "That night," he wrote, "I slept the sweet sleep of one returned to his home." He kept his promise to the general: In a letter to Ould, he reported his conversation with Butler and requested Richardson's release.

"It is not only on account of my promise," Pollard wrote, "that I ask of you the concession of Mr. Richardson's exchange for myself but because I have been deeply moved by a just and natural sympathy in his case. It is true that he is an attaché of the *New York Tribune*. That, I have been assured by his friends, was merely a professional and very subordinate connection, as he neither controls its columns, nor is known as a politician. I truly believe that this unhappy man has suffered penalties which have given him the strongest claim I have ever yet heard of, on the part of any Federal prisoner, upon the humanity of this government. He has been more than eighteen months a prisoner. I learned in the North that while he had been in this long captivity, his wife has died—insane I was told; then his child had died; and thus his family has gone to the grave, while he lingered in prison. Why not let this miserable man go?"

When Pollard wrote that letter, neither he nor Ould knew that Richardson had escaped.

Ould quickly quashed this latest plea for mercy. "I am inclined by a sense of duty to decline the proposed exchange," he wrote back. "I have already refused to exchange Richardson for a half-dozen different named parties. It would be unjust to them if a proposal heretofore declined were accepted now."

This time, though, it didn't matter what Ould thought.

RICHARDSON'S TELEGRAM from Strawberry Plains arrived at the *Tribune* office on Friday, January 13, and Horace Greeley shared the news in his editorial column the next day:

> The very many friends of our correspondent A. D. Richardson
> will read with the same satisfaction that we did the following
> dispatch received from him yesterday afternoon:

Knoxville, Friday, Jan 13, 1865

"Out of the jaws of death; out of the gates of hell."

    Albert D. Richardson

Mr. Richardson, with another correspondent of *The Tribune*, Mr. Brown, and one of *The World*, was taken prisoner in the spring of 1863, while attempting to run by Vicksburg in a tug, which was blown up. The prisoners were paroled and sent to Richmond for exchanges. On their arrival there, the correspondent of *The World* was immediately released, but their paroles were taken from Messrs. Richardson and Brown, and they were immediately consigned to Libby Prison.

Greeley reported that his two correspondents had since been transferred to Salisbury Prison, and that the Rebels had refused several offers to exchange them. And then, characteristically, he couldn't resist the urge to use that information to clobber an enemy he seemed to loathe far more than mere Confederates—the rival *New York Herald*.

In the meantime, correspondents of the *Herald* have been captured, and, like the gentleman of the *World*, almost immediately released. In one instance, this was brought about by the representation of a prominent Democratic politician of this city, who assured the Rebel authorities that it would better serve the purposes of the Rebel Government to release this representative of that journal than to keep him a prisoner. The last exchange offer for Mr. Richardson was Mr. Pollard, and he, we presume, was accepted. Mr. Brown still remains a prisoner.

On Sunday, January 16, the *Tribune* received another telegram from Knoxville, this one from Junius Browne, and Greeley shared it with his readers the next day:

We received, last evening, the following dispatch from our correspondent, Julius H. Browne, who has followed his companion, Richardson, "out of the jaws of death, out of the gates of hell" at Salisbury, North Carolina.

Knoxville, Jan. 14, 1865

Arrived here safe this morning. Leave for New York tomorrow. Escaped from Salisbury Dec. 18.

  Julius H. Browne

Mr. Browne, it seems, has been nearly a month in making his way to Knoxville, and has probably met with many interesting adventures, of which we shall hear in due season. The families and friends of our correspondents will accept our hearty congratulations at the termination of their long imprisonment. Whether Mr. Richardson effected his own escape or was exchanged for Mr. Pollard we have not yet learned.

Those two short items in the *Tribune* provide a valuable lesson about the glamour and the glory of a career as a newspaper reporter: Junius Browne risked his life covering a war. He was captured by the enemy and imprisoned for 20 months. He escaped and trudged 300 miles over snow-covered mountains. And when he finally reached safety, his own newspaper misspelled his name. Several times. On several days. First name *and* last name.

FLAGS HUNG FROM THE CHANDELIERS. Silverware sparkled in the candlelight. Wineglasses were filled and emptied and filled again. Course after sumptuous course of elegant food arrived, and was dispatched—oyster soup, quail, and "every delicacy that sea, land or air could furnish," the *Cincinnati Gazette* reported, "served in the best style of Epicurean fancy."

It was Saturday night, January 21, a week after Junius Browne trudged into Strawberry Plains, and Cincinnati's reporters had organized a full-blown testimonial dinner for Browne, Richardson, and Davis. The Bohemian escapees, all veterans of Cincinnati newspapers, had arrived in the city after stops in Knoxville, Nashville, and Louisville. Browne was staying at his family's home, Richardson in a hotel. They planned a trip to Washington to lobby the government to free the Salisbury prisoners, but they were happy to pause long enough to be feted by old friends, among them several dozen reporters, including Richard Colburn—the *New York World* correspondent who'd been captured with them at Vicksburg and quickly released from Libby Prison. The dinner's official host, Thomas Weasner, president of the Cincinnati City Council, apologized that the mayor was out of town and unable to attend.

When dinner had been devoured, the waiters marched in bearing a special dessert—a foot-high statue of George Washington sculpted out of ice cream. "The Father of his Country was soon beheaded, and presently his whole body was distributed and disposed of according to the customs observed in such cases," the *Cincinnati Commercial* reported. "Then the wine corks flew, the nut-crackers were brought into requisition, and Mr. Weasner gave the first regular toast."

Toasts were the glory—and the bane—of the nineteenth-century testimonial dinner. These dinners, nearly always stag affairs, ended with five or ten or even 20 toasts, each one followed by a formal response—a carefully prepared oration on the subject of the toast. The speeches ranged from the brief to the interminable and from the witty to the bathetic. Frequently, the final toast of the long night was "To Women," with the responder uttering hideously sentimental praise to the gender that hadn't been invited to the dinner. Veterans of these affairs learned to fortify themselves with strong liquids before the toasting began. Of course, newspapermen figured their toasts and responses were far more entertaining than those of less literary mortals.

Weasner stood to propose the first toast: "To the President of the United States—America needs no other ruler." A local congressman responded with a brief paean to President Lincoln, and then announced that he'd rather listen to the honored guests than continue speaking. Weasner proposed the second toast: "To the Army and Navy—Invincible in attack, impregnable in defense" and a brigadier general responded by expressing confidence in a Union victory before saying that he, too, wanted to hear from the escapees.

"To our heroic and distinguished guests," Weasner said, proposing the third toast. "Their bravery in capture and their fortitude in captivity are equaled only by the daring of their escape. Out of the jaws of death, out of the mouth of hell!"

When Richardson rose to deliver the response, the diners stood and cheered. "Mr. President and guests," he began. "I can say little to interest you. My blood is too sluggish and my brain too dull."

That was rhetorical nonsense. Despite his recent ordeal, Richardson's brain was plenty sharp and he'd prepared a carefully constructed comic ode to his fellow fugitives. He began by announcing that Davis had spent his prison days laboring under two delusions. His first delusion was that he suffered from a severe spinal disorder. In Salisbury, Richardson said, Davis frequently took to his bunk, complaining of back pain. The man was so sickly that Browne and Richardson worried that he would collapse during their escape and they'd have to leave him behind, groaning in pain on some forlorn mountainside.

"We found the hardships incomparably greater than we anticipated, but do you fancy that he succumbed to them?" Richardson asked. "On the contrary," he answered. "He was constantly at the head of the column, and nearly killed us all with his inexhaustible and irrepressible pedestrianism." Then came the punch line, delivered with Richardson's characteristic deadpan: "I expect to suffer to my dying day from the effects of walking behind this unfortunate invalid."

That got a laugh. Richardson was rolling.

"His other delusion, which he cherished with profound sincerity, was that he was a total abstinence man," he continued. "But when—footsore and wet, hungry and cold—he came within reach of a certain beverage of which I presume you gentlemen have never heard but which is concocted in the mountains of North Carolina and Tennessee, and called, in the language of the natives, apple brandy"—Richardson paused for a beat or two—"the delusion, and the brandy, vanished simultaneously."

Finished with Davis, Richardson turned to "my friend and Siamese brother during these long 20 months—Dr. Browne." He called his friend *doctor*, he explained, because that is what he was called by the sick prisoners he treated in the yard at Salisbury. "Every prisoner knew him as *doctor*, and I cheerfully certify to his professional popularity. One day, in reply to a question, he said he was an *amateur* physician, and the remark went through the garrison from one soldier's mouth to another. It puzzled them a good deal. The general impression seemed to be that it signified something a little ahead of the regular profession—perhaps an additional or higher degree. One of them asked me, 'At what college do these amateur physicians graduate? I prefer them a hundred times to the common doctors. They seem to know so much more about their profession.'"

Richardson invited his audience to study *Dr.* Browne, who sat before them, freshly bathed, shaved, shorn, and clad in an impeccable suit. This was not how he looked during his recent trip through the mountains, Richardson informed the audience. Then he described Browne's traveling garb. "Overcoat, he had none. Pantaloons had been torn to shreds and tatters by the brambles and thorn bushes of the mountain paths. He had a hat, which was not a hat. It was given to him after he had lost his own in a Rebel barn by a warm-hearted African—by an African who felt with the most touching propriety that it would be a shame for any correspondent of the *Tribune* to go bareheaded as long as a single Negro in America was the owner of a hat. It was a white wool relic of the old sandstone period with a sugarloaf crown and a broad brim drawn down closely over the ears like a bonnet. His boots were a splendid refutation of the report that leather is scarce among the Rebels. The small portion of his body that was visible between the top of his boots and the bottom of his hat was robed in an old gray quilt of secessionist proclivities."

Richardson paused to let his friends ponder that portrait of the man most of them knew as a fastidious, dapper, and supremely cultured gentleman. Then he unleashed his punch line. "With his pale, nervous face and his remarkable costume, he looked like a cross between the Genius of Intellectuality and a Rebel bushwhacker."

The audience hooted and cheered. "The description of Mr. Browne's personal appearance in crossing the mountains was rich," the *Cincinnati Commercial* reported. "Nothing would do it justice but a good wood cut."

After Richardson sat down, there were toasts to "The Press," to "The Nation," to "Literature and Art," to "The Veteran Soldier," and to the city of Cincinnati. And then Weasner proposed a toast to "The Union People of the South—White and Black," and Junius Browne rose to deliver the response.

"I am glad to know that public opinion has so far developed that the Negro can be toasted on an occasion such as this without explanation or apology," Browne said. "When Mr. Richardson and myself were incarcerated at Castle Thunder, one of the Rebel officers gave us a reason for some new injustice toward us—that we were abolitionists before the war. Thank God I was an abolitionist before the war, and I am proud to say so."

Richardson had opted to go for laughs in his remarks, but Browne—whose usual mode of communication was the sardonic joke—chose to deliver a heartfelt speech in praise of the mountain Unionists who'd saved their lives.

"Everywhere, they aided and befriended us—white and black, young and old, men, women and children," Browne said. "Though entirely strangers, they sheltered us and fed us and protected us as if we were their nearest of kin. Through long and weary and tempestuous nights, we passed from the dwelling of one Union man to another, receiving food and concealment at every instance at the most imminent risk to themselves. There was nothing they would not do for us. . . . The Negroes were not a whit less zealous than the white Loyalists. Though confident they would be cruelly beaten, perhaps murdered by their 'chivalrous' masters if they were known to have sheltered Yankees, they never hesitated a moment to administer to our relief. They rose from their beds on bitter cold and extremely inclement nights to direct us to stables, furnish us stealthily with food and guide us to places where we would be secure from danger. The name of 'Union man' or 'Yankee' is sufficient at any time to awaken their deepest interest and transform them, through the spirit of self-sacrifice, into heroes. God bless them!"

When Weasner offered a toast to "Our Special Correspondents"—the phrase most newspapers used to identify war reporters—Colburn rose to deliver the response and the reporters in the room perked up. Not only was Colburn the correspondent captured with Browne and Richardson at Vicksburg, he was also the reporter who had, along with Browne, concocted elaborately bogus eyewitness accounts of the battle of Pea Ridge from a hotel room 200 miles away. Those hoaxes had become legendary among journalists, who regarded them as hilarious parodies of war reporting. Would Colburn, known for his dry wit, mention them? What would he say?

"Mr. President and gentlemen," he began. "I regard it as an infelicity of gatherings of this sort that one is frequently called upon to say something complimentary about his own calling. It is human nature to prefer almost any other profession than the one we follow. I see about me several whose places I might desire rather than my own—for instance, that of a brigadier general, or an office holder or a poet, or a government contractor. In fact, I think that to run an oil well would suit me."

The reporters laughed and cheered, indulging their perennial fondness for pretending to disdain their trade.

"Until recently, I have held a poor opinion of newspaper war correspondents and was disposed to look upon them as a doomed, unfortunate lot," Colburn continued. "They seem to be regarded, like many public servants, as a necessary evil. They are expected to do miracles—and I really believe they come as near to succeeding as men can. They must be able to see very clearly what is taking place at a great distance. And this I believe they do pretty well—and describe it, too."

The reporters in the room laughed.

"Pea Ridge!" shouted a heckler, and the reporters laughed again.

After winning his laughs, Colburn turned his attention to the men who'd been captured with him at Vicksburg. "I am glad to welcome these gentlemen back to life, light and liberty because they are my friends, companions, comrades and, for a short period of time, my fellow prisoners. I witnessed the heroism of their capture, sympathized with their long course of suffering and admired their perilous march toward freedom. I needed no such demonstrations to convince me that they were made of the right stuff. Both are gentlemen. But they are more. They are philosophers. They return to us, let us hope, with intellects and constitutions unimpaired."

Without ever mentioning Richardson's name, Colburn reminded the audience that the man who'd been so funny a few minutes earlier had suffered the loss of his wife and daughter during his long imprisonment. "A tinge of sadness runs through the joy which one of them experiences at his escape," Colburn said. "The heavy load of affliction has been laid upon him in sad bereavement. The congratulations of friends, the favor of fortune, the smiles of affection, all of which await him, cannot make up to him the infinite love of that which he has lost. We will rejoice with him in his rejoicing and mourn with him in his affliction."

Before the long night ended, there were many more toasts—including the inevitable nod "To Women"—and then the crowd of old acquaintances, by then liberally lubricated, staggered to their feet and sang "Auld Lang Syne."

24

THE ONE WHO WASN'T THERE

"**WE HAVE BEEN OVERWHELMED** with kindness and attention," Richardson wrote to his boss, Sydney Gay, from Cincinnati. But he admitted that he couldn't fully savor the "champagne and speeches" knowing that his wife was not alive to share them. "Looking toward home, I am constantly haunted by the thought of my own irreparable loss—the absence of that one love which was dearer to me than all the world beside."

His feet were frostbitten, every joint in his body ached, and he was exhausted, he told Gay. He promised to write an article about his adventures, but first he and Browne were heading to Washington to demand action to save the Salisbury prisoners. "The situation of our prisoners of war at Salisbury is so utterly horrible that we could never rest in our beds again if we omitted any possible efforts for their relief. It is our first duty and I feel it is the utmost obligation that ever rested upon me. Hopeless as the task seems, we do believe we can do something."

Richardson and Browne boarded an eastbound train in Cincinnati and, after missing several connections and spending an unscheduled night in Harrisburg, Pennsylvania, they finally arrived in Washington on Thursday, January 26. They quickly arranged to testify on Monday before Congress's Joint Select Committee on the Conduct of the War. Richardson also learned that the U.S. Christian Commission—a charitable group that provided food, medical care and Bibles to Union troops—was gathered in convention in Washington and he delivered an impassioned speech to the group on Saturday.

"I spoke an hour before it this morning, giving in detail the condition of the Salisbury prisoners," he wrote to Gay. "The narration made a profound impression. Almost every person in the hall was in tears and a resolution was adopted pledging the Commission to work on the matter unremittingly till something is accomplished."

Afterwards he focused on convincing the congressional committee to demand that the army make a deal to repatriate the Salisbury prisoners before they all starved or froze to death. "My only hope is Congress. The committee will very soon—early next week—report some measures and it is of supreme importance that these measures be wise and efficient."

On Monday, January 30, Richardson and Browne arrived in the committee room, eager to testify. Albert was sworn in first. "I understand that you are one of the newspaper correspondents who lately escaped from Salisbury," said Senator Ben Wade, the committee chairman. "Will you give the committee a statement of such matters as you may deem important in relation to your experience as a prisoner, and what you have observed in reference to the treatment of our prisoners by the Rebel authorities?"

"After confinement in six different prisons, I was sent to Salisbury on February 3, 1864 and kept there until December 18, when I escaped," Richardson replied. "For several months, Salisbury was the most endurable rebel prison I had seen. The 600 inmates exercised in the open air, were comparatively well fed and kindly treated. But in early October, 10,000 regular prisoners of war arrived there, and it immediately changed into a scene of cruelty and horrors."

Albert recounted those horrors, describing prisoners living in holes in the prison yard, freezing because their coats—and sometimes their boots—had been confiscated when they were captured. Their rations were barely sufficient to sustain life, he said, and some days they received no rations at all. "Sometimes they were without a morsel of food for 48 hours. The few who had money would pay from $5 to $20, Rebel currency, for a little loaf of bread. Most of the prisoners traded the buttons from their blouses for food."

His job as clerk of the prison hospitals enabled him to provide the committee with detailed statistics. "During the two months between October 18 and December 18, the average number of prisoners was about 7,500. The deaths for that period were fully 1,500—or twenty percent of the whole. . . . I brought away the names of 1,200 of the dead. Some of the remainder were never reported, the others I could not procure on the day of my escape without exciting suspicion. I left about 6,500 remaining in the garrison on December 18 and they were dying then at the average rate of 28 a day, or 13 per cent a month."

Nearly every week, Rebel recruiters promised food to prisoners willing to join the Confederate army, Richardson testified, "and between 1,200 and 1,800 of our men enlisted in two months." The horrors of the prison were deliberately designed to aid the recruiters: "The simple truth is that the Rebel authorities are murdering our soldiers at Salisbury by cold and hunger, while they might easily supply them with ample food and fuel. They are doing this systematically and, I believe, intentionally, for the purpose of either forcing our government to an exchange or forcing our prisoners into the Rebel army."

When Richardson finished, Senator Wade called Browne to testify. "I understand that you were a prisoner at Salisbury and escaped at the same time as Mr. Richardson," Wade said. "You have heard his testimony. Will you state whether you concur with him in what he has stated?"

"I concur with Mr. Richardson in all his statements," Browne replied. "It was so barbarous and inhumane at Salisbury for the two months previous to my escape that I regard the exposure thereof a duty I owe to the thousands who still remain there."

Browne testified that his prison job was "medical dispenser," bringing medicine to hundreds of sick prisoners living outside in crude, makeshift tents or holes in the ground. Every day, between 25 and 45 prisoners died. "The marvel was that anyone survived," he said. "Starved and freezing, with hardly water enough to drink, much less wash their persons or the scant clothes they wore, the poor fellows naturally and necessarily despaired, and not a few of them were anxious to die, to escape from the slow torture of their situation."

Browne reminded the committee that he'd covered the war and seen many battlefields and military hospitals, but none of those sights prepared him for what he witnessed at Salisbury. "The air was full of pain and pestilence," he said, with characteristically florid rhetoric, "and all the horrors of imagined hells seemed realized in that most wretched place, of which I shall never think without a shudder and an augmented faith in the naturally abhorrent doctrine of total depravity."

★

THEY'D KEPT THE SOLEMN PROMISE they made to each other in the Welborn barn: They'd traveled to Washington to bear witness to what they'd seen in Salisbury. Would it save any lives? They didn't know. But they'd done their duty and now they were free to go to New York and return to work. Richardson fired off a letter to Gay, promising to arrive ready to write "whatever you want, as much as you want & I hope as soon as you want it."

In New York, their first task was to reveal the list of more than 1,200 dead prisoners that Richardson had secretly copied on the day before their escape, then carried across the mountains hidden in his clothes. The *Tribune* published it on February 1 under a simple headline: THE DEAD AT SALISBURY.

> Alexander, John, Co. K, 7th Michigan, shot by guard, Nov. 22, 1864.
> Applegate, L., Co. B. 112 Pa., shot by guard, Nov. 26, 1864.

The names, printed in small type, ran down the length of the front page, and filled most of page two, a roll call of classic American names of the era: Baker, Carpenter, Cooper, Cook. Black, Brown, Green, White. O'Brien, O'Connor, O'Neal, O'Reilly. Fitzpatrick, Fitzenmeyer, Quackenbush, Whitefoot. There were three men named Jackson, four named Kelly, seven named Johnson, eight named Jones, and 27 Smiths. Two of the dead were named Richardson, which must have given Albert pause when he furtively copied the list on his last day in Salisbury.

All 1,200 men had died *inside* the hospitals, Richardson explained in a brief introduction. Many other men died *outside*, in the yard, and their deaths frequently were not reported to prison authorities because their starving mess-mates knew that the dead man's rations would be subtracted from their meager daily allotment of food: "They voluntarily withheld the names so that, pinched with hunger as they were, they might draw the rations of their late comrades."

In this way the unnamed dead had helped keep their friends alive.

Once the list was published, Browne and Richardson turned their attention to their own stories, each writing a lengthy account of his adventures. Both pieces appeared a week later, on February 8, under a stack of front-page headlines:

TWENTY MONTHS IN THE SOUTH
—
EXPERIENCE IN SEVEN REBEL PRISONS
—
NARRATIVE OF THE TRIBUNE CORRESPONDENTS
—
A THRILLING CAPTURE, A LONG CONFINEMENT, AND A MARVELOUS ESCAPE
—

Running the Vicksburg Batteries—The Expedition Bombarded, Blown Up and Burned up—The Survivors in the River— Exultation of the Rebels—Libby Prison—Castle Thunder—Pen Pictures!—The Horrors of Salisbury—Restoration to Freedom.

Browne's account came first and he began by promising to relate his adventures "in what the ancients would have regarded as the underworld." Then he launched into a long, droll account of the Bohemians' ill-fated moonlight cruise past the guns of Vicksburg, describing how the Rebels blasted them off the barge and then scooped them out of the Mississippi like "colossal cat-fish."

He used so much space recounting their capture that he didn't have much room left to describe life in Libby Prison. It was the "least obnoxious" jail they endured, he noted, but that didn't stop him from vilifying the three men who ran the place—Commandant Thomas Turner, guilty of "dastardly conduct and extreme cruelty," his assistant, Richard Turner, "a vulgar brute," and Erasmus Ross, "a little puppy." Actually, Ross was a Union spy who secretly helped prisoners escape, but Browne didn't know that when he added a sentence advocating vengeance: "Albeit generally opposed to violence I trust some of our officers will be able to make their threats good, and hang one or all of that trio."

Browne skipped quickly over their five-month sojourn in Castle Thunder before describing the horrors of Salisbury: " . . . a reign of pain and horror such as I had not believed could exist in the Republic under any circumstances. . . . Ghastly corpses were borne to the dead house, and piled up as hogs are in pork-packing establishments of the West."

He quickly sketched their escape and then, finding he'd reached the end of his allotted space, he hastily passed the baton to Richardson: "After many an adventure and narrow escape, which I will leave to my collaborator to relate, we reached our lines at Strawberry Plains."

Richardson's story began right below Browne's, beneath another block of breathless boldface headlines:

> How Men Feel Under Bombardment—Thrilling Experiences—A Moment of Suspense—Rebel Perfidy—How Union Victories Affect Prisoners—The Tribune Correspondents to be Kept During the War—Particulars of Their Escape—Stirring Adventures Among Black and White Unionists—An Unknown Hero—Dan Ellis, the Union Guide—"Out of the Jaws of Death, Out of the Mouth of Hell."

"The seven weeks since we escaped seem to me longer than all the rest of my life, they are so crowded with stirring scenes," Richardson began. "But the twenty months in Rebel prisons, with their fearful dreariness and vacancy, appear brief indeed—a wound in the memory, which, when the balm of Freedom was applied, instantly healed."

While Browne used his story to settle scores with the petty tyrants of Libby Prison, Richardson directed his rage at the Union officials who released Edward Pollard instead of demanding that the Confederates exchange him for the *Tribune* reporters. "When Pollard, the most obnoxious of them all, and belonging to the most malignant journal in the whole South, fell into our hands, he was treated with incredible leniency. While in Fort Warren, he was permitted to visit Boston, and dine with friends there. Afterward, when we had been for sixteen months in foul, loathsome, vermin-infested Rebel prisons, and were sick in the hospital at Salisbury, what was done with him? He was paroled to Brooklyn, one of the pleasantest cities in the world, where he was a thousand times better off than he would have been in Richmond."

Richardson devoted much of his space to the part of their adventure that Browne had barely reached—the long trek through the mountains.

He quickly sketched the story of Dan Ellis, portraying him as a larger-than-life character, the Union's Paul Bunyan: "Ellis is a genius, and his life is a romance. . . . He is wary, vigilant and sleepless as an Indian, and knows every secluded path and every Union man through an immense range of country." But Richardson couldn't resist making a joke about Ellis's flinty asceticism. "Dan declares that parched corn is just as good to travel on as the most luxurious food if a man only thinks so. But I feel bound to say that I have tried it, and don't think so."

Like Browne, Richardson ran out of space before he ran out of story, and he found that he couldn't do justice to the tale of Melvina Stephens. "The heroism of that Union girl, who mounted a horse at midnight, and piloted us for seven miles through devious paths out of a very hot nest of Rebels into which we had involuntarily stumbled, must wait for a future record."

The two reporters' narratives proved popular enough to insure that such a "future record" would soon exist: Publishers quickly contracted with both men to expand their stories into books.

AFTER FINISHING HIS ARTICLE, Richardson left on a lecture tour, speaking about the plight of the Salisbury prisoners in Philadelphia, Boston, Providence, Bangor, Portland, and Chelsea. He was no doubt sincere in his desire to raise public awareness about the prisoners, but there was another reason for his trip: He was afraid to go home.

"I shrink from going there at all," he confessed in a letter to his brother Charles. He was eager to see his children, who were living with Charles, but he was tormented with guilt that he'd abandoned them. How would they react when he arrived? Leander, who was now nine, would certainly remember him. But Maude, who was five, and Albert Jr., who was three, might not even recognize him. And his house was haunted by his memories of Lou, who had died before he could say goodbye, and the baby Mary Louisa, who had died before he could even say hello.

Nervous about his homecoming, he begged Charles not to invite his old friends and neighbors to any kind of reception for him. "I don't want any whatever. I will go home by some unlooked for route if it is insisted upon. I wouldn't go there at all if I could avoid it. If you only knew how bitter all this welcome and rejoicing seems to me when I think of the one who is not there to share it."

He did go home, of course, and he did reunite with his children. But he stayed only three days before hustling back out on the lecture circuit. His brief return left him feeling hollow and depressed because "my nearest and dearest one was not there to share it," he wrote in a letter to Gay. "Three nights in my desolate house, surrounded by her books & pictures & writing—with everything there just as she left it— have taught me more even than I knew before, how dark it is there now that the perpetual sunshine of her presence is gone—how dull it is when her abounding humor no longer illuminates it—how bitter it is with her love forever lost."

He told Gay that he'd found letters she'd written to him in May 1863 but didn't send because she learned that he'd been captured. "One of the first passages in them makes me almost think I hear her voice again, it is so like her: 'Leander came home from school today covered all over with mud from head to foot—the result of one of those accidents which *will* occur to the most quiet children when mud-puddles fly up and splash them in the face!'"

Richardson enclosed a photo of Lou in his letter to Gay. "Here is a picture taken 3 or 4 months before our marriage." And then he added another thought: "I have no heart to look at her papers yet."

It would take months before he worked up the courage, and when he did, he was filled with guilt. "For five days, I have been engrossed in the letters, papers & other articles left by my dear wife," he told Gay. "It has been full of painful & bitter memories. I think I *meant* to be a tender & kind husband to her; but I was always selfish, often ex-acting, & sometimes harsh & unjust. The memory of two or three occa-sions of the latter will fill me with bitterness & self reproach to the last hour of my life. When I think of the perfect loyalty, the undying pa-tience, the utter & unselfish love, for which I made so poor a return, & above all of that last terrible week, when she went down into the dark valley *alone*, I almost wish that I was among those untroubled sleep-ers who rest beside the old Salisbury garrison."

25

THE STUFF OF HEROES

WILD RUMORS SPREAD through Salisbury Prison for days and then, on February 21, the commandant confirmed them: The inmates would leave the next day, heading home. The prisoners erupted in cheers. "Such shouting and singing!" Benjamin Booth wrote in his diary. "No tongue nor pen can describe the joy and happiness."

Some weeks earlier, the Confederate government finally consented to an exchange program that included both black and white prisoners, and the Federals agreed to resume the exchanges. But for the Salisbury prisoners, there was a catch: Only those inmates who were too sick to walk would be shipped to Richmond by railroad. The rest would have to march to Greensboro, where they would board a train heading south to the Union-occupied coastal city of Wilmington, N.C. Greensboro was more than 50 miles away.

The sick prisoners—1,420 men—hobbled out the gate, past a crowd of curious townspeople, and climbed into railroad boxcars. "It was a pitiable spectacle to see the haggard, staggering patients marching to the train," recalled prison chaplain A. W. Mangum. "Some faltered along alone; some walked in couples, supporting one another; now and then three would come together, one in the middle dragged along by the other two; and occasionally several would bear a blanket on which was stretched a friend unable to walk or stand. Deeply was every heart stirred which was not dead to sympathy, as the throng gazed at the heart-rending pageant."

After the trainload of sick men departed, the rest of the prisoners were issued three days' rations—three loaves of bread—and shortly after noon they marched out the gate, guarded by Rebel soldiers. There were 3,634 of them.

"It looked more like an army of skeletons than an army of men," Booth wrote in his diary. He also noted what he was wearing that day—an Army cap, ripped pants, two shirts, each missing an arm, and "a pair of moccasins made out of the legs of an old pair of pants, taken from the dead body of a comrade."

They marched north along the railroad tracks until dark, then stopped to build fires, eat some bread, and sleep in the cold woods. The next morning, they set out again. Around noon, they came to a stream too swollen with swift-running water to wade across. Instead, they had to traverse a narrow railroad bridge that was slippery with frozen mud. The men tiptoed or crawled across it. Booth watched as two prisoners slipped off, fell into the rushing current, and drowned.

At dark, they made camp again, and when they awoke the next morning, they discovered that ten prisoners had died overnight. The living marched on, walking past farmhouses where women and children stood watching them pass. "Many comical, and not very flattering remarks were made concerning our appearance," Booth noted. When the guards weren't watching, prisoners begged for food. One woman handed Booth two sweet potatoes, another gave him two ears of corn.

The prisoners reached Greensboro on February 25 after four days of marching. They boarded an overnight train to Raleigh, where a crowd surrounded them, gawking at the human scarecrows. On the walk from one train depot to another Booth hobbled on bare feet, his makeshift moccasins having disintegrated along the way. A little girl, perhaps six years old, ran up and handed him two aged boots with the tops cut off.

"Here, soldier, is an old pair of boots," she said. "They are not very good ones but they will keep your feet off the stones."

Booth laid a hand on her head and asked God to bless her. He was grateful for the footwear, of course, but almost as thankful for the way she'd addressed him. "She did not say, as all Southerners do, 'Yank,' she said 'Soldier,' a royal term of which I was never more proud than at that moment."

Stuffed into crowded boxcars, the prisoners bounced slowly south for four days. When they finally disembarked near Wilmington, they discovered another eight dead men among them. The living lined up, waited to sign their official parole papers, and then marched towards the Union lines. About a mile down the road, they spotted an American flag, and erupted in cheers. In his diary, Booth described what happened next:

> We drew near to headquarters and saw that poles had been erected on each side of the road, which were wreathed in evergreens and a banner drawn across the road from pole to pole, on which was inscribed in large gilt letters, these words:

> WE WELCOME YOU HOME, OUR BROTHERS

> A band was standing at its base playing "Home Sweet Home." This was more than we could bear. The sight of the Flag, the cordial welcome extended to us, the touching strains of the dear old song, unmanned us. Men fell down by the side of the road and wept like children—wept tears of joy, joy that could be expressed only in tears. The band had to cease playing before the column could be induced to move forward.

The waiting Union soldiers embraced the emaciated prisoners and led them to a mess hall stocked with plenty of meat, bread, and, best of all for Booth, real coffee with real sugar.

The next day, the prisoners stepped on a scale to be weighed. A week before he was captured on October 19, Benjamin Booth had weighed 181 pounds. On March 3, in Wilmington, he measured 87.5 pounds. In 20 weeks in Salisbury, he'd lost 94 pounds. More than half of his body had vanished.

B Y THEN, THE CONFEDERACY was collapsing and the war nearing its end. On February 17, Sherman's army, having already ravaged Georgia, captured Columbia, the capital of South Carolina. On the same day, Union forces seized Charleston, including Fort Sumter, where the war had begun. "*This* disappointment," said Jefferson Davis, "to me is extremely bitter." On March 11, Sherman took Fayetteville, North Carolina, and pushed north, planning to help his friend Ulysses Grant capture Richmond. Two days later, the desperate Confederate Congress voted to permit slaves to fight in the Rebel army, much to the disgust of General Howell Cobb, a former Georgia governor. "If slaves will make good soldiers," Cobb said, "our whole theory of slavery is wrong."

In New York, Junius Browne followed the war news from a hotel room on Broadway, where he was writing a memoir of his wartime adventures. He began the book with the cheeky Bohemian confession that he was writing it for money: "I would state that this unpretending Volume owes its parturition to the request of my publishers, who, unsolicited, offered me such terms as a gentleman of very slender income (his estates in Castile being entirely inconvertible in Wall street) and somewhat expensive habits, could ill afford to refuse."

The book is simply a record of "personal observation and experience, without any attempt at high coloring," he announced, "merely plain facts homely grouped together." That was balderdash: Junius Browne was incapable of writing a page devoid of "high coloring," and he rarely wrote one without a splash of purple, a multi-syllable synonym for a simple word, and an abstruse allusion to classical literature. That was his style and he was sticking to it.

As he sat writing in an armchair in his hotel room, listening to the bells of Trinity Church and watching crowds thronging Broadway, the horrors of prison seemed unreal: "All that somber Past appears now like a nightmare dream, and this restoration to a free and normal condition the glad awakening."

In the book, he defended war reporters as "brave, loyal, talented and honorable gentlemen" and he proclaimed that the "romance of war" was a cruel myth: "What is war, after all, but scientific assassination, throat-cutting by rule?" He also enjoyed describing his wartime dreams, which often featured the two things he missed most during his ordeal —beautiful women and gourmet food.

Of course, the most exciting part of his story was the trek across the mountains. He'd read enough adventure yarns to recognize the dramatic appeal of Melvina Stephens, the beautiful maiden who rode to the rescue of the struggling heroes just when the Rebels threatened to capture them. He dubbed her "The Nameless Heroine" and milked her story for all it was worth—and maybe more—summoning his polysyllabic powers to describe her sitting on her steed, surrounded by the wretched men she was leading to safety: "I confess I looked at her with some degree of admiration as she sat there, calm, smiling, comely, with the warm blood of youth flushing in her cheek, under the flood of mellow moonlight that bathed all the landscape in poetic softness and picturesque beauty. . . . That scene was a good theme for a picture. The girl mounted, and the central figure, with some 18 men in half military, half civilian garb, with bronzed faces and a certain wild appearance, travel-stained, ragged, anxious-eyed, standing around her in groups, listening to what she said in a low but earnest and pleasantly modulated tone."

A few pages later, after describing how Stephens led the men to safety and then calmly rode off, Browne could not resist a literary flight of fancy:

> If I were not a conscientious journalist and a veracious historian. . . . I should tell how I, or somebody else, took her hand and kissed her lips in the moonlight, and saw the tears start in her eyes; how my heart, or some other person's heart, beat wildly for a moment, as that vision of beauty, more beautiful in its sorrow, beamed upon the wintry, Luna-lighted night, and then faded away forever.
>
> But as nothing of the kind occurred, I shall say nothing of the kind. I shall only wish the dear, devoted girl the tenderest of lovers, and the brightest and happiest of lives. Upon her youthful head may the choicest benisons of Heaven fall unstinted! May violets of beauty and lilies of sweetness bloom ever in her pathway, and fill with fragrance all her coming days.

BROWNE WAS DEEP INTO HIS MEMOIR before Richardson finally began writing *his* book. Albert had spent most of February either lecturing or visiting his family in Massachusetts. Still weak from his ordeal in the mountains, he nearly fainted while lecturing in Albany and grudgingly spent several weeks in bed recuperating, hiring a stenographer to help him answer the many letters he received from worried relatives of Salisbury prisoners.

"I am beginning to get at it a little on the book; but make slow work of it," he told his sister-in-law, Jennie, on March 20, writing from the room he'd rented in a boarding house near the *Tribune*. "I have an excellent stenographer; and after tomorrow shall 'rush' it. Have contracted to give the printer 450 to 500 pages before April 20, and so far have given them just 2! I will pour it on them when I begin!"

Faced with the preposterous task of writing a book in a month, Richardson had no time to craft and polish the kind of flowery prose that Browne was producing a few blocks away. Instead, he wrote—and sometimes dictated—the story in his own plainspoken voice, beginning with his opening sentence: "Early in 1861, I felt a strong desire to look at the Secession movement for myself; to learn, by personal observation, whether it sprang from the people or not; what the Revolutionists wanted, what they hoped, and what they feared."

Necessity led Richardson to create the kind of straightforward, unadorned writing that would later—in the hands of Mark Twain, Stephen Crane, and Ernest Hemingway, among others—become the essential sound of American prose, overthrowing the reigning, quasi-British florid style practiced by Junius Browne and most of his contemporaries. Richardson enlivened his writing with droll one-liners. He described Castle Thunder's prissy Presbyterian chaplain: "He would have given tracts on the sin of dancing to men without any legs." In a sentence that still rings true, he captured the folly of the reporters who dismissed Grant as inept: "The journalistic profession tends to make men oracular and severely critical." And he captured Grant himself in a few choice sentences, describing the general in the days after Shiloh: "He rarely uttered a word upon the political bearings of the war; indeed he said little upon any subject. With his eternal cigar, and his head thrown slightly to one side, for hours he would sit silently before the fire, or walk back and forth, with eyes upon the ground, or look on at our whist table, now and then making a suggestion about the play."

But there was one thing Richardson couldn't—or wouldn't—describe. His Victorian reticence prevented him from even mentioning that his wife and daughter had died while he was in Salisbury Prison. The closest he came to the subject was a paragraph about the pain of prisoners who received letters revealing the death of loved ones:

> During the long prison hours, such [prisoners] had nothing
> to think of but the vacant place, the hushed voice, and the

desolate hearth. Hope—the one thing which buoys up the prisoner—was gone. That picture of home, which had looked before as heaven looks to the enthusiastic devotee, was forever darkened. The prisoner knew if the otherwise glad hour of his release should ever come, no warmth of welcome, no greeting of friendship, no rejoicing of affection, could ever replace for him the infinite value of the love he had lost.

Of course, those readers who knew Richardson recognized that passage as a muted cry from his broken heart.

He was halfway through the book on April 14, when Abraham Lincoln was assassinated, and he paused in his narrative to tell how he'd seen Lincoln deliver a speech in Kansas on a cold night in 1859. "In a conversational tone, he argued the question of Slavery in the Territories, in the language of an average Ohio or New York farmer. I thought, 'If the Illinoisans consider this a great man, their ideas must be very peculiar.' But in ten or fifteen minutes, I was unconsciously and irresistible drawn by the clearness and closeness of his argument. . . . In his plain, moderate, conciliatory way, he would urge upon his auditors that this matter had a Right and a Wrong—that the great Declaration of their fathers meant something."

By then, Browne had already sent his manuscript to the publisher. A month later, he was correcting the page proofs when he learned that Jefferson Davis had been captured while fleeing from Union soldiers in Georgia. That news rekindled his memories of the countless Confederates who'd sworn that they'd rather "die in the last ditch" than surrender. Now thousands had surrendered, and the much-ballyhooed ditch remained empty. He couldn't resist taunting the hated Rebels in a sneering "Conclusion" that he tacked to the end of his book:

Where is the last ditch? Where are the men, women and children who were to die so delightedly and so melodramatically before they would submit to the "Yankee" yoke?

Tell me, gentle shepherd; tell me where!

Never was so vast a bubble as that of the pseudo-Chivalry pricked before; never was such pompous assumption so effectually extinguished; never was such lofty arrogance so deeply humiliated. Give the Rebels their wish at this final hour—all but the prominent leaders at least—and leave them alone. If they

> do not go and hang themselves—and they wont by any
> means—they are as devoid of sensibility and a sense of fitness
> as they are of chivalry and shame.

After venting his anger, Browne concluded the book on a more up-lifting note: "The end of the War has been obtained. The Republic has fulfilled its destiny. Slavery, the plague spot upon the fair body of our Country, is dead. . . . America for the first time is truly free. For the first time, her people can sing her national songs without a blush; and the poorest of her sons can declare 'I am an American!' with, not un-covered head, but with mien erect and a glow of purest satisfaction be-fore the proudest potentates of the admiring world."

Richardson didn't end *his* book with any such flights of rhetoric. He simply stopped the story when he reached the Union lines in Strawberry Plains, concluding with his now-legendary telegram to the *Tribune*.

Both men's publishers quickly hustled their books into print in the summer of 1865. Browne titled his memoir *Four Years in Secessia,* and appended the kind of subtitle that nearly renders the book superflu-ous—"Adventures Within and Beyond the Union Lines: Embracing a great variety of facts, incidents and romance of the war, including the author's capture at Vicksburg, May 3, 1863, while running the Rebel batteries; his imprisonment at Vicksburg, Jackson, Atlanta, Richmond and Salisbury; His escape and perilous journey of four hundred miles to the Union lines at Knoxville."

Richardson called his book *"The Secret Service, the Field, the Dun-geon and the Escape"*—a title that rendered a subhead superfluous. He dedicated it "To Her Memory, Who Was Nearest and Dearest, Whose Life was Full of Beauty and Of Promise."

Both books were enormously successful: Richardson's sold 100,000 copies; Browne's, not quite as many. Both books made their authors fa-mous, and both became popular volumes in Northern libraries for decades. In 1883, the story of their escape was recounted for a younger generation in D. M. Kelsey's "Deeds of Daring By Both Blue and Gray," a bestselling book of Civil War adventure stories for boys. Meanwhile, their accounts of Melvina Stephens' heroics inspired an Ohio songwriter named B. R. Hanby to immortalize this Union Joan of Arc in a popular tune he called "A Song for the 'Nameless Heroine.'"

Out of the jaws of Death,
Out of the mouth of Hell,
Weary and hungry and fainting and sore,
Fiends on the track of them,
Fiends at the back of them,
Fiends all around but an angel before.

Out by the mountain path,
Down through the darksome glen,
Heedless of foes, nor at danger dismayed,
Sharing their doubtful fate,
Daring the tyrant's hate,
Heart of a lion, though form of a maid.

Hail to the angel who goes on before,
Blessings be thine, loyal maid, evermore!
Hail to the angel who goes on before,
Blessings be thine, loyal maid, evermore.

★

THE CIVIL WAR KILLED MORE THAN **700,000** Americans and changed the lives of millions more, including many of the people Albert Richardson and Junius Browne encountered during their adventures.

Richard T. Colburn, the New York *World* reporter captured with Browne and Richardson, quit the newspaper business to become a public relations man for Fisk & Hatch, a prominent Wall Street firm. He became an expert on railroad bonds and made a fortune. When he died in 1913, at the age of 80, he left more than $300,000 to two scientific groups to fund research into "psychic demonstrable sciences."

Thomas P. Turner, the commandant of Libby Prison, fled Richmond on the day the Union army arrived and made his way to Cuba, accompanied by Confederate General Jubal Early. Turner sailed to Canada, and remained there for ten years, before moving to Tennessee, where he became a dentist. He died in 1901.

Libby's much-hated second-in-command, Richard Turner, was captured by Union soldiers and imprisoned in Libby's dungeon. Using a knife smuggled in by his wife, he escaped, but was recaptured a month later and locked into a more secure facility for a year. When he died in 1901, Turner was a county chairman of Virginia's Democratic Party.

Louis Napoleon Beaudry, the prisoner who organized the Libby Lyceum and edited the *Libby Chronicle*, moved to Albany, N.Y., and served that city's Methodists as a minister, teacher, and tireless advocate for the Band of Hope Temperance Union. He died in 1892.

George Washington Alexander, the pirate, playwright, songwriter, and corrupt commandant of Castle Thunder, fled the United States after Appomattox, spending several years teaching French in Canada. He returned to the United States in 1873, and became editor of the *Sunday Gazette*, a Democratic weekly published in Washington, D.C. In 1880, he moved to Baltimore and listed his occupation as a "sanitary engineer." He died in 1895.

Alexander's enormous black dog, Nero—who terrified Castle Thunder prisoners and appeared on stage in his master's play—was captured by Union soldiers in Richmond in 1865, and auctioned off on the steps of the Astor House hotel in New York to raise money for a soldiers' charity.

Pryce Lewis—the Union spy who shared quarters with Browne and Richardson in Castle Thunder's comfy "citizens' room" before bribing his way out of the prison—became a private detective after the war. In 1911, sick, broke, and 83 years old, he took a train from his New Jersey home to Manhattan, then rode an elevator to the top of the city's tallest building and jumped off.

John H. Gee, the commandant of Salisbury Prison, was arrested in November 1865 and tried on charges that he had violated "the laws of war and customs of war" by failing to provide sufficient food, shelter, and medical treatment to his prisoners. He was acquitted, and returned to his Florida home, where he resumed his career as a physician until his death in 1876.

Luke Blackmer, the Salisbury attorney who sent books, food, and money to Browne and Richardson and then helped them escape, was later elected to the Salisbury school committee and the state legislature. He died in 1889.

Benjamin Booth, the Union soldier who kept a diary in Salisbury Prison, returned to his Iowa home, delirious and nearly dead from typhoid fever. Nursed by his wife, he recovered, and he worked as a mechanic and inventor of farm equipment until his death in 1927. His diary, self-published in 1897, sold poorly and for years he used the pages of unsold copies to start fires in his kitchen stove.

Thomas Wolfe—the Connecticut sea captain who escaped with Richardson and Browne—returned to the sea after the war, working for a steamship company based in Galveston, Texas. In 1875, he captained the steamer *City of Waco* when it exploded and burned, killing 56 people including Wolfe.

Robert Ould, the Confederate agent for prisoner exchange who steadfastly refused to exchange Browne and Richardson, practiced law in Richmond after the war, and wrote several essays defending the Confederate government (and himself) against accusations of cruelty to prisoners. He died in 1882 and is buried in Richmond's Hollywood cemetery, beneath a headstone describing him as a man "who loved the gospel and died in its faith."

Edward Pollard, the Richmond newspaperman captured by the Union navy, chronicled his rather cushy imprisonment in *Observations in the North: Eight Months in Prison and on Parole*. He also wrote *The Lost Cause*, which proclaimed the "inferiority of the negro," touted the South's "well-known superiority in civilization," and urged Southerners to continue to struggle for "States Rights" and against "negro equality" and "negro suffrage." He died in 1872, but the views he expressed in *The Lost Cause* dominated Southern politics for another century.

Sydney Gay, managing editor of the *New York Tribune*, fell out of favor with Horace Greeley, who fired him in 1866. Gay became managing editor of the *Chicago Tribune*, then an editorial writer for the *New York Evening Post*. He died in 1888. In 1950, his granddaughters discovered a trunk in Gay's stable on Staten Island. It contained nearly a thousand letters written to him during the Civil War, including many from Browne and Richardson.

Horace Greeley ran for president in 1872, challenging incumbent Ulysses S. Grant as the candidate of the Democratic Party, which he had vilified for decades. Greeley's wife died a week before election day, then Grant won in a landslide, and Greeley suffered a nervous breakdown, scribbling a rambling note that began: "I stand naked before my God the most utterly, hopelessly wretched and undone of all who ever lived." His doctor put him in a home for mental patients in Pleasantville, N.Y., and he died there three weeks later. He was 61.

Dan Ellis joined the Union army on January 14, 1865, the day after he led the group that included Richardson and Browne to Strawberry Plains. Commissioned a captain in the Tennessee Volunteer Cavalry, he led raids on Confederates in the mountains of Tennessee. He mustered out in September 1865 and went home to his family. Ten months later, his wife gave birth to their sixth child, and Dan named the boy Ulysses S. Grant Ellis. In 1866, Congress awarded Ellis $3,060 in payment for his service during the war. In 1867, he published his memoir, *The Thrilling Adventures of Daniel Ellis*. The book was ghostwritten by a Tennessee journalist who translated Ellis's plain talk into preposterously pretentious sentences, such as the one that began, "Although they were cut down in the very spring-time of their proud manhood by Rebel tyranny like young flowers which are nipped in their buds by some cold, untimely blast, yet the recollections of their noble deeds of patriotism will always occupy a green spot upon the panorama of memory . . . " and then continued for 63 more words of equally wretched prose. Ellis died in 1908 and is buried in a family plot in the mountains of Tennessee.

Unfortunately, the postwar activities of Melvina Stephens, the "Unknown Heroine," are lost to history, as are the fates of the slaves and the white mountaineers who fed and sheltered Browne and Richardson on their long walk to freedom.

AFTER THE WAR, JUNIUS HENRI BROWNE worked as a newspaper editor, first at the *Tribune* and later at the *New York Evening Gazette*, while leading an active social life, escorting young ladies to the theatre and the opera and enlivening dinner parties with his erudite wit. In 1867, the *Cincinnati Gazette* described him for readers in his hometown:

> He is a critical Greek, Latin and French scholar; a brilliant
> conversationalist; full of epigram, of startling theories and
> extravagant statement; picturesque, imaginative, entertain
> ing; always ready to maintain an opinion, prompt to defend
> the weaker side, whatever it may be; in age about thirty-
> four, unmarried; slender in figure, graceful in movement,
> and, like so many journalists, prematurely bald. In private

> life he is the soul of integrity, generosity and tenderness;
> beloved by all; refined and sensitive as a woman, and holding
> the friends who know him by "hooks of steel." . . . It is under-
> stood that his new book proved liberally remunerative.

The book that proved "liberally remunerative" was followed by two others. In 1869, he published *The Great Metropolis: A Mirror of New York*. A jaunty, witty boulevardier's view of the city, it included chapters on Manhattan's rich and famous and their favorite restaurants, theatres, and churches as well as chapters on the city's thieves, beggars, and prostitutes and the jails, gambling dens, and slums they inhabited. When that book was completed, Browne sailed to Europe, traveling through England, Ireland, France, Spain, Germany, and Italy. After returning in 1871, he wrote *Sights and Sensations in Europe,* a book that is partly a comic account of his travels and partly a sketch of the continent's history and politics. The book's dedication illustrates the author's mischievous wit: "To those who have been to Europe, and to those who have not, this volume (such as it is), in the hope that the two classes may become its purchasers, is mercenarily inscribed."

During the war, Browne enjoyed amusing the Bohemians with his comic mockery of marriage, but after returning from Europe, he married Lillian Gilbert, after a courtship that had lasted years. "Short courtships make long miseries," Browne joked. Daughter of a prosperous accountant, Lilly was the younger sister of Lucia Gilbert Calhoun, one of the *Tribune*'s star writers. After their marriage, Junius and Lilly lived with her parents in Manhattan, first on West 45th Street, then on West 57th Street, while they raised their three sons, Junius, Gilbert, and Curtis. Browne kept writing, turning out articles for America's top magazines, mainly travel pieces and literary essays.

"I have excellent health as I have always had, and I still continue my old trade of ink wasting," Browne wrote in a letter to Luke Blackmer in 1889. He hadn't seen Blackmer since the night he and Richardson escaped and hid in the attorney's barn, but he remembered Blackmer's kindness and invited him to visit if he ever traveled to New York. "I am usually to be found at this address, as I write mostly at home. I sincerely hope you are well and reasonably prosperous. Where is your cousin Major Blackmer?—whom I have not seen since he handed us a canteen of water when we came out of your barn on the night of Dec. 19th 1864, and bid us God speed on our flight to freedom. Could those times ever have been? They seem to have belonged to another life; and yet, in another view, to be part of yesterday."

Browne's invitation to visit arrived too late; Blackmer had died a few weeks earlier. Junius Browne lived another 13 years, long enough to see the twentieth century. He died on April 2, 1902, at the age of 68.

☆

A FTER THE WAR, ALBERT DEANE RICHARDSON became a best-selling author and one of the most famous reporters in America.

In the summer of 1865, while thousands of Americans were reading his war memoir, Richardson traveled across the West in a stagecoach. The trip was a junket sponsored by the Overland Mail and Stage Line, and Richardson was invited to come along by Schuyler Colfax, who was the Speaker of the House. Also along for the free ride was Samuel Bowles, editor of the *Springfield Republican*, who thought Richardson seemed more like a preacher than a Bohemian: "He does not chew tobacco, disdains whisky, but drinks French brandy and Cincinnati Catawba, carries a good deal of baggage, does not know how to play poker, and shines brilliantly among the ladies."

The stagecoach bounced across Kansas and rumbled to Denver, Salt Lake City, and the mining camps of Nevada before crossing the Sierras and rolling into San Francisco. Thrilled to be back in the West, Richardson chronicled the trip in travel pieces that ran in the *Tribune* and were reprinted in newspapers across the country.

He spent the winter with his brother and his children on the family farm in Massachusetts, where he began his next book, reworking his prewar Western dispatches and the accounts of his recent trip into a book called *Beyond the Mississippi*. A joyous ode to the American West, it was published in 1867 and proved even more popular than his war memoir.

Richardson bought a house in Woodside, New Jersey, just outside Manhattan, with bedrooms for his three children and his housekeeper. He began work on a new book, a biography of Ulysses S. Grant, who was soon to run for president. And in the midst of all these activities, Albert Richardson fell in love with a beautiful woman.

Her name was Abby Sage McFarland. She was 30 years old, the author of a book of poems, and an actress who entertained audiences with dramatic readings from Shakespeare, Tennyson, Longfellow, and Browning. Unfortunately, she was married, and the mother of two young sons. Her husband, Daniel McFarland, was a lawyer, a failed land speculator, and a mean drunk who beat his wife when he drank and begged forgiveness when he sobered up. She left him in February 1867, not long after meeting Richardson at a dinner party hosted by *Tribune* writer Lucia Gilbert Calhoun.

A month later, in March 1867, Richardson was walking Abby home from the Winter Garden theatre, where she had performed that night, when a voice called out, "Libertine!" Daniel McFarland stepped out of the shadows and fired three shots at Richardson. Two missed, but one hit him in the thigh. Richardson wrestled McFarland to the ground, and held him until two cops arrived and took both men to a police station.

Ignoring his friends' advice, Richardson refused to press charges against McFarland, hoping to avoid a public scandal that would inevitably taint Abby's reputation. Terrified of her unstable husband, Abby fled with her sons, moving to her parents' house in Massachusetts.

"I want you always," Richardson wrote to her while he recuperated from his wound. "If heaven shall ever grant me the last blessing of calling you mine, by the most sacred name of wife, it will compensate me for all waiting and sorrow. . . . My whole heart, my whole life, go out to you. I think I see a happy future, sunny days, love of children, love of home, good to others. I *know* I see a loyalty nothing can shake, a trust that is absolute, a love that is utter and vital."

In 1868, Abby moved to Indiana, one of the few states where a woman could obtain a divorce for a reason other than adultery. By law, she had to live there for a year, and she did, earning a living by writing articles for newspapers and magazines. To avoid tarnishing Abby's reputation or endangering the divorce, Richardson stayed away. In October 1869, an Indiana court granted Abby her divorce. Finally free of McFarland, she traveled to Massachusetts to spend Thanksgiving with Richardson and his extended family. Reunited, the lovers planned to marry and talked of moving to the West to start a new life. Albert was ecstatic. "I feel as if I could leap a five-barred gate in one bound," he said.

A week later, he was back in New York, strolling into the offices of the *Tribune* late in the afternoon of November 25. He was thumbing through his mail when Daniel McFarland walked up and fired a bullet into his belly.

Richardson collapsed on a couch, bleeding profusely. His colleagues summoned a doctor, who administered a shot of morphine and said there was nothing else he could do. Richardson's friends carried him on a chair two blocks to the Astor House hotel and put him to bed in a room on the second floor. Junius Browne wrote a notice and posted it on the door: "Mr. Richardson's condition is now critical, and will be for some days, and his recovery is largely dependent upon perfect rest and quiet. Consequently, we particularly request that his friends will refrain from calling at his room."

Abby received the news by telegram in Massachusetts and took a night train to New York. She arrived to find Albert dying. He asked her to marry him. She said yes.

On Tuesday, November 30—the fifth day after the shooting— Henry Ward Beecher, the famous abolitionist minister, performed the ceremony in Richardson's hotel room before a small group of family and friends. The groom's brother, Charles, attended, along with the bride's mother. Junius Browne was there with Lillian Gilbert. Albert lay in the bed, his head propped on pillows, while Abby sat in a chair, holding his hand.

"Do you take this woman, whom you have by your side now, in this hour, standing near the heavenly land, and renew to her the pledges of your love?" Beecher asked. "Do you give your heart to her, and your name? Is she, before God and these witnesses, your beloved, your honored and your lawful wife?"

"Yes," Albert said.

"Do you accept him as your head in the Lord?" Beecher asked Abby. "Are you now to him a wife, sacred and honored, bearing his name? And will you love him to the end of your life?"

"I do," Abby replied. "And I will."

The marriage lasted 60 hours. Albert D. Richardson died on December 2, 1869. He was 36 years old.

"I knew from the first the almost necessarily fatal character of his wound but I would not and did not surrender hope until I saw the stamp of death on his face," Browne wrote to Sydney Gay. "Thru all his sufferings he bore himself with a calmness and courage almost super-human. All my sorrow could not repress my admiration for the noble fellow. I hope that when I take the train for the cemetery that I shall be half as philosophic as he. There was a good deal of the stuff of which heroes are made in our departed friend."

ACKNOWLEDGMENTS

Many kind souls helped with the research and writing of this book and I'd like to thank them here.

It's funny how these things begin: My old boss, Steve Petranek, editor-in-chief of the Weider History Group, made a caustic comment about the quality of Civil War journalism, which inspired me to investigate the subject, which led me to stumble across a mention of Browne and Richardson's adventures, and I was soon hooked on the story.

My colleagues at *American History* and other Weider magazines encouraged my interest in this story and suggested sources of information—David Grogan, Chris Kreiser, Wendy Palitz, Jon Guttman, Mike Robbins, Gene Santoro, Steve Harding, Sarah Richardson, Bill Horne, Barbara Justice, and Sarah Cokeley.

Allen Ellis, who has written extensively about his great-great-grandfather, Dan Ellis, generously shared his research with me. So did George Cooper, the author of *Lost Love*, a wonderful book about Albert Richardson and Abby Sage. Bob Blackmer provided biographical information on his relatives Luke and Elon God Blackmer. Skip Tate and Father Thomas Kennealy of Xavier University provided information on Junius Browne's days at what was then called St. Xavier College. Junius H. Browne IV kindly spent hours talking to me about his great-great grandfather and the history of the Browne family.

Roger Wingler, an amateur historian of Wilkes County, N.C., guided me on a day-long tour of the places where Browne and Richardson hid out. Then he took me to a great barbecue joint, where we feasted on pork and cornbread, the foods that kept Albert and Junius alive.

Many good friends provided food, shelter, wine, and warm hospitality during my research trips—Gay Daly, Jay Lovinger, Renee Loth,

Bert Seager, Jon Garelick, Clea Simon, and Beatrice Oehl. My friend Bob Thompson frequently met me at an Irish pub in Washington to drink beer and commiserate while we were both writing books. George Ramick provided emergency computer assistance. He also took the author photo, insisting that I stop grinning like an idiot and look serious. John DiNella kept me laughing with his hilarious noctural phone calls and bizarre pseudonymous postcards.

The irrepressible Miriam Kleiman steered me through the daunting terrain of the National Archives. Gretchen Witt and her staff at the Edith M. Clark History Room in the Rowan Public Library in Salisbury, NC, dug countless documents out of obscure files I never could have found without their expert assistance. Arlene Balkansky and her colleagues in the Library of Congress's periodicals reading room went out of their way to help me find old newspaper articles. Audrey C. Johnson, senior rare-book librarian at the Library of Virginia, unearthed obscure Confederate documents on the Libby and Castle Thunder prisons. Anna J. Cook, a librarian at the Massachusetts Historical Society, provided valuable assistance with the letters of Albert Richardson and his family, and the staff at the Columbia University's Rare Book and Manuscript Library helped me find the letters Albert and Junius wrote to their editor, Sydney Gay.

Scott Mendel, my agent, encouraged me to write this book, and Clive Priddle, its skillful editor, made it better. The two Melissas of PublicAffairs Books—Melissa Raymond and Melissa Veronesi— guided me through the intricacies of the production process. Jennifer Blakebrough-Raeburn copyedited the manuscript, correcting my mistakes and unearthing hidden follies.

My beautiful daughters Caitlin and Emily amused and charmed me during the writing of this book, as they have all their lives. And of course, the lovely and talented Kathy Oehl, my wife and best friend, helped me more than anyone, reading rough drafts, suggesting changes, proofreading, and keeping me (relatively) sane. In fact, she's looking over my shoulder right now, pointing out my errors—a talent she has honed to perfection over these past 34 years.

NOTES ON SOURCES

Junius and Albert's Adventures in the Confederacy is a work of nonfiction: Everything in it is true—or as close to the truth as I could reconstruct 150 years after the events occurred. I didn't fictionalize anything; all facts, quotes, and dialogue were taken from historical sources. This isn't an academic book so I see no need for footnotes, but I believe curious readers deserve a documentation of my sources. First, I'll give a general overview, then a chapter-by-chapter breakdown.

Obviously, the best source for Browne and Richardson's adventures is their memoirs—Browne's *Four Years in Secessia* (O.D. Case and Company, 1865), and Richardson's *The Secret Service, The Field, The Dungeon and The Escape* (American Publishing Company, 1865). Both men also wrote accounts of their adventures that were published in the *New York Tribune* on Feb. 8, 1865. And they wrote letters to their editor, Sydney Gay, which are available in the Sydney Howard Gay papers in the Rare Book and Manuscript Library at Columbia University. Richardson's letters to his family are in the "Richardson family papers" at the Massachusetts Historical Society in Boston.

Other Civil War reporters wrote about adventures they shared with Richardson and Browne. Richard Colburn described their capture and early imprisonment in *The New York World* on May 28, 1863. William E. Davis described his escape with Richardson and Browne in the *Cincinnati Gazette* on Feb. 7, 1865. Several members of the Bohemian Brigade wrote memoirs—Franc B. Wilkie's *Pen and Powder* (Ticknor and Company, 1888), Thomas Knox's *Camp-Fire and Cotton-Field* (Da Capo Press, 1969), and Sylvanus Cadwallader's *Three Years with Grant* (Bison Books, 1996).

Three books on Civil War journalism provided valuable background: *Bohemian Brigade* by Louis M. Starr (Knopf, 1954), *A Bohemian Brigade* by James M. Perry (John Wiley & Sons, 2000), and

257

The North Reports the Civil War by J. Cutler Andrews (University of Pittsburgh Press, 1985).

Several books provided valuable information on the Confederate prisons where Browne and Richardson were incarcerated: *Libby Prison Breakout* by Joseph Wheelan (PublicAffairs, 2010), *George W. Alexander and Castle Thunder* by Frances H. Casstevens (McFarland & Company, 2004), and *The Salisbury Prison* by Louis A. Brown (Broadfoot Publishing, 1992). I also used memoirs by former inmates of these prisons, which I cite in the notes for specific chapters.

Several excellent books provided background on the Civil War in the mountains of North Carolina and Tennessee: *Bushwhackers* by William R. Trotter (John F. Blair, 1988), *Mountain Partisans* by Sean Michael O'Brien (Praeger, 1999), *A South Divided* by David C. Downing (Cumberland House, 2007), and *The Civil War in North Carolina* by John G. Barrett (University of North Carolina Press, 1963).

For general information on the war, I relied on James McPherson's magnificent *Battle Cry of Freedom* (Oxford University Press, 1888), as well as *The Civil War* by Geoffrey C. Ward (Knopf, 1992), the companion volume to Ken Burns' classic documentary on the war. In quoting documents from the war—including letters to and from Robert Ould, the Confederate agent of exchange—I used the multivolume *"Official Records of the War of the Rebellion"*—known to Civil War scholars as "the OR."

One other book was invaluable to my research: *Lost Love* by George Cooper (Vintage Books, 1995), a moving account of the doomed romance of Albert Richardson and Abby Sage McFarland.

———

Chapter 1: A Magnificent Man-Trap

The Bohemians' capture is described in Browne's *Secessia,* pages 229–241, and Richardson's *Secret*, pages 337–349, as well as in Colburn's *World* story and in Cadwallader's memoir, pages 57–59.

Chapter 2: Very Perilous Business

Browne's account of meeting Richardson comes from *Garnered Sheaves* by Abby Sage Richardson, Albert's widow (Columbian Book Company, 1871), as does my account of Albert's early life. Browne's studies at St. Xavier are documented in "The Catalogue of St. Xavier

College, for the Academical Year 1846–7," available on the website of the school, now called Xavier University. The courtship of Albert Richardson and Mary "Lou" Pease is recounted in *Lost Love*. Richardson chronicled his adventures in "Bleeding Kansas" in *Beyond the Mississippi* (American Publishing, 1867). His letter about "bogus laws" is from *Garnered Sheaves*, page 41. His letter on "New England ways" is quoted in *Lost Love*, page 95.

Richardson recounted his trip with Horace Greeley in *Beyond the Mississippi*, pages 161–178, and Dee Brown fleshed out that story in *Wondrous Times on the Frontier* (Harper Perennial, 1992), pages 39–44.

My description of the *Tribune* offices comes from Starr's *Bohemian Brigade*, pages 13–15. Richardson recounted his conversation with Dana and his secret reporting trip through the South in *Secret*, pages 17 through 205. His articles about the trip appeared in the *Tribune* on March 11, 15, 21, 23, 28, 29, April 2, 4, and 9, 1861.

Chapter 3: No One Here Seems to Have Any Knowledge About Anything

Browne chronicled his befuddlement in Jefferson City in *Secessia*, pages 23–28. He described his writing as "sesquipedalian fustian" in *Garnered Sheaves*, page 28. His account of his naked ride is in *Secessia*, pages 33–37, and his story of traveling with Bohemian women is on pages 57–58. Wilkie described Browne in *Pen and Powder*, pages 52–53 and 75. Richardson wrote about the Bohemian life in Missouri and quoted the *Gazette*'s pillow fight story in *Secret*, pages 189–195.

The Grant quote and the background on Fremont comes from *Pathfinder*, a biography of Fremont by Tom Chaffin (Hill and Wang, 2002), pages 460–473.

Richardson wrote about the battle of Fort Henry in *Secret*, pages 213–218, and in the *Tribune* on Feb. 14, 1862. Browne wrote about Fort Donelson in *Secessia*, pages 66–80, and in the *Tribune*, Feb. 22, 1862. Wilkie's description of Browne's shooting appears in *Pen and Powder*, pages 105–108.

The best account of the Pea Ridge hoax is "The Enemy Were Falling Like Autumn Leaves: Fraudulent Newspaper Reports of the Battle of Pea Ridge," by David Rose in the *Arkansas Historical Quarterly*, Autumn 1995. Browne's bogus story appeared in the *Tribune* on March 20, 1862. Colburn's appeared in the *World* on March 19, 1862.

Chapter 4: Slouching Towards Vicksburg

Greeley's anger with his reporters' missing the Battle of Shiloh is re-counted in Starr, page 100. Richardson's explanation is from his let-ter to Gay, April 27, 1862. Richardson described Grant and his underlings in *Secret*, pages 243–246. Browne describes the fickle prostitutes in *Secessia*, page 133–134, and the boring prayer meet-ings on page 152.

Richardson recounts the battle, and occupation, of Memphis in *Se-cret*, pages 260–270, and in a letter to Gay, June 20, 1862. Browne tells that story in *Secessia*, pages 179–191, and in the *Tribune* on June 11, 1862. Browne's *Tribune* article of the Battle of White River appeared on June 25, 1862. Richardson informed Gay of Browne's ill-ness in letters dated Aug. 5, 7, 12, 16, and Sept. 1 and 11, 1862.

Starr told the story of the *Tribune*'s coverage of Antietam in *Bo-hemian Brigade*, pages 137–149. Richardson's account is in *Secret*, pages 275–303.

Richardson wrote about his meeting with Lincoln in *Secret*, pages 314–324, and in a letter to Gay on March 20, 1863. Starr tells the story, quoting Winchell's account, in *Bohemian Brigade*, pages 118–119, 162, and 180–182.

Browne revealed his reporting frustrations in letters to Gay on Sept. 16, Nov. 8, and Nov. 23, 1862, and Jan. 3, 1863.

Richardson told Gay about Rosecrans and Streight in a letter dated April 11, 1863. His letter to Gay on the "romance & picturesqueness" of war is quoted in Starr, page 184.

Chapter 5: Impudent Scamps

This chronicle of the reporters' journey across the Confederacy is based on the accounts in *Secret*, pages 347–363, *Secessia*, pages 240–256, and Colburn's article in the *World*.

The bizarre story of John McClanahan and his *Memphis Appeal* is recounted in B. G. Ellis's *The Moving Appeal* (Mercer University Press, 2003). The story of Grant's attack on Jackson is recounted in Duane Schultz's *The Most Glorious Fourth* (W.W. Norton, 2000).

The *Southern Confederacy*'s editorial urging the lynching of the Yankee reporters is quoted in *Secret*, pages 362–363.

Chapter 6: Fresh Fish! Fresh Fish!

For descriptions of life in Libby, I used diaries and memoirs by Libby prisoners, including Federico Cavada's *Libby Life* (King & Baird, 1864), Louis Di Cesnola's "Ten Months in Libby Prison" (unidentified publisher, Philadelphia, 1865), and William D. Wilkin's "Forgotten in the Black Hole: A Diary from Libby Prison," in *Civil War Times*, June 1976.

Richardson's account of his early days at Libby is in *Secret*, pages 365–371, Browne's is in *Secessia*, pages 257–267, Colburn's is in his *World* article.

The story of Abel Streight's ill-fated invasion of the Confederacy is told in Wheelan's *Libby Prison Breakout*, which also chronicles the adventures of Elizabeth Van Lew, the Union spy, and Erasmus Ross, her collaborator inside Libby.

Lincoln's telegram to Ludlow is quoted in Starr's *Bohemian Brigade*, page 187. Ludlow's letter to Ould on June 2, 1863, appears in the O.R., Series II, Vol. 5, page 657. Ould's reply, on June 5, 1863, is in the same source, page 746. Ould's "let them suffer" letter, dated Mar. 21, 1863, appears in the O.R. Series II, Vol. 5, page 855.

Chapter 7: The General's Dance

The prisoners' Fourth of July celebration is described in *Secret*, page 371, in *Libby Prison Breakout*, pages 55–57, and in Louis Beaudry's *The Libby Chronicle*, available on microfilm at the Library of Congress.

The story of Sawyer and Flinn is chronicled in *Libby Prison Breakout*, pages 58–60, in *Secret*, pages 373–374, in *Secessia*, pages 273–275, and in a four-part series by Jacob Schaad Jr., in the New Jersey newspaper *Shore News Today*, in August and September 2011.

The General's dance and the Vicksburg victory celebration are described in *Secret*, pages 375–376, in *Secessia*, pages 264–265, and in *Libby Prison Breakout*, pages 60–61.

The New York draft riot was covered in long stories in the *Tribune* on July 14 and 15, 1863, and chronicled in Starr's *Bohemian Brigade*, pages 220–225, and in McPherson's *Battle Cry of Freedom*, pages 609–611. The list of rich Yankees who bought their way out of the war comes from Ward's *The Civil War*, page 242. The Richmond *Dispatch*'s gleeful reaction to the riot was published on July 18, 1863.

My brief synopsis of prisoner-exchange issues is based on the more detailed account on pages 791 through 802 of *Battle Cry of Freedom*, which is also the source for Ould's "last ditch" quote. The correspondence between Ould and Meredith is from the O.R. Series II, Vol. 6, pages 232 and 237. The *Dispatch*'s bloodthirsty editorial on Yankee prisoners appeared on July 16, 1863.

Chapter 8: Raise Your Left Foot and Swear

Browne described his dream in *Secessia*, page 267. Both Browne and Richardson gleefully recount soldiers' freakish survival stories in many places in their books. Browne's wry "saved by a Bible" quote appears on page 104 of *Secessia*.

Browne's comic riff about cooking in Libby appears in *Secessia*, pages 277–283, and Cavada wrote about it in his memoir, pages 161–165. Richardson described the desperate men in the dungeon in *Secret*, pages 378–379.

My account of the amazing Louis Beaudry, creator of the Libby Lyceum and *The Libby Chronicle*, is based on his diary, *The War Journal of Louis Beaudry* (McFarland, 1996) and on his *Libby Chronicle*, which he reconstructed and self-published in 1889, available at the Library of Congress. The poem "Castle Thunder" is in the *Chronicle*'s August 28, 1863, issue.

Chapter 9: What Have I Done, Mr. Anti-Christ?

Richardson and Browne described their sojourn in Castle Thunder in *Secret*, pages 381–399, and *Secessia*, pages 284–312. *New York Herald* reporters Leonard Hendrick and George Hart recounted their Castle Thunder experiences in the *Herald*—Hendrick on Jan. 30, 1864, and Hart on Feb. 10, 1864.

My minibiography of Captain Alexander is based on Casstevens' *George W. Alexander and Castle Thunder*, which is also the source for his song lyrics and the scathing review of his play. The transcript of the Confederate Congress's investigation of Alexander—"Evidence Taken Before the Committee of the House of Representatives Appointed to Enquire Into the treatment of Prisoners at Castle Thunder"—is available in the Library of Virginia in Richmond.

The system of bribery in Castle Thunder's "citizens' room" is described in *Double Death* (Walker & Company, 2010), Gavin Mortimer's biography of Union spy Pryce Lewis, and in Lewis's unpublished memoir, available at the Pryce Lewis Collection at St. Lawrence University in Canton, N.Y.

The story of Caphart as "Mr. Anti-Christ" comes from *Southern Lady, Yankee Spy* (Oxford University Press, 2003), Elizabeth R. Varon's biography of Elizabeth Van Lew.

Mrs. Richardson's letters to Sydney Gay, dated Aug. 27, Sept. 23, Oct. 13, Oct. 27, Nov. 4, and Nov. 30, 1863, are in Gay's papers at Columbia University.

The story of the reporters' botched escape and time in the dungeon is recounted in *Secret*, pages 393–396, in *Secessia*, pages 284–329, and in Hendrick's *Herald* story, also my source for Alexander's "duty to escape" quote. Richardson's question—"what do these learned gentlemen think about Dante?"—is from *Garnered Sheaves*, page 62.

Chapter 10: Captivity Dries Up the Heart

The information on food shortages in Richmond comes from *Libby Prison Breakout*, pages 8–13. Van Lew's quote is from her papers, available on microfilm at the Library of Virginia. Sneden's quote on corpse-tossing appears in his diary, *Eye of the Storm* (Free Press, 2000).

Alexander's firing is chronicled in Casstevens, pages 128–131. The "bowling alley" quote is from Hendricks' *Herald* story.

Browne's description of Spencer Deaton is from Secessia, page 310. Deaton's background is recounted in Oliver Perry Temple's *East Tennessee and the Civil War* (Clarke, 1899). The Richmond *Dispatch* and the Richmond *Examiner* described Deaton's hanging on Feb. 20, 1864.

Chapter 11: The Heavy Blow

Browne and Richardson described the trip to Salisbury and their early days there in *Secessia*, pages 301–319, and in *Secret*, pages 401–410. The story of the great escape from Libby Prison is recounted in *Libby Prison Breakout*, pages 144–187.

Richardson's thoughts after his wife's death are taken from *Secret*, pages 402–403, *Lost Love*, pages 97–98, and from the letter he wrote to his brother Charles on May 24, 1864. That letter never reached Charles. Years later, it ended up in the hands of a stamp collector and was featured in the July 26, 1952, issue of *Stamps* magazine.

Chapter 12: Heroes of America

Luke Blackmer's background comes from files in the local history collections in the Edith M. Clark History Room at the Rowan Public Library in Salisbury, N.C.

The story of the Heroes of America and Holden's antiwar campaign for governor is recounted in *Battle Cry of Freedom*, pages 695–698, in William R. Trotter's *Silk Flags and Cold Steel* (J.F. Blair, 1988), pages 181–205, and in "The Heroes of America in Civil War North Carolina" by William T. Auman and David D. Scarboro in the October 1981 issue of the *North Carolina Historical Review*. William E. Davis revealed that he joined the Heroes—and initiated Browne and Richardson—in his article in the *Cincinnati Gazette* on Feb. 7, 1865.

Edward Pollard told the story of his capture in *Observations in the North: Eight Months in Prison and on Parole* (E. W. Ayres, 1865). Richardson's letter about Pollard's parole is in *Garnered Sheaves*, pages 64–68. Richardson chronicled the reporters' second botched escape and Browne's transformation into "No Go" in *Secret*, pages 409–410.

Chapter 13: The Dead Cart

Booth recounted his dream and his trip to Salisbury in his diary, published as *Dark Days of the Rebellion* (Meyer Publishing, 1996).

My description of Salisbury Prison after the influx of nearly 10,000 prisoners comes from *Secret*, pages 411–418, *Secessia*, pages 321–332, Booth's diary, pages 97–131, and several prisoners' diaries and memoirs in the "Salisbury Confederate Prison Materials" collection in the Rowan Public Library, which is the source of Drummond's description of Browne and Richardson helping prisoners.

The story of Browne describing himself as an "amateur physician" is in *Garnered Sheaves*, page 61, as is Browne's recollection that "brave men often sent for Richardson." Albert Richardson's letter praising Junius Browne, dated Feb. 27, 1865, and addressed to "My Dear Madam," is in the Richardson family papers at the Massachusetts Historical Society.

Chapter 14: Insurrection

The story of the failed insurrection is based on Richardson and Browne's books, Booth's diary, Louis A. Brown's *The Salisbury Prison*, and the diaries and memoirs of prisoners E. W. McElroy, Archibald McCowan, George W. Swift, Richard A. Dempsey, and James Eberhart—all found in the Rowan Library's prison collection.

My account of the prisoner exchange issues is based on *The Salisbury Prison*, pages 57–68, and *Battle Cry of Freedom*, pages 791–802.

Pollard recounted his dinner with Butler in *Observations in the North*, pages 101–112. Ould's letter to Bragg is from the O.R. Series II, Vol. 7, pages 1298–1299.

The incident of guards shooting at black prisoners is mentioned in *Secret*, page 421, and is described in Dempsey's memoir. Browne's quote on the difficulties of walking to the Union lines is in *Secret*, page 428, also the source on Richardson's talks with Welborn.

Chapter 15: Sweet Goddess of Liberty

The story of how the reporters slipped out of prison is recounted in *Secessia*, pages 358–362, and in *Secret*, pages 427–437, as well as Davis's story in the *Cincinnati Gazette*.

Chapter 16: God Bless the Negroes

The reporters chronicled the first days of their journey in *Secret*, pages 437–445, in *Secessia*, pages 362–371, and in Davis's *Gazette* story.

Browne recalls meeting Elon God Blackmer in his March 4, 1889, letter to Elon's cousin Luke Blackmer, reprinted in *The Salisbury Prison*, page 208. Elon's military record is available online in the "Civil War Soldiers and Sailors Database." His relative, Bob Blackmer, provided more biographical information on both Elon and Luke in his correspondence with me.

Benjamin Booth's quote about the news of Richardson's escape appears in his diary, pages 152–153.

Chapter 17: War in the Mountains

The Sheldon Laurel massacre is the subject of Phillip Shaw Paludan's *Victims: A True Story of the Civil War* (University of Tennessee Press, 1981), and is recounted in William R. Trotter's *Bushwhackers*, which is also an excellent source on the sociology of the war in the mountains. Gov. Vance's quote on violence appeared in O'Brien's *Mountain Partisans*, also my source for statistics on mountain counties voting against secession. Parson Brownlow's quote on "a hateful aristocracy" appeared in *Bushwhackers*, as did the stories about the Highland Legion, Keith and Malinda Blalock, and Jack Vance. The Champ Ferguson story is recounted in much greater detail in *Mountain Partisans*.

Browne and Richardson recount their journey into Wilkes County in *Secessia*, pages 369–376, and in *Secret*, pages 446–448.

Chapter 18: Christmas

The story of the reporters' sojourn with the Welborns is told in *Secret*, pages 449–461, and in *Secessia*, pages 375–385.

Maberry Welborn's quotes appear in *Secret*, pages 451 and 452. I identified Maberry as the patriarch of the family through census records and his 1874 affidavit to the Southern Claims Commission. The affidavit—and others by various Welborns—supports a claim (#13528) by his nephew Thomas V. Welborn, and reveals that Maberry hid Browne, Richardson, and Davis in his barn. These affidavits are available on ancestry.com and at the National Archives.

Chapter 19: No One Ever Reaches There

The story of the fugitives crossing the Yadkin and meeting bush-whackers is recounted in *Secret*, pages 461–467, and in *Secessia*, pages 350–357 and 386–390.

Chapter 20: Anything for Freedom

Most of the information in this chapter comes from *Secret*, pages 467–487, *Secessia*, pages 391–403, and Davis's *Gazette* story.

Booth's account of gruesome events in Salisbury is from his diary, pages 160–161. Richardson mentions Lafayette Jones in *Secret*, pages 391 and 479–480, and Jones' story is recounted in greater detail in "The Private War of Lafayette Jones: A Civil War Tragedy in North-east Tennessee," by Ed Speer in the *Tennessee Historical Quarterly*, Winter 2002. The story of Canada Guy is recounted in *Bushwhackers*, pages 171–173, and in Dan Ellis's memoir, *Thrilling Adventures of Dan Ellis* (Harper & Brothers, 1867), pages 291–295.

Chapter 21: Chasing the Old Red Fox

My profile of Dan Ellis is based on his memoir, as well as information on Ellis in *Bushwhackers* and *A South Divided*, and on two magazine articles by Allen Ellis—"Yankee Captain Dan Ellis" in *Blue & Gray* magazine, April 1992, and "The Lost Adventures of Dan Ellis" in *The Journal of East Tennessee History*, number 74, 2002.

The reporters' travels with Ellis are recounted in *Secret*, pages 487–502, *Secessia*, pages 403–419, and in Ellis's memoir, pages 352–362.

Chapter 22: Melvina

The story of Melvina Stephens' heroic ride and the reporters' arrival in Strawberry Plains is told in Davis's *Gazette* article, in Ellis's memoir, pages 357–360, in *Secret*, pages 501–509, and in *Secessia*, pages 420–430.

Chapter 23: Life, Light, and Liberty

Pollard's account of his talk with Butler and his return to Richmond appears in *Observations in the North*. His letter to Ould, and Ould's reply, are in that book's appendix.

The *Tribune*'s accounts of Richardson and Browne's telegrams appeared in the issues of Jan. 14 and Jan. 16, 1865.

The testimonial dinner for Browne, Richardson, and Davis was covered in the January 23, 1865, editions of the *Cincinnati Commercial*, and the *Cincinnati Gazette*, which printed transcripts of the speeches and the heckler's cry of "Pea Ridge!"

Chapter 24: The One Who Wasn't There

The transcript of Richardson and Browne's testimony before the Joint Committee on the Conduct of the War is printed in Senate Report 142/12, Serial Volume 1214, 38th Congress, 2nd Session, available at the National Archives.

Richardson's speaking tour and his visit to his family in Massachusetts are chronicled in *Lost Love*, pages 90–99, and in letters to Sydney Gay and Charles Richardson in January and February 1865. His anguished letter to Gay about his failures as a husband is quoted in *Lost Love*, pages 97–98.

Chapter 25: The Stuff of Heroes

My account of the long march of the Salisbury prisoners is based on accounts in *The Salisbury Prison*—the source of Mangum's quote—and from Booth's diary, pages 196–231.

Jefferson Davis's quote on "this disappointment" appears in Ward's *The Civil War*, page 360. Cobb's quote on slaves appears on page 835 of *Battle Cry of Freedom*.

Browne joked that he wrote *Secessia* for money in the book's preface. His purple prose on the "Nameless Heroine" is on pages 421–426. His pugnacious "Conclusion" is on pages 449 and 450.

Richardson's description of Grant is in *Secret*, page 244; his description of Lincoln is on pages 312–314. The lyrics to "Song for the Nameless Heroine" are in *Secret*, pages 510–512.

Information on the postwar fate of this book's characters comes from various sources. On Colburn: *New York Times*, Sept. 1, 1915. On Thomas Turner and Richard Turner: *Libby Prison Breakout*, pages 221–222. On Louis Beaudry: the website "Louis Napoleon Beaudry's Family." On Alexander and his dog Nero: Casstevens' biography, pages 153–154 and 159–164. On Lewis: *Double Death*, pages 1–3. On Gee: *Salisbury Prison*, pages 29 and 184. On Blackmer: files in the Brawley Collection at the Rowan Library. On Booth: his diary, pages vii and 250. On Wolfe: *The New York Times*, Nov. 15, 1875. On Ould: Southern Historical Society Papers, Vol. 1, number 3, 1876. On Pollard: *Lost Cause*, pages 749–753. On Gay: Starr, pages xvii and 353–354. On Greeley: *The General and the Journalists* by Harry J. Maihafer, pages 243–247. On Ellis: *Blue & Gray*, April 1992.

The gloriously florid description of Junius Browne—"like so many journalists, prematurely bald"—appeared in the *Cincinnati Gazette* on July 24, 1867. The information on his wife is from *Lost Love*, page 116. His addresses and family information is from census records. His letter to Blackmer is in *The Salisbury Prison*, page 208.

Albert Richardson's romance with Abby Sage McFarland and his murder are the subjects of George Cooper's book, *Lost Love*, which was the source for my account of the tragedy. Browne's letter to Gay about "the stuff of which heroes are made" is on page 137.

Readers seeking more information on my sources—or anything else—can e-mail me at kblowstop@gmail.com.

Peter Carlson is the author of *K Blows Top*, which has been optioned for a feature film, and *Roughneck: The Life and Times of Big Bill Haywood*. For 22 years, he was a reporter and columnist for the *Washington Post*. Now he is a columnist at *American History* magazine. He has also written for *Smithsonian*, *Life*, *People*, *Newsweek*, *The Nation*, and the *Huffington Post*. He lives in Rockville, MD.

PublicAffairs is a publishing house founded in 1997. It is a tribute to the standards, values, and flair of three persons who have served as mentors to countless reporters, writers, editors, and book people of all kinds, including me.

I. F. STONE, proprietor of *I. F. Stone's Weekly*, combined a commitment to the First Amendment with entrepreneurial zeal and reporting skill and became one of the great independent journalists in American history. At the age of eighty, Izzy published *The Trial of Socrates*, which was a national bestseller. He wrote the book after he taught himself ancient Greek.

BENJAMIN C. BRADLEE was for nearly thirty years the charismatic editorial leader of *The Washington Post*. It was Ben who gave the *Post* the range and courage to pursue such historic issues as Watergate. He supported his reporters with a tenacity that made them fearless and it is no accident that so many became authors of influential, best-selling books.

ROBERT L. BERNSTEIN, the chief executive of Random House for more than a quarter century, guided one of the nation's premier publishing houses. Bob was personally responsible for many books of political dissent and argument that challenged tyranny around the globe. He is also the founder and longtime chair of Human Rights Watch, one of the most respected human rights organizations in the world.

• • •

For fifty years, the banner of Public Affairs Press was carried by its owner Morris B. Schnapper, who published Gandhi, Nasser, Toynbee, Truman, and about 1,500 other authors. In 1983, Schnapper was described by *The Washington Post* as "a redoubtable gadfly." His legacy will endure in the books to come.

Peter Osnos, *Founder and Editor-at-Large*